EDWARD IRVING AND HIS CIRCLE

EDWARD IRVING
From a drawing by A. Robertson

[*Frontispiece*

EDWARD IRVING AND HIS CIRCLE

INCLUDING SOME CONSIDERATION OF THE
'TONGUES' MOVEMENT IN THE LIGHT
OF MODERN PSYCHOLOGY

By

ANDREW LANDALE DRUMMOND

Ph.D., B.D., (*Edin.*) S.T.M., (*Hartford Theol. Seminary, U.S.A.*)

"A man of one thought, the Gospel of Christ;
A man of one purpose, the glory of God;
Content to be reckoned a madman—for Christ."
—EDWARD IRVING

WIPF & STOCK · Eugene, Oregon

Wipf and Stock Publishers
199 W 8th Ave, Suite 3
Eugene, OR 97401

Edward Irving and His Circle
Including Some Consideration of the 'Tongues' Movement in the Light of Modern Psychology
By Drummond, Andrew Landale
Copyright©1937 James Clarke & Co
ISBN 13: 978-1-60608-766-4
Publication date 6/9/2009
Previously published by James Clarke & Co, 1937

Copyright©James Clarke & Co1937
First English edition 1937 by James Clarke & Co
This edition published by arrangement with James Clarke & Co

To
MY MOTHER

PREFACE

The centenary of Edward Irving's death in 1934 was celebrated in many ways, but not by the appearance of a biography. I have not been forestalled and cannot complain that "while I am coming, another steppeth down before me". The centenary offers an appropriate opportunity for setting Irving in the perspective of a century. Mrs. Oliphant's *Life* will remain a classic, one of the better Victorian biographies, containing many of his letters in full. But the viewpoint of 1934 is very different from that of 1862 and new material has accumulated—notably, Carlyle's *Reminiscences*, which Stevenson discerningly called "the most *attaching* of his books". Modern psychology throws a good deal of light on the "unknown tongues" that used to puzzle an earlier generation. Readers who grow weary of "the manifestations" and "the gifted persons", are advised to "skip" Chapters XI and XII.

Professor David Masson used to say there were two types of Scottish genius, (*a*) those who devoted themselves to arduous intellectual investigation, e.g. Reid, Hume, Mill and Hamilton; (*b*) in contrast to metaphysical aloofness, a more popular type, "partaking of the metaphysical tendency or not, but drawing their essential inspiration from the sentimental depths of the national character", e.g. Burns, Scott, Chalmers, Irving and Carlyle. Irving is a great representative Scotsman, not merely a great divine. His personality abounds in human interest.

I am indebted to Professor James Mackinnon, Edinburgh University; Principal Hywel Hughes, Scottish Congregational College, Edinburgh; Mr. R. B. Pattie, of the Catholic Apostolic Church, Edinburgh; Mr. Frank Miller, F.S.A. Scot., Annan; Professor P. E. Shaw, Hartford, Conn., U.S.A.; Miss L. W. Kelley, M.A., Archivist of the Presbyterian Historical Society of England; and particularly to Mr. J. C. S. Brough, an Elder of Regent

Square Presbyterian Church, London, who has spared no pains in putting material at my disposal.

I have to thank the Carnegie Trust for the Universities of Scotland for a grant towards the cost of publishing this book, which is based on a thesis accepted by the University of Edinburgh for the degree of Doctor of Philosophy.

The following abbreviations are used :—

Froude: J. A. Froude's *Carlyle's Early Life* (1891).
Ol.: Mrs. Oliphant's *Life* (2nd. ed., 1862).
C.R.: Carlyle's *Reminiscences* (Everyman ed.).

CONTENTS

CHAPTER		PAGE
	PREFACE	vii
I.	A SON OF ANAK	13
II.	"SCOTTISH UNCELEBRATED IRVING"	24
III.	"THE CELEBRATED IRVING"	44
IV.	THE ORATOR FOR GOD	58
V.	"TWO STRINGS?"	75
VI.	HOME AND FRIENDS	88
VII.	"CLOUDCAPT TOWERS"	102
VIII.	GATHERING CLOUDS	117
IX.	LIGHT FROM FERNICARRY	136
X.	CHARISMATIC CHRISTIANITY	152
XI.	THE TONGUES: VARIOUS VIEWS	165
XII.	THE STRANGE CASE OF ROBERT BAXTER	185
XIII.	DARK DAYS	208
XIV.	SHRINES OF MEMORY	229
XV.	THE IRVINGITE MOVEMENT IN THE LIGHT OF PSYCHOLOGY	236
XVI.	THE IRVINGITE MOVEMENT IN THE LIGHT OF PSYCHOLOGY (CONTINUED)	253
XVII.	IRVING'S PERSONALITY	271
	APPENDIX:	
	GLOSSOLALIA IN HISTORY; PARALLELS	278
	BIBLIOGRAPHICAL NOTE	298
	INDEX	301

ILLUSTRATIONS

1. EDWARD IRVING . . . . . *Frontispiece*
   From a drawing by A. Robertson

                                          FACING PAGE
2. REGENT SQUARE CHURCH 102
   Exterior in 1829

3. REGENT SQUARE CHURCH 154
   Interior in Irving's day

4. PORTRAIT OF EDWARD IRVING . . . 211
   By Faithful Pack, 1832

NOTE

Landseer painted Irving's portrait. A print is in the possession of the Presbyterian Historical Society. Edward Armitage represented Irving along with Crabb Robinson and other "founders of London University," in fresco on the Walls of the Hall of Residence (now Dr. Williams' Library). This is strange, considering Irving denounced London University as a synagogue of Satan! (P. 120).

Wilkie had Irving's features in mind in his well-known picture of *John Knox preaching before Queen Mary.*

EDWARD IRVING AND HIS CIRCLE

CHAPTER I

A SON OF ANAK

"These are busy times for religion. Puseyism puts on its beaver and walks abroad. The old Kirk shakes herself and gets up, ashamed to have lain so long among the pots."—
CARLYLE.

IT is significant that the first statue the stranger sees on entering Scotland from Carlisle is erected to the memory, not of a nobleman or statesman, poet or soldier, but of a simple Christian minister, "who, with distinguished gifts and prophetic voice and chastened spirit and amid trying scenes, was enabled to endure hardness as a good soldier of Jesus Christ."

This statue, by J. W. Dods of Dumfries, was unveiled on 4th August, 1892, the centenary of Irving's birth, by Dr. Charteris, Moderator of the General Assembly of the Church of Scotland, in the presence of a vast crowd including the niece of Edward Irving and not a few who had heard him preach sixty years before. It stands in a commanding position in the middle of the broad High Street, and in the opinion of the late Principal Martin Irving of Melbourne, is an excellent likeness of his father. Forty years later, on 7th December, 1934, a great company assembled to celebrate the centenary of Irving's death. The statue was floodlit, likewise the church where he had been deposed from the ministry by the light of a tallow candle (13th March, 1833). In the presence of distinguished visitors, Dr. A. J. Carlyle of Oxford, Irving's grand-nephew, delivered a memorial address. The Presbyteries of Annandale and London North were officially represented, the latter recording their high appreciation of Irving in their Minutes. Centenary articles appeared in the leading newspapers and reviews.

But nowhere was his name more revered than in Annan, his birthplace. Every organisation from the Town Council to "the Edward Irving Tent of Rechabites" took active part in the celebration. That was to be expected, for even in his hour of dereliction Irving knew that he was a prophet not without honour in his own country.

Annan to-day is a prosperous-looking country town of about five thousand inhabitants. It has a broad main street, with pleasant houses of red sandstone. The coming of the motor has brought Annan into easy touch with Carlisle and the south. In the last decade of the eighteenth century it was not much more than a village of thatched houses. Most of the burgesses enjoyed "a competent portion of the things of this world", to use the words of the *Shorter Catechism*. They had little concern with politics, as the magistrates elected their "sixth part of an M.P.", along with other burghs. The weekly newspaper resounded with distant echoes of the French Revolution—which only assumed reality when Britain declared war on France. That meant the sailing of more corn-laden sloops from the Waterfoot, where the Annan flows into the Solway two miles from the burgh. It also meant more droves over the Border, past many a ruined peel tower which in the days of the reivers had witnessed the forcible driving north of English cattle. The shadows crept slowly over the sundial on the wall of the Buck Inn; and men had leisure to read the Bible and Patrick Walker's *Covenanting Lives*, and to listen to scraps of ancient Border Ballads at the hearth. Mrs. Oliphant asserted that religion was dormant in Annan at the close of the eighteenth century—apart from a few "Seceders". She wrote her classic biography of Irving in 1862—when "Disruption Orthodoxy" still attributed every spiritual ill to the malign influence of "Moderatism". Mr. Frank Miller, F.S.A., Scot., has corrected this impression in a lucid article on "Edward Irving and Annan":—

"It is true that there was no feverish activity in religious circles at that time. But the good old custom of family worship was maintained, and every Sabbath morning grave-looking men and women, carrying well-thumbed Bibles and little sprigs of southernwood, crowded to the parish church. There was much genuine, if unobtrusive piety in Annan when our modern Saint Edward first knelt in prayer at his mother's knee" (Scottish Ch. Hist. Socy., *Proceedings*, vol. I, pt. 1).

Edward Irving was born on 4th August, 1792, in a plain two-storied house in Butts Street, near the old Fish Cross of Annan (not the Town Cross, as stated by Mrs. Oliphant). The house is still there and is marked by a tablet with this inscription: "He left neither an enemy nor a wrong behind him". Here Carlyle in his old age was one day seen standing, his eyes fixed on the place where was cradled "the best man" he had ever "after trial enough found in this world". A medical friend of Irving's used to tell him that his squint was due to having lain in a wooden cradle, with one eye in the shade and the other exercising itself in the light which poured in through the long, low window!

Edward's father, Gavin Irving (pronounced Ga-yin), was a tanner who carried on his unsavoury trade in a neighbouring yard. Gavin may have had the blood of Border chiefs in his veins, but he was an unromantic figure—"a prudent, honest-hearted, rational person, with no pretensions to superior gifts of mind" (according to Carlyle). He was for many years a member of the Town Council and was a bailie when the election took place celebrated in Burns' ditty, "There were five Carlins in the South". Edward's mother, Mary Lowther, was a native of the neighbouring parish of Dornock where her father was a "bonnet laird" or small landowner. She was a great granddaughter of the Rev. Thomas Howys, minister of Annan (1703–53), said to be of Huguenot extraction.

Mary Lowther had far more personality than her easygoing husband. She had brilliant black eyes and a fine figure. She was active, cheerful and high-spirited. Edward used to say long after: "Evangelicalism has spoiled both the minds and the bodies of the women of Scotland—there are no women now like my mother."

Both parents lived to a good old age and were buried in Annan kirkyard. The father died in 1832 in his seventy-fourth year, the mother in 1840 in her seventh-sixth year. They had three sons and six daughters. John (the eldest) and George (the youngest) became doctors; both died in early manhood. The eldest daughter, Janet (very like Edward in appearance, said Carlyle), married Provost Dickson, a brother of Dr. Dickson the African explorer. Another daughter, Agnes, married Warrant Carlyle, a missionary in the West Indies; she was the mother of the Rev. Gavin Carlyle, the editor of Irving's Collected Works.

Edward Irving was baptised in Annan Parish Church—a substantial square building with a gallery round three sides dating from 1789 (the steeple added later). His first teacher was an old woman named Peggy Paine, supposed by Mrs. Oliphant and earlier biographers (without good reason) to be a near relative of "the unfortunate tailor-sceptic, author of *The Age of Reason*".

When Edward had learnt to read he was removed to a school kept by Adam Hope:

"rigorously solid teacher of the young idea so far as he could carry it," says Carlyle in his graphic sketch of the dominie; "a strong-built, bony, but lean kind of man, and a pair of the sharpest, not the sweetest black eyes. Walked in a lounging, stooping figure; in the street, broad-brimmed, and in clean frugal rustic clothes; in his classroom, bareheaded, hands usually crossed over back, and with his effective leather 'cat' hanging ready over his thumb, if requisite anywhere" (*C.R.*, p. 173).

We are indebted to Mr. Frank Miller for correcting Mrs. Oliphant's incomplete and inaccurate account of Irving's school-life. She does not mention Hope's school, which he attended till the new Annan Academy was opened when he was nearly twelve. He was only at the Academy for about a year. Mrs. Oliphant does not mention the Rev. William Dalgliesh, the headmaster, and seems to have thought that Hope was headmaster; actually, he was English teacher there after giving up his own school. The Academy had come into existence through an endowment set apart when a vast common in the neighbourhood of the burgh was divided among the burgesses. Dalgliesh was related to Irving and was a fine scholar, but Hope seems to have set his mark on the boy more decisively.

Hope was a staunch "Burgher Seceder" and every Sabbath led a small band of austere worshippers across the moor to Ecclefechan (*Ecclesia Fechani*—forgotten shrine of some shadowy Celtic saint). The boy Edward often accompanied his master. He loved the freedom of that walk over the hills, with their slopes of springy turf, where the sheep pastured and where shepherds of an antique type pondered the ways of God with men. For as he timed his elastic footsteps to the heavy tread of his elders, he unconsciously attuned his ear to the terms of high metaphysical theology and old-world stateliness of speech. Could he ever forget the disciplined fervour, the moral intensity of these good people who claimed to carry on the Covenanting tradition of Annandale?

Reverence and reality blended as they worshipped gravely in a thatched meeting-house without a ceiling, while in wet weather their steaming plaids hung up to drip. Gladly did Irving in later years acknowledge his indebtedness to the Rev. John Johnston of Ecclefechan, "a most holy father of the Burgher Communion". He was one of those venerable Secession ministers whom Carlyle described—"men so like evangelists and poor scholars and gentlemen of Christ I have nowhere met with among Protestant or Papal clergy in any country". Carlyle's parents belonged to this congregation, and young Edward must often have worshipped near Tom, three years his junior.

"That poor temple of my childhood is more sacred to me than the biggest cathedral," wrote Carlyle in 1866,—"rude, rustic, bare, no temple in the world was more so; but there were sacred lambencies, tongues of authentic flame which kindled what was best in one, what has not yet gone out."

Edward's elder brother John refused to follow him to Ecclefechan. Bailie Irving did not approve of these wanderings from the parish church—"Why run into these ultra courses, sirrah?"

The easy-going father had probably little fault to find with Edward, especially as the boy did not fall a victim to the narrow, gloomy religiosity which was the darker side of Seceder piety. Cheerful sociability was expected in Annan and Edward never allowed religion to make him a recluse. The most Victorian biographer would find it hard to prove him precociously bookish or a prig. His good looks were developed in the open air and a tremendous reserve of strength and energy was built up. He did not have to go far afield for "ploys". There were hills to climb, a hospitable and friendly country to explore, a river close at hand and the miniature port at the Waterfoot, where the Solway and its boats tempted forth the adventurous boyhood of Annan. When the tide is full, a nobler firth is not to be seen than the Solway, with Skiddaw glooming behind the soft slopes of Cumberland and Criffel standing sentinel on the Scots side. When the tide is out, the shrunken Solway meanders through vast stretches of sand and dreary mud-flats; stake-nets raise their heads where great ships might

B

have passed a few hours earlier and there are parts where you can ride or even drive a cart across. "When, however, Solway sets about his daily and nightly reflow, he does it with a rush and impetuosity worthy of the space he has to fill, and is a dangerous play-fellow when 'at the turn'." Edward and his brother John discovered this for themselves one day. They had gone down to the sands to meet their uncle, George Lowther, who was to cross at the ebb. In the happy wilderness of sand and shingle, with salt-water pools full of curious creatures, the boys became so absorbed that they thought neither of their uncle nor of the rising tide. Suddenly a horseman appeared, seized first one, then another of the astonished children, and throwing them across the neck of his horse, galloped on without a word. Out of the reach of the pursuing tide, he pointed back breathlessly to where he had found them; only then did he discover it was his nephews whom he had saved. Mrs. Oliphant draws the obvious moral:—

"Had George Lowther been ten minutes later, one of the noblest tragic chapters of individual life in the nineteenth century need never have been written; and his native seas, less bitter than the sea of life that swallowed him up at last, would have received the undeveloped fortunes of the blameless Annan boy" (Ol. I. 16f.).

Irving's first friendship was with Hugh Clapperton, afterwards a famous African explorer—the first European to throw light on the semi-civilised Hausa Empire. The same elm-shaded yard was common to both families. The boys often shared meals and a fireside corner. They were both of an adventurous temperament, and it was to his old schoolfellow that Clapperton sent a farewell message as he lay dying at Sokoto in 1827. When one thinks of the energy and high spirits of Irving's boyhood and the troubled years that lay ahead, one remembers the name of another native of Annan who died a year before Irving's birth—Thomas Blacklock, the blind poet who befriended Burns at the turning-point of his life. It was Blacklock who wrote the sixteenth Paraphrase, sung in Irving's time in many a Scottish parish church:—

> "In life's gay morn, when sprightly youth
>   With vital ardour glows,
> And shines in all the fairest charms
>   Which beauty can disclose. . . ."

Irving's whole youthful being "glowed with vital ardour." But alas! the words of the pessimist were to bring to nought these high hopes.

> "For soon the shades of grief shall cloud
>   the sunshine of thy days;
> And cares, and toils, in endless round,
>   encompass all thy ways." (*Ecclesiastes* 9.)

Edward Irving in his thirteenth year set out for Edinburgh accompanied by his brother John, aged fifteen. Edward was to go through the usual Arts curriculum, as a prelude to Divinity. John was destined for the Medical profession. The life of these boy-students belongs to a past era in the history of Scottish Universities. Even by the middle of the nineteenth century the old order had undergone but slight modification, as Dr. A. K. H. Boyd revealed in his classic essay on "College Life at Glasgow" (*Leisure Hours in Town*, x). In 1805 the academic régime of "plain living and high thinking" was taken for granted. Students came up from the country to poor lodgings in town, where they subsisted on oatmeal, cheese and ham, sent by the carrier from home or by some "private opportunity". For six months in the year they attended lectures and managed their education with a minimum of academic supervision.

One wonders how boys of that age ever concentrated in such a fascinating city as Edinburgh! From their high tenement window they would be lured by the sunshine on the Braid Hills and the flashing of the Forth, not to speak of the nearer attractions of crowded, picturesque Old Edinburgh and the "elegance" of the New Town then steadily stretching northwards from Princes Street.

It was a lonely, individualistic life for young students without money or friends in the Capital. The University had its library and classrooms but not much else, though the Dialectic Society pointed to a corporate intellectual life with its noble motto, "*Gloria Hominis Ratio et Oratio*". Students learnt independence no doubt in the stern school of self-discipline—but at the expense of deep scholarship, for the professors had often to teach the elements of their subject as if masters of some grammar school.

Irving graduated A.M. in April, 1809, and paid a visit to Annan. Some thought him "rather a showy young man", but the general impression was favourable.

He had come to see his old master, Mr. Hope. He stood talking to him for ten minutes or so in the Latin class-room. Among the pupils who listened eagerly that bright forenoon (supposed to be preparing their lessons) was Thomas Carlyle. Fifty-seven years later he recalled the scene:—

"Irving was scrupulously dressed, clerical black his prevailing hue; and looked very neat, self-possessed and enviable; with coal-black hair, swarthy clear complexion; very straight on his feet; and, except for the glaring squint alone, decidedly handsome. . . . We didn't hear everything; gathered that the talk was all about Edinburgh, of this Professor and of that ('Wonderful world up yonder;—and this fellow has been in it and can talk of it in that easy cool way!'). The last Professor touched upon, I think, must have been mathematical Leslie; for the one particular I clearly recollect was something 'concerning the circle', pronounced 'cir*cul*' with a certain *preciosity*, which was slightly noticeable in other parts of his behaviour. Shortly after this, he made his bow; and the interview instantly melted away. For seven years I don't remember to have seen Irving's face again" (*C.R.*, p. 180).

Actually, the academic record of "the blooming young man" was not outstanding. But his imagination was fired, and if his reading was desultory it was enthusiastic. He discovered *The Arabian Nights*. He would carry in his waistcoat pocket a miniature copy of *Ossian*, which he read aloud to a friend on walks "with sonorous elocution and vehement gesticulation". He devoured a copy of Hooker's *Ecclesiastical Polity* which he happened to come across in an Annandale farmhouse; later on in life, he would refer to "the venerable companion of my early days, Richard Hooker". He seems to have had no doubt about the Ministry, as his vocation. He only spent one complete session in the Divinity Hall. For the remainder of his theological course he became a "partial student", so that he could support himself by teaching; his father had a large family to provide for. This meant that instead of taking four winter sessions in the Divinity Hall, a student was allowed to matriculate, attend for a few weeks annually, sit the necessary examinations and deliver the prescribed "discourses". The Divinity Hall was thronged with students, but the lamp of theological learning burnt low. Rampant pluralism left the professors scant time or energy for original research. Dr. William Ritchie, "with the piercing gaze of an old eagle", sat in the Divinity Chair, which he combined with the pulpit of St. Giles'. It was quite common for a professor to divide his time between his students and his rural parishioners (not to mention his glebe and poultry). So there was not much to attract Irving to attend lectures as a "regular" student.

Through the kindly interest of Professor Christison and Sir John Leslie, he was appointed master of a new school at Haddington (1810). Sir John was Professor of Mathematics—perhaps it was named "the Mathematical School" as a compliment to him, for there was nothing peculiarly mathematical in its curriculum! As a distinguished physicist, Professor Leslie fostered in Irving an interest in science which he was able to cultivate during his schoolmaster years, a training that ought to have corrected his later tendency to "over-belief". One can imagine how Irving's generous sympathies went out to Leslie when his appointment to the Edinburgh Chair was contested by a narrow-minded clerical party who raised the convenient cry of "heresy" (*v.* Cunningham's *Ch. Hist. of Scotl.* II., 430ff.).

Haddington is a sedate, old-fashioned county town that has changed little with the years. Its cobbled streets and small shop-windows still testify to its conservatism. Education was at a low ebb in 1810, and the new teacher was not only welcomed by the community but admitted into the best society of the town and neighbourhood. According to one of his pupils, he was "a tall, ruddy, handsome youth, cheerful and kindly disposed". His only fault was that he was too argumentative. At a supper party he would broach fancies strange in a healthy young man. He would love to speak of the high destinies of the human race in heaven, where the saints were not only to be made "kings and priests unto God", but were to rule and judge angels. Dr. Lorimer, the senior minister of the town, would suggest that there were more profitable subjects for a Divinity student than these speculations. Irving was up in arms: "Dare either you or I deprive God of the glory and thanks due to his name for this exceeding great reward?" To which the doctor readily replied: "Well, well, my dear friend, both you and I can be saved without knowing about that." On Saturdays Irving and his college friend Robert Story (afterwards minister of Rosneath) would walk to Bolton Manse, a few miles out of Haddington. The minister,

Andrew Stewart, had once been a doctor; he was a pioneer in the open-air treatment of phthisis, and in that capacity cured the Hon. Margaret Stuart, supposed to be far gone in consumption. Physician and patient fell in love and duly married. Her brother, Lord Blantyre presented the "beloved physician" to Bolton.

A beautiful oval music-room was constructed in the Manse for the bride—a room I used to admire as a boy. My grandfather, the Rev. Thomas Drummond, was minister of Bolton from the Disruption till 1883.

A new church had been built just before Irving's arrival in the neighbourhood—"a neat Gothic structure" with a tower that was a credit to such a small parish as Bolton. In Mr. Stewart, Irving found a cultured and eminently reasonable minister, doubly useful to his people as pastor and physician. (He had been secretary to the blind poet-preacher, Thos. Blacklock, a native of Annan.) In Irving, Mr. Stewart discerned a young man of fine qualities who would probably outgrow his impatience and love of argument. Our hero thought nothing of walking eighteen miles into Edinburgh and back, the same day. One summer afternoon, when school was over, he set out with several older pupils to hear the great Dr. Chalmers preach at St. George's. Tired with their long walk they made their way to a gallery. One pew was vacant, but a man stretched his arm across the door and said it was engaged. Irving remonstrated in vain. Soon his patience gave way and he thundered, "Remove your arm, sir, or I will shatter it to pieces!" Terrified, the man slunk off and the boys took possession of the pew. Several other incidents of a similar type are related.

It was in the home of Dr. Welsh, the principal doctor of Haddington, that "the Annandale youth came into a little world of humanising graces", as Mrs. Oliphant says. The doctor's little daughter, Jane, had overheard her parents discussing her education. Her father, disappointed that she was a girl, was anxious that she should have the advantage of being educated like a boy. Jane's ambition was roused—she would show what she could do! On her tenth birthday she burnt her doll on a funeral pyre. Then she unearthed an old Latin grammar, mastered the first declension and with dramatic instinct concealed herself under the table while her father was in dressing-gown and slippers, sipping his after-dinner coffee. When all was still, came the words from under the table, "*penna, pennae, pennam*". Of course Dr. Welsh was delighted and was only too ready to engage the new schoolmaster as tutor. The hours were 6 a.m. to 8 a.m. and again after school hours.

"A life-long friendship sprang out of that early connection. The pupil, with all the enthusiasm of childhood, believed everything possible to the mind which gave its first impulse to her own; and the teacher never lost the affectionate, indulgent love with which the little woman, thus confided to his boyish care, inspired him" (Ol. I. 39).

One can imagine him pausing at the end of the day's work before writing his "report". The pupil is sitting on the table, one evening rather apprehensively. The teacher glances quickly at her downcast face and lingers remorsefully over his verdict. Then he cries sympathetically, "Jane, my heart is broken! but I *must* tell the truth,"—and writes "*pessima*". Irving was afterwards to be confronted with many another dilemma, in which his affection tugged one way and his conscience the other.

Jane Welsh was ten years and three months old when Irving first gave her lessons and just over eleven when he left Haddington. Sir James Crichton-Browne, editor of her *New Letters and Memorials*, asks how she could possibly have "fallen passionately in love with Irving" at this age (Vol. II, 207). His reply is that Jane was precocious and developed beyond her years; he instances her falling in love with the only son (aged 12–13) of an artillery officer stationed in Haddington (Vol. II, 47). One may safely say that as Jane grew up she thought of Irving in an affectionate way as a real friend and not simply as a tutor whose presence in the house was past history. That friendship survived separation, disapproval and outward estrangement to the end of his life.

CHAPTER II

"SCOTTISH UNCELEBRATED IRVING"

"One day we will both shake hands across the brook, you as a first in Literature, I as first in Divinity—and people will say, ' Both these fellows are from Annandale. *Where* is Annandale?'" (Irving to Carlyle, "in a tone of self-mockery, saving it from barren vanity.")

AFTER two years in Haddington Irving was promoted (again through the good offices of Sir John Leslie) to the mastership of a new academy at Kirkcaldy, an ancient burgh on the Fifeshire coast. "The lang toun" was in need of higher education than that afforded by the parish school, so in 1812 the minister and residenters decided to look out for a suitable schoolmaster. Irving was installed in two rooms in a narrow wynd, with a small classroom adjoining. The conditions were not promising and it is obvious no young man could manage a number of boys and girls in such cramped quarters without rigorous discipline—especially when he claimed to teach Italian and French as well as Latin. Neighbours soon got used to hearing cries.

On one occasion a brawny joiner appeared at the schoolroom door with an axe on his shoulder, asking with grim irony, "Do ye want a hand the day, Mr. Irving?" On another occasion the neighbours heard sounds of pain, but discovered to their discomfiture that they came from a beast under the hands of a neighbouring butcher, not from a schoolboy under the hands of the dominie.

Outside the classroom, however, Irving was as popular with his pupils as he had been at Haddington. On Saturdays he would accompany them on all sorts of ploys—swimming, boating and climbing. Kirkcaldy had its fishing and weaving industries in those days, but was still a small town. It was picturesque with its weatherbeaten breakwater and "salt pans"; from the steep, red-tiled roofs rose curious blue-painted wheels turned by the wind (flax-mill machinery).

The sands were unspoilt. The Firth of Forth was a splendid background, with its green isles gleaming in the sunlight and Arthur's Seat looming out through the Edinburgh smoke in the distance, a moody lion. On moonlight nights he would gather his pupils round him and discourse on the stars, with many a mysterious gesture and swing of his long arms, till sometimes superstitious townsmen would rush down to the shore and collect their offspring, upbraiding the dominie with wild threats of peril to his immortal soul. Irving was undoubtedly an educational pioneer in getting his pupils to observe nature for themselves and in teaching them the use of such scientific instruments as he could command. Perhaps it was his unusual manner, his commanding figure that daunted parents; his tartan coat in which "red predominated"—was that not the garb of a charlatan?

The flamboyant note, however, was appreciated by his pupils, who became known as "Irvingites" (a special and affectionate bond of fraternity). The boys caught much of their master's chivalrous spirit in their relation to "the Academy lasses". Respectful affection was always mingled with awe. It is related that one girl coming too early for a lesson on *Paradise Lost*, found Mr. Irving alone and reciting one of Satan's speeches with so terrible an emphasis and aspect that she fled in dismay! He had a sombre delight in the mysterious and the grandiose, which blended strangely with a frank, cheerful nature.

A rival academy was established—not *entirely* due to the dissatisfaction of parents. Kirkcaldy was a town of over 4,000. To Thomas Carlyle, the new dominie, Professor Christison wrote: "Mr. Irving has the Academy, not the parish school, but in a town and neighbourhood so populous there is field enough for you both" (16th May, 1816).

Carlyle, as a schoolboy, had once met Irving when he returned to Annan with high hopes and college prizes. They met again about Christmas, 1815, in a Mr. Waugh's house in Rose Street, Edinburgh. In a rather superior manner, Irving asked his junior a series of questions about Annan:—

"You seem to know nothing!" Carlyle was provoked. "Sir, by what right do you try my knowledge in this way? I have had no interest to inform myself about the births in Annan; and care not if the process of birth and generation there should cease altogether!" "That would never do for me!" cried Irving's friend Nichol (a teacher who needed pupils). So the thing passed off with a laugh. (*C.R.*, p. 183f.).

The situation scarcely seemed to promise friendship and Carlyle was not the kind of man likely to make friends easily. But Irving welcomed him like a brother with the words "Two Annandale people must not be strangers in Fife."

Both young men were "intending" the ministry of the Church of Scotland rather than that of the Seceders, for by this time the Evangelical Revival was sweeping like a great purifying wave over the National Kirk. The "Moderate" ascendancy had definitely come to an end; consequently dissent was arrested—till the Disruption finally rent the Church in two. There was some truth in Carlyle's statement that "all dissent in Scotland is merely stricter adherence to the national kirk at all points." The Church of Scotland was rallying to its side strong Calvinists who believed in the old Covenanting traditions, and younger men, too, who believed that the Gospel must be applied in a new way to meet the changing needs of the nineteenth century. The Divinity Halls were crowded. "Patronage" was still the law of the Church, but the right of congregations to have a voice in the appointment of ministers was receiving increasing support. Carlyle and Irving were not the only young men of promise who had to face the possibility that without "influence" the temporary expedient of school-mastering might long outlast their Divinity Course. "Livings" were hard to find.

The two Annandale men saw much of each other. In Carlyle's *Reminiscences* (p. 186 ff.) you can read how Irving kept his word; how he opened his house, his library and his heart to him ("Upon all these, you have *will and waygate!*"—an Annandale phrase of completest welcome). On summer evenings they walked together on Kirkcaldy sands. Irving proved a real friend to the youth whose dyspeptic irritability made friendship difficult. Carlyle has given a vivid account of some of their excursions. One day they climbed the Lomond Hills to see the famous Theodolite then being used for a Trigonometrical Survey. The official in charge was "coldly monosyllabic", even to "County people". But Irving was so courteous and well-informed that the official *had* to melt and invited them to inspect his instrument, through which they saw the Signal Column on the top of Ben Lomond, sixty miles off.

One sunny afternoon, on the Kirkcaldy sands, they were watching ships outward bound from Leith. They were sure that "Burgher" friends from Annan, the Glens, were on one of these ships (they were leaving as missionaries for Persia). Might they not intercept the ship in "Robie Greg's yawl" and have a last word with the Glens? They soon realised it was a case of the tortoise and the hare and landed on the isle of Inchkeith, where they were so hospitably entertained by the lighthouse-keeper that it was 11 p.m. before they returned to their alarmed friends in Kirkcaldy. (*C.R.*, p. 188–193.) Carlyle also describes a walking-tour with Irving and two of his friends—Pears, schoolmaster at Abbotshall, near Kirkcaldy ("born i' Dunse") and Brown, his successor at Haddington. Pears was to secure beds at Torryburn on the Forth, but only turned up at 6 a.m. after they had been four hours in a wretched inn; greeted with satirical "ah-ah's", he departed into the rain and did not join the party till they reached Stirling.

"I remember the squalor of our bedroom; and how little we cared for it in our opulence of youth; the sight of giant Irving, in a shortish shirt, on the sanded floor, drinking patiently a large tankard of 'penny-wheep' (the smallest beer in Creation), before beginning to dress, is still present to me as comic; much more memorable . . . the night before, a mysterious red glow which had long hung before us in the murky sky; growing gradually brighter and bigger, till at last we found it must be *Carron Ironworks*, on the other side of Forth River" (*C.R.*, p. 197).

And so on along the Forth by Culross and Kincardine to Stirling and the Trossachs. Irving was the acknowledged Captain, but the party split into two, for the rains and the bad oatcakes and whisky of Highland inns got on their nerves; he took Pears and Carlyle took Brown; at the Falls of Clyde, near Robert Owen's new mill, they joined forces again amicably.

Another walking-tour Irving enjoyed with Carlyle was by Yarrow and St. Mary's Loch to Moffat. With only an extra shirt and a comb and often barefoot, they would tramp from one shepherd's cottage to another. The talk of these *canty* shepherds was wholesome for young men inclined to take life rather seriously. Back in Kirkcaldy, the two friends gradually diverged in point of view. Irving began to gravitate to "over-belief", and away from the sceptical tendency to which he had sometimes inclined at Haddington; had not Dr. Welsh once remarked, "This youth will scrape a hole in everything he is called on to believe?" As for Carlyle, his "grave, prohibitive doubts" about entering the Ministry were greatly strengthened by the reading of Hume, and especially Gibbon, in Irving's library.

Neither of the two young men were sorry when in 1818 they finally "kicked the schoolmaster functions over". Carlyle departed to seek a livelihood in literature. His last link with the Ministry snapped when he called on the Professor of Divinity ("Dr. Ritchie not at home"—"Good, let the omen be fulfilled!"). Irving realised that if he was to avoid being "a stickit minister" he must return to Edinburgh.

In 1815 he was "licensed to preach the Gospel" by the Presbytery of Kirkcaldy, having completed his "partial" Divinity Course after six winters. He was now able to "exercise his gift" in Kirkcaldy and elsewhere. The "haill toun" turned out to hear his first sermon. When the sermon was in full current, an incautious movement of the young preacher tilted aside the Bible, and his manuscript fluttered down upon the precentor's desk underneath. A rustle of excitement ran through the church—the critics held their breath. Calmly Irving reached over the pulpit, grasped his notes, crushed them, thrust them into his pocket and went on as fluently as before. This act would have taken most Scottish congregations by storm; he had triumphantly proved he was no "paper minister". But Kirkcaldy folk were not as others and offered him little encouragement when he tried his wings in the parish church from time to time. Shrewd sermon-tasters opined that he had "ower muckle gran'ner". The kirk was "thin" whenever it was known that the young probationer was to preach. When he did appear in the pulpit he could generally count on "that thrawn baker Beveridge" kicking open his pew door and dourly tramping down the flagged passage and out of church! It seems likely that a style so rich and splendid as Irving's may have sounded bombastic and flashy in youth, before the harmonious keynote had been found.

There was something fatal about Kirkcaldy kirk. For when he returned in June, 1828, as a great London preacher, a terrible tragedy occurred in the church that he had known in the days of his humiliation. Long before the bells began to ring the building was overcrowded with eager sermon-tasters bent on hearing the young man who had turned out such an unexpected credit to Kirkcaldy. Irving made his way from the adjacent manse through the rose garden in the Sabbath evening sunshine. Suddenly, the great door of the church was flung open and a frenzied crowd poured out. A man rushed at the cloaked preacher, shaking a clenched fist in his face, denouncing him as the cause of the catastrophe. It was a dishonest builder that he should have denounced. A gallery had collapsed with a terrific sound of rending timbers and a suffocating cloud of lath and plaster. Wounded to the heart, Irving rushed in and with titanic energy tried to rescue the victims. Thirty-five were killed. When everything possible had been done for the sufferers that survived, and the anxious manse family were assembling for evening prayers, his grieved soul broke into words—"God hath put me to shame this day before all the people". In silence and in secrecy he left the town, never to return to his father-in-law's manse.

It was during his schoolmaster days that he had become intimate with Isabella Martin, the minister of Kirkcaldy's eldest daughter, who had been one of his pupils. The Rev. John Martin (1769–1837), whom he sometimes assisted, was an earnest if unimaginative Evangelical clergyman, "living a domestic patriarchal life in the midst of the little community under his charge, fully subject to their observation and criticism, but without any rival; bringing up his many children among them, and spending his active days in all that fatherly close supervision of morals and manners which distinguished and became the old hereditary ministers of Scotland" (Ol. I. 61f.). The manse seems to have been the only house in Kirkcaldy where Irving could feel in the slightest degree at home. Carlyle recollects:—

"I was willing enough to step in—though various boys and girls went cackling about. The girls were some of them grown up . . . yet even these, strange to say, in the great rarity of the article and my ardent devotion to it, were without charm to me. Martin himself . . . a clear-minded, brotherly, well-intentioned man."

Mr. Martin's influence did not extend as far as contact with influential persons who could help Irving to secure a parish. So in his twenty-sixth year he betook himself to Edinburgh and settled in lodgings in Bristo Street, near the College. He felt the stimulus of living in the capital in the days of Scott, Jeffrey and Cockburn. The Napoleonic Wars had been over for three years; the public turned with fresh interest to the arts and sciences and to Church affairs. J. G. Lockhart, in *Peter's Letters*, gives a lively, satirical picture of Edinburgh at this period. During the winter of 1818–19 Irving took classes at the University in Chemistry and Natural History. These studies he prosecuted with enthusiasm, though in a note to his friend, the Rev. Robert Gordon, he humorously confessed that he had learnt from mineralogy "as little about the structure of the earth as he could have learned about the blessed Gospel by examining the book of *kittle* Chronicles!" He also read much French and Italian. The day of Teutonic enthusiasm had not yet dawned, or Irving would certainly have learned German and found treasure-trove in German theological literature, then so little known in either Scotland or England. He loved to discuss the universe with congenial friends and was instrumental in founding a new debating society of a more mature kind than the "Philomathic" to which he had once belonged. This was "the Philosophical Association". It was intended for post-graduate students, and of the seven or eight members, Carlyle was one and Irving another. Irving supplemented his modest means by giving lessons in Mathematics to Captain Basil Hall, famous for his travels in America and the Far East.

Deciding to profit by fresh observation and new experience, he determined to burn his Kirkcaldy sermons. But his services were unsolicited by friendly ministers and congregations, in spite of every effort to fit himself more adequately for his vocation. No doubt *that* had something to do with his growing distaste for the Evangelicalism of the capital, which was steadily ousting Moderatism (now threadbare) from the leading pulpits.

"Rejected by the living, I conversed with the dead." He dived into the older divines (Puritan, Anglican and Presbyterian) with a zeal that would have delighted the heart of the late Dr. Alexander Whyte. Too deeply did he drink of these sixteenth and seventeenth century writers. Old-world ways of thought and expression were absorbed quite sincerely, but this to outsiders seemed distinctly affected. The Romanticism of that day would send an enthusiastic student back to those authors, sacred and secular, who flourished before eighteenth century "Enlightenment" prescribed clarity and order.

Would that Irving had been able to undertake the travel and study in Germany that he hinted in his letter to the Rev. John Martin! In his lodgings in dusty Bristo Street, he remembered the kindly comfort of Kirkcaldy Manse, urged Andrew and David to keep up their reading and begged Mrs. Martin to accept the present of a bed, "a cumbrous and inelegant memorial but the first article of furniture of which I was possessed". "But let me dignify it what I can," he adds quaintly, "by the fervent prayer that while it appertains to your household it may always support a healthful body, and pillow a sound head, and shed its warmth over a warm and honest heart."

His heart, however, was turning back to Haddington. His despondency was somewhat alleviated by visits to his friends there. His "dear and lovely pupil" had by this time grown into a charming girl of eighteen, more fascinating than any of the maidens of Fife. As a matter of fact, he had only entered into a kind of half-engagement to Isabella Martin. Much more was made of this in Scotland a century ago than to-day, especially in old-fashioned manses like the Martin's. Mr. Martin distrusted the unconventional streak in Irving's character, though he could not help liking him. He refused to release him from what he considered an engagement—an unwise act, surely. Pledges given at Kirkcaldy bound Irving's honour, but could not bind his heart. He was uneasy but felt that in course of time he might be honourably released from this obligation. But with his poor prospects, this uneasiness sometimes caused him acute depression.

At times he thought vaguely of the Mission Field. He could be no conventional missionary, returning periodically to an expectant Exeter Hall, with his due tale of conversions. But might he not be a missionary of more apostolic spirit, "without scrip and without purse"? (after a winter in Edinburgh his savings were coming to an end). These thoughts were passing through his mind when he received an unexpected invitation to preach for Dr. Andrew Thomson in the fashionable Charlotte Square church where he had once brought his pupils from Haddington. This invitation was supported by the information that the great Dr. Chalmers would be present and was wanting an assistant. He preached at St. George's (quite acceptably, he thought), but day after day passed without a word from Chalmers. He decided that the only thing to do was to pack up and leave for Annan, by one of the coasting vessels that called at the Solway ports. Sick at heart and buried in his own thoughts, he took the wrong boat at Greenock and had to come ashore. He saw a steamer (still a novelty in 1819) in all the bustle of departure. With sudden caprice he went on board, feeling that he must *do* something. He discovered that the boat was bound for Belfast. On arrival he was arrested on suspicion of being a notable criminal who was *wanted* by the police. Appearances were certainly against the brawny stranger, travelling with only a knapsack and without any confessed motive. Fortunately a Presbyterian minister, Mr. Hanna (father of Dr. Chalmers' biographer) intervened and took him off to his hospitable manse. He then spent some weeks in Ireland, walking from place to place (as the crow flies) and sharing the peasant's milk and potatoes with abandon. He had no idea what course to take and felt that at all costs he must have a breathing-space. To his surprise he found at Coleraine a bulky enclosure from his father; it contained a letter from Dr. Chalmers.

The date was several weeks back and the invitation to go to Glasgow by no means as definite as he would have liked. "It was enough, however, to stir the reviving heart of the young giant, whom his fall, and contact with kindly mother earth, had refreshed and re-invigorated"(Ol. I. 96). He returned to Glasgow, to find the Doctor out of town. There was nothing to do but to await his return. In this state of suspense he wrote a characteristic letter to the Martins at Kirkcaldy.

"Glasgow, 1st September, 1819.

". . . Here, then, I am a very sorry sight, I can assure you. You may remember how disabled in my rigging I was in the Kingdom (i.e. of Fife); conceive me, then, to have wandered a whole fortnight among the ragged sons of St. Patrick, to have scrambled about the Giant's Causeway, and sailed in fish-boats and pleasure-boats, and driven gigs and jaunting-cars, and never once condescended to ask the aid of a tailor's needle. Think of this, and figure what I must be now. But I have just been ordered a refit from stem to stern, and shall by to-morrow be able to appear amongst the best of them; and you know the Glasgow bodies ken fu' weel it's merely impossible to carry about with ane a' the comforts of the Sa't Market at ane's tail, or a' the comforts of Bond St. either. I shall certainly now remain till I have seen and finally determined with Dr. Chalmers. . . ."

In October, 1819, at the age of twenty-seven, Irving began his work as assistant to the great Dr. Chalmers in St. John's parish, Glasgow. At last he had scope for his titanic energy. His figure was not long in attracting attention. "*That* Mr. Irving! That Dr. Chalmers' helper! I took him for a cavalry officer!" "I think he maun be a Hieland chief." "Do you know, Doctor, what people are saying about your new assistant? They say he's like a brigand chief." "Well, well," said Dr. Chalmers with a smile, "whatever they say, they never think him like anything but a leader of men." There was a note of authority in Irving's manner which seemed "very peculiar" to the matter-of-fact citizens of Glasgow. They had never come across a minister (still less an assistant) who, when calling, gave the apostolic blessing, "Peace be unto this house!" and laid his hands on bairns' heads with the words, "The Lord bless thee and keep thee!" Irving was diffident when it came to preaching, however; "I will preach to them if you think fit, but if they bear with my preaching they will be the first people who have borne with it." (Had he not been sincere, he would surely have changed his style to suit the popular fancy.) Whenever he was to preach, groups of people could be seen leaving the church, disappointed that it was not "the doctor himsel'". The assistant, however, was not greatly mortified; he quite realised the natural preference that would be accorded to such a shining light. But he did not like the patronising attitude of the congregation, who were well enough pleased with the "helper" since the Doctor had chosen him. The Doctor's own opinion was: "Irving's preaching is like Italian music, appreciated only by connoisseurs" (an occasional student in a scarlet gown could be seen in the gallery drinking in every word Irving said). The assistant's temperament was so different from the minister's that there could never be complete understanding.

"The statesman and philosopher watches the poet-enthusiast with a doubtful, troubled, half-amused, half-sad perplexity;— likes him, yet does not know what he would be at; is embarrassed by his warm love, praise and gratitude;—vexed to see him commit himself;—impatient of what he himself thinks credulity, vanity, waste of power; but never without a sober, regretful affection for the bright unsteady light that could not be persuaded to shine only in its proper lantern." (Ol. I. 116f.).

Irving's opinion of Chalmers is expressed in a letter to Carlyle which makes clear the fact that he realised the danger of popular applause:—

"Every minister in Glasgow is an oracle to a certain class of devotees. . . . Dr. Chalmers, though a most entire original by himself, is surrounded with a very prosaical sort of persons, who please me something by their zeal to carry into effect his philosophical schemes, and vex me much by their idolatry of him. My comforts are in hearing the distresses of the people, and doing my mite to alleviate them. . . ." (14th March, 1820.)

The year 1819 was a time of great hardship in Glasgow. Unemployment and underpayment were rife; industrialism was making for the most degraded conditions of labour and housing; discontent came to a head in the "radical rising" at Bonnymuir. There was talk of "midnight meetings, pikes and secret committees". Elderly gentlemen with powdered hair would speak in an exultant undertone about "Cordon of troops, sir". Every reasonable reform was confused with "sedition" by the authorities. The Town Council was a municipal oligarchy, self-appointed.

Chalmers was hard at work trying to adapt the parochial system to the complex needs of a great city—one of the bravest anachronisms in social history. He would take over the burden of poor-relief in his parish, and other parishes would follow his example. He would minister to the physical, educational needs of the people and meet the cost, partly by appealing to the independence of those he sought to help, partly by collections at the church "plate". St. John's parish, with its 10,000 souls, was divided into manageable districts under elders and deacons, who were to be assisted by teachers and social workers. It is impossible here to describe that noble experiment (*v.* Chalmers' *Problems of Poverty*, Nelson's Selection). One can only refer to Irving's share. He had no economic or ecclesiastical theories as to the cure of social problems. He was only aware of human need, as he went in and out of the three hundred families whose pastoral care he had undertaken.

Such an experience, you say, would have made a realist of any potential visionary. "Peace be with you here!"—"Ay, sir, if there's plenty wi't!" cried an angry little weaver. But the ugliness, filth and ignorance of Glasgow slums only served to draw out Irving's antique chivalry. How he endeared himself to the poverty-stricken Calton weavers! He would go into the most wretched wynds and up the dirtiest stairs and would sometimes be "the partaker of their miserable cheer"; he would help a tired pedlar to carry his heavy pack; he would distribute a pound a day of a £100 legacy till it was all spent (an act of Quixotic generosity at which Chalmers the economist must have smiled sadly). I like the story of Irving and the radical, infidel shoemaker. This worthy would turn his back when the "helper" called, while his wife made her deprecating curtsy in the foreground. One day Irving took up a piece of patent leather (then a recent invention) and remarked upon it in technical terms. The shoemaker paid no attention and went on working with redoubled energy, exasperated by this pretence of knowledge.

"What do ye ken about leather?" he demanded without raising his eyes. That was just the opportunity that Irving wanted, for he was a tanner's son though minister and scholar. Gradually mollified, the cobbler slackened work and listened intently as his visitor described some process of manufacturing shoes by machinery. At last came the remark, "Od, you're a decent kind o' fellow! do *you* preach?" The advantage was discreetly pursued. On the following Sunday the rebel made a shy, defiant appearance at church. Next day Irving encountered him in the Gallowgate, and laying his hand on the shirt-sleeve of the shrunken, sedentary workman, he walked by his side along the busy street. By the time they parted not a spark of resistance was left in the shoemaker. His children hence forth went to school. His deprecating wife went in peace to church and he accompanied her—in "Sabbath blacks". He would always say, when Irving's name was mentioned, "He's a sensible man, yon; he kens aboot leather!"

Irving's attitude in higher circles was as commanding and dignified as among "the lower orders". There was something sacerdotal in his manner that surprised and impressed. Some witling at a Glasgow dinner party, after profanity that would hardly be tolerated nowadays, directed his offensive discourse to Irving, as the representative of priestcraft and superstition. Irving heard him out in silence and turned to the other listeners. "My friends, I will make no reply to this unhappy youth, who hath attacked the Lord in the person of His servant; but let us pray that this his sin may not be laid to his charge." Then, with a solemn motion of his hand (which the awe-struck guests instinctively obeyed) he rose up to his full majestic height and solemnly commended the offender to the forgiveness of God.

During his Glasgow days the vigorous assistant seems to have realised that "the bow too tensely strung is easily broken". He would recruit his strength by excursions —now down the Clyde with Robert Story of Rosneath, now in the depths of Ayrshire, now in distant parts of Ireland. He was enjoying himself in Ireland so hugely that he quite forgot he had agreed to meet a Glasgow friend at Annan, with a view to showing him the moors and mosses of Dumfriesshire. The friend arrived at the Irvings' house and waited on, day after day. Mrs. Irving was hospitable but anxious. The friend, however, did not "weary", for he became very interested in Edward's youngest sister who had been detailed to show the stranger the beauties of Annan. When Edward turned up in a fortnight's time, he discovered an engaged couple waiting to be congratulated! It was a happy conclusion to his own carelessness. One could tell innumerable stories of the impression he made by his splendid physique. A ferryman once mistook him for a man on horseback. A family rising from their knees after prayers were affrighted by the surprising apparition of a tall figure, who uttered the blessing, "Peace be unto this house!" On one occasion he leaped ashore at Govan Ferry—with success but at the cost of damage to his nether garments. Hard by stood a cottage tenanted by a certain Nanny Campbell, whose husband was a tailor. There he sat for an hour charming the rustic couple with his discourse till the rent was repaired, garbed meantime in "Nanny's best Sunday petticoat" (according to local tradition). He was a frequent visitor at Govan manse when Govan was a sequestered rural place, not yet a grim industrial area. He had met the minister, Matthew Leishman, at Bolton manse. Leishman in after days had many a tale of Irving, both grave and gay. One wishes his friendship had been even closer, for Leishman's influence was salutary for Irving's temperament.

Irving was always a welcome guest at Haddington. The doctor had died in 1819 ("A very valiant man," said Irving). Mrs. Welsh felt that the former tutor was a link with old times. Towards the end of May, 1821, Irving took Carlyle out to Haddington and introduced him to the Welshes. Carlyle could not remember much about the journey, but never forgot the *end* of it.

"Ah me, ah me!—I think there had been, before this, on Irving's own part some movements of negotiation over to Kirkcaldy for *release* there, and of hinted hope towards Haddington, which was so infinitely preferable! And something (as I used to gather long afterwards) might have come of it, had not Kirkcaldy been so peremptory, and stood by its bond (as spoken or as written), 'Bond or utter Ruin, Sir!'—upon which Irving had honourably submitted and resigned himself. He seemed to be quite composed upon the matter by this time. I remember in our inn at Haddington that first night, a little passage: we had just seen, in the Minister's house (whom Irving was to *preach* for), a certain shining Miss Augusta,—tall, shapely, airy, giggly, but a consummate fool, whom I have heard called 'Miss *Disgusta*' by the satirical;—we were now in our double-bedded room, George Inn, Haddington, stripping, or perhaps each already in his bed, when Irving jocosely said to me, 'What would you take to marry Miss Augusta now?' 'Not for an entire and perfect chrysolite the size of this terraqueous Globe!' answered I at once, with hearty laughter from Irving.—'And what would you take to marry Miss Jeannie, think you?' 'Hah, I should not be so hard to deal with there I should imagine!' upon which another bit of laugh from Irving; and we composedly went to sleep. I was supremely dyspeptic and out of health, during those three or four days; but they were the beginning of a new life to me" (*C.R.*, p. 223f.).

Carlyle returned to Edinburgh and wrote his first letter to Jane Welsh on 4th June. He could not have appeared at a more propitious moment, Jane was an heiress on a small scale and had many suitors. Yet she wrote to her friend Bess Stodart on 8th March: "A visit from any man with brains in his head would be an act of mercy here"; and at the end of May, within seven weeks of her twentieth birthday, she wrote to her, "I'll die a virgin if I reach twenty in vain" (*Early Letters of J. W. Carlyle*, ed. D. G. Ritchie, pp. 25 and 31).

Carlyle never forgot Irving's "crowning kindness". He had introduced him to Jane Welsh and afterwards encouraged the couple to meet in London, knowing Mrs. Welsh's antipathy to Ecclefechan manners. Irving was sure that keen-witted Jane would enjoy the original genius of Carlyle. She did so to such an extent that he was alarmed at the possibility of her being "indoctrinated" by the heterodox writers they were studying together. During the summer of 1821 he wrote to Carlyle:—

"I would like to see her surrounded with a more sober set of companions than Rousseau (your friend), and Byron and such like. They will never make different characters than they were themselves, so deeply are they the prototypes of their own conceptions of character. And I don't think it will much mend the matter when you get her introduced to Von Schiller and Von Goethe[1] and your other nobles of German literature. I fear Jane has dipped too deep into that spring already, so that unless some more solid food be afforded I fear she will escape altogether out of the region of my sympathies and the sympathies of honest, home-bred men. In these feelings I know you will join me; and in giving to her character a useful and elegant turn you will aid me as you have opportunity."

This letter reveals Irving's singular lack of jealousy. Carlyle was spending a good deal of time with Jane and Jane's intellect was showing affinity to Carlyle's. But it was only the intellectual side of the companionship that Irving objected to—it was too heterodox! In the same letter, he passes directly to the friendship that meant so much to the two young men:—

"I have been analysing, as I could, the origin of my esteem and affection for you. You are no more a favourite than I am, and in the general points of character we are not alike, nor yet alike in the turn of our general thoughts; and we are both too intrepid to seek in each other pity or consolation, and too independent to let anything sinister or selfish enter into our attachments. How comes it to pass then, that we have so much pleasant communion? I'll tell you one thing. High literature is exiled from my sphere, and simple principle is very much exiled from yours. Thus we feel a blank on both sides, which is supplied in some measure when we meet. I'll tell you another thing. Severed from the ordinary stays of men, influence, place,

[1] Irving regarded Goethe as an idle Singer, a neo-pagan. But he read *Wilhelm Meister* and observed to Dr. John Carlyle: "Very curious—here are some pages about Christ and the Christian Religion, which, as I study and re-study them, have more sense than I have found in all the Theologians I ever read!" T. Carlyle comments: "Was not this a noble thing for such a man to feel and say?" (*C.R.*, p. 306f).

fortune, each in his way has been obliged to hang his hopes upon something higher; and though we have not chosen the same thing, in both cases it is pure and unearthly, and next to his own the thing which the other admires most. I can easily see that in the progress of our thoughts and characters there will be ample room for toleration and charity, which will form the touchstone of our esteem" (Froude, I, 137f.).

Irving's austerity was mingled with light-heartedness: Carlyle's lacked relief. An old Haddington nurse, speaking of Mrs. Carlyle before her marriage, said:—

"Ah! when she was young, she was a fleein', dancin', light-heartit thing, Jeanie Welsh, that naething would hae dauntit. But she grew grave a' at once. There was Maister Irving, ye ken, that had been her teacher; and he cam aboot her. Then there was Maister——. Then there was Maister Carlyle himsel'; and he came to finish her off like. . . . (quoted by Mrs. A. Ireland, *Life of Jane Welsh Carlyle*, 1891, p. 106f.).

In the previous spring Carlyle had spent a few days with Irving in Glasgow. He had watched the opulent merchants sauntering about and reading their newspapers in the Tontine. He had seen for himself the appalling condition of the poor and agreed with Irving that "if timeous remedies come not soon they will sink into the degradation of the Irish poor". But he thought his friend scarcely did Chalmers justice: "Never preacher went so into one's heart." They had some private talk, the doctor explaining to him "some new scheme for proving the truth of Christianity, all written in us already *in sympathetic ink ;* Bible awakens it, and you can read". Irving accompanied his friend fifteen miles on his long tramp to Ecclefechan. They started early and breakfasted at the manse of a Mr. French. Their way lay over Drumclog Moss, a silent moor brown with "peat hags", its Covenanting memories lately renewed by Scott's description of the battle—"the bog probably wetter in those days," observed Carlyle, "clearly a good place for Cameronian preaching, and dangerously difficult for Claverse and horse soldiery if 'the suffering remnant' had a few old muskets among them!" On they went, holding high converse and forgetful of the passing of time.

"The talk had grown ever friendlier," said Carlyle. "At length the declining sun said plainly, You must part. . . . We leant our backs to a drystane dyke, and looking into the western radiance continued in talk yet a while loth both of us to go. It was just here as the sun was sinking, Irving actually drew from me by degrees, in the softest manner, the confession that I did not think as he of the Christian religion, and that it was vain for me to expect I ever could or should. . . . He had pre-engaged to take well of me like an elder brother, if I would be frank with him, and right loyally he did so, and to the end of his life. we needed no concealments on that head, which was really a step gained. The sun was about setting when we turned away each on his own path. Irving would have a good space further to go than I . . . and would not be in Kent Street till towards midnight. But he feared no amount of walking, enjoyed it rather, as did I in those young years. I felt sad, but affectionate and good, in my clean, utterly quiet little inn at Muirkirk. . . ." (*C.R.*, p. 225f.)

Dark days lay ahead for Carlyle. He was living in poverty in Edinburgh, subsisting on irregular fees for articles and German translating. His range of ideas was so extended as to make him impatient of the trammels of any profession but letters. Adversity was embittering his life and he badly needed a faithful friend. He had good cause to say in later life, "But for Irving I had never known what the communion of man with man meant." He found in Irving an elder brother. As for Irving, he was alarmed for his friend's future; he saw that his faults of peevishness and cynicism were fostered by a lack of real faith in God. In December, 1821, he pressed him to come to Glasgow and be his guest for an indefinite time. In these days it was Carlyle, not Irving, who was nervous and abnormal, and needed to be told to "pull himself together". A few examples may be quoted out of many:—

"You live too much in an ideal world, and you are likely to be punished for it by an unfitness for practical life."

"I pray you may not again talk of your distresses in so desperate, and to me, disagreeable, manner. My dear Sir, is it to be doubted that you are suffering grievously the want of spiritual communion, the bread and water of the soul? and why, then, do you, as it were, mock at your calamity or treat it jestingly? I declare this is a sore offence." (Letter, 15th March, 1821.)

Irving had the insight to recognise Carlyle's genius when he was unknown and discouraged. We find him writing on 26th April, 1821:—

"I am beginning to see the dawn of that day when you shall be plucked by the literary world from my solitary, and therefore more clear, admiration; and when from almost a monopoly. I shall have nothing but a mere shred of your praise. They will unearth you, and for your sake I will rejoice, though for my own I may regret. But I shall always have the pleasant superiority that I was your friend and admirer, through good and through bad report, to continue, so I hope, unto the end. Yet our honest Demosthenes (Dr. Chalmers), or shall I call him Chrysostom (Boanerges would fit him better), seems to have caught some glimpse of your inner man, though he had few opportunities; for he never ceases to be inquiring after you. You will soon shift your quarters, though for the present I think your motto should be, 'Better a wee bush than na bield'."

On 23rd February, 1823: "Remember London is your destination . . . Scotland breeds men, but England rears them."

Irving's own prospects at this time were none too bright. He had a secure assistantship, but was merely one of a horde of probationers who swooped down on available "livings" every year. There were loaves and fishes in the Church, but what were these among so many? There was no more unworldly probationer than Edward Irving. He was uninterested in fat stipends and glebes. He had no liking for the system of Patronage that made the minister the nominee of a laird or Town Council. But he did long for a free field in which he might sound his own clarion, fight his own battle and lead his own followers. He was overshadowed by mighty Chalmers and unsatisfied by the social ideals and consecrated personality of even so great a Scotsman. He had seen something of Scottish Evangelicalism at its best in Edinburgh, but it failed to appeal to him. He felt that in Scotland there was too much dull formalism, timid orthodoxy, and unworthy compromise. His thoughts turned to a ministry abroad. He would have accepted a call from a Presbyterian congregation in Kingston, Jamaica, but for the opposition of his friends. He was spoken of as a likely successor to Dr. Mason in New York. What really fired his imagination was an unexpected call in the spring of 1822 to the Caledonian Chapel, London. It was an insignificant congregation, but was not London the metropolis? To the vacancy committee he wrote, after preaching as candidate: "If you desire my services among you, then I am ready at any call and almost on any conditions, for my own spirit is bent to preach the Gospel in London." In tense expectancy and yet in weariness he wrote to the Rev. John Martin, of Kirkcaldy: "There are a few things that bind me to the world, a very few; one is to make a demonstration for a higher type of Christianity—something more heroical, more magnanimous than this age affects. God knows with what success."

The call accepted, Irving spent a week with his friend, the minister of Rosneath. Full of vitality as usual, he leaped a gate near the manse. "Dear me, Irving," Story exclaimed, "I did not think you had been so agile!" Irving turned on him. "Once I read you an essay of mine and you said, 'Dear me, Irving, I did not think you had been so classical'; another time you heard me preach, 'Dear me, Irving, I did not know you had so much imagination'. Now you shall see what great things I will do yet!" And so the friends talked on, chaffing each other, and Irving made his usual witticisms at the expense of "the common stock of dry theology" and "the certificated soundness of dry men." As they crossed the Gairloch, he remarked: "You are content to go back and forward on the same route like this boat, but as for me, I hope yet to go deep into the ocean of truth."

So Irving returned to Glasgow and preached his farewell sermon at St. John's, telling his hearers of the "imperfections which had not been hidden from their eyes" and thanking them for their forbearance. Mrs. Chalmers thought his panegyric on the doctor rather fulsome, for she laid hands on the manuscript and toned it down before it reached the printer's hands! The minister-elect was then presented with a watch; at his request it was the work of a watchmaker whose chief qualification was the fact that he was an Annandale man! Then followed his ordination by the Presbytery of Annan in the parish church where he was baptised and was to be finally deposed. He had the good sense to take a thorough spring holiday at home before leaving for the south. To his friend, Mr. David Hope, he wrote on 28th May, 1822:

"I am snugly seated in this Temple of Indolence, and very loath to be invaded by any of the distractions of the busy city. I would fain . . . meditate from a distance the busy scene

I have left and the more busy scene to which I am bound. My mind seems formed for inactivity. I can saunter the whole day from field to field, riding on impressions and the transient thoughts they awaken, with no companion of books or men, saving, perhaps, a little nephew or niece in my hand."

His last evening he spent with Carlyle in the coffee-room of the Black Bull Hotel, Glasgow, just before Christmas, 1821; he was to start by early coach next day.

"He showed me old Sir Harry Moncrieff's Testimonial; a Reverend old Presbyterian Scotch Baronet, of venerable quality (the last of his kind) whom I knew well by sight, and by his universal character for integrity, honest orthodoxy, shrewdness and veracity; Sir Harry testified with brevity, in stiff firm, ancient hand, several important things on Irving's behalf; and ended by saying, 'All this is my true opinion, and meant to be understood as it is written!' At which we had our bit of approving laugh, and thanks to Sir Harry. Irving did not laugh that night; laughter was not the mood of either of us. I gave him as road-companion a bundle of the best cigars I almost ever had: he had no practice of smoking; but could a little, by a time, and agreed that on the Coach-roof, where he was to ride night and day, a cigar might be tried with advantage. Months afterwards, I learnt he had begun by losing every cigar of them,—left the whole bundle lying on our seat in the Stall of the Coffee-room;— this cigar-gift: being probably our last transaction there. We said farewell: and I had in some measure, according to my worst anticipation, *lost* my friend's society (not my friend himself ever), from that time." (*C.R.*, p. 231f.)

CHAPTER III

"THE CELEBRATED IRVING"

> "A singular phenomenon appeared in the religious world. . . . A Presbyterian minister came to an obscure place of worship in the metropolis and took all ranks by storm. Irving went far beyond Whitefield in attracting the notice of lords, ladies and commoners. His name was on every lip; newspapers, magazines and reviews discussed his merits; and caricatures in shop windows hit off his eccentricities."—
> Dr. Stoughton, Church Historian.

THE Caledonian Chapel, Cross Street, Hatton Garden (in the wastes of Holborn) was one of the newest but least notable congregations in the Scots Presbytery of London, which included churches like Crown Court, London Wall, and Swallow Street. It has passed through various hands. Erected in 1796 as the first Swedenborgian Temple in London, and tenanted by Baptists and Anglican seceders in turn, it was purchased by managers of a fund for Gaelic preaching and was taken over in 1816 by the Caledonian Asylum, an orphanage for Scottish children. The Asylum directors thought it possible to start a new congregation, the minister to act as chaplain to the institution, to preach on Sundays in English and also in Gaelic as required. The relation of the "Asylum" to the congregation was rather complicated, especially in view of the Gaelic Preaching Fund. A lucid account is given by Mr. John Hair in his interesting history of Regent Square Church (Nisbet, 1899). The author explains the origin of the Caledonian congregation, describes its eventual transfer to Regent Square and corrects some of Mrs. Oliphant's inaccuracies (v. p.33n.). The real difficulty was to find a good bilingual preacher. The first minister, the Rev. James Boyd (father of the better known "A.K.H.B.") preached acceptably in Gaelic and English, but after a year was presented to the parish of Auchinleck. Before leaving London he baptised John Ruskin, who was born on 8th February, 1819. His successor, the Rev. Allan Macnaughton, possessed the necessary qualifications, but resigned in 1820.

After a year's vacancy (v. p.111) the congregation had dwindled to about fifty and the committee was willing to recommend a non-Gaelic preacher if the language difficulty could be surmounted. They were glad to ask Dr. Chalmer's assistant "to make trial and proof of his gifts". So on 24th December, 1821, Irving came up to London. He was cordially received and preached his trial sermon, with the Duke of York (president of the Caledonian Asylum) as one of his hearers. After a month in London he wrote in high spirits to Jane Welsh:

"My Dear and Lovely Pupil . . . know now, though late, that my head is almost turned with the approbation I received—certainly my head is turned; for from being a poor desolate creature, melancholy of success, yet steel against misfortune, I have become all at once full of hope and activity. My hours of study have doubled themselves; my intellect, long unused to expand itself, is now awakening again, and truth is revealing itself to my mind. And perhaps the dreams and longings of my fair correspondent may yet be realised. I have been solicited to publish a discourse which I delivered before the Duke of York, but have refused till my apprehensions of truth be larger, and my treatment of it more according to the models of modern and ancient times. The thanks of all the directors I have received formally—the gift from the congregation of the Bible used by His Royal Highness. The elders paid my expenses in a most princely style. My countrymen of the first celebrity, especially in art, welcomed me to their society and the first artist in the city drew a most admirable half-length miniature of me in action."

The artist was Andrew Robertson, an enthusiastic member of the Highland Society of London, an originator of the Caledonian Asylum and Chapel. We reproduce his fine likeness of Irving, representing him in the Caledonian pulpit in the prime of early manhood.

It is a contrast to turn from the hopeful young minister to the embarrassed office-bearers, anxious to appoint the man who would redeem their church from failure, but held in the meshes of a legal document which the Gaelic trustees refused to relax. How were they to get round the Trust Deed which insisted on Gaelic preaching? Irving intervened.

"Now here is what I propose," he wrote (22nd February, 1822), "that if the directors do wish me, and will wait for me till by dint of all my powers I can acquire Gaelic, I shall forthwith remove myself to Glenfinlas, near the Trossachs, where I am well known, and domesticate myself among the hospitable Stewarts there, and apply myself to the Celtic tongue."

Happily the committee did not need to consider seriously this magnanimous proposal! Pending the passage of a Bill through Parliament, the congregation decided to rent the Caledonian Chapel from the Asylum directors and invite Mr. Irving to begin his ministry. Standing on the threshold of this ministry, he was rather depressed and distrustful of the future; the delay would have much to do with it. To one of the office-bearers he wrote:—

"There is a sea of troubles, for my notions of a clergyman's office are not common, nor likely to be in everything approved. There is a restlessness in my mind after a state of life less customary, more enterprising, more heroical, certainly more apostolical. My notions of pulpit eloquence differ from many of my worthy brethren. In truth I am an adventurer on ground untried, and therefore am full of anxieties. . . . Oh! many things distress me which cannot be told, and kill all ambitions, at least denude them of their glare. These also the Lord will help me through, if I trust Him."

This letter reveals Irving's visionary bias. It reveals undue self-consciousness. It reveals also the danger of undefined aims of heroic achievement. Even at this early stage in his career, with surprising success ahead, one can observe an erratic strain in his personality that was later to prove his ruin.

At length, all obstacles overcome, Irving was inducted on 16th October, 1822, as ordained minister of the Caledonian Chapel. His first sermon was from a text unforgettable under the circumstances (Acts 10, 29): "Therefore came I unto you without gainsaying, as soon as I was sent for: I ask therefore for what intent ye have sent for me?" Those who heard this sermon were the fifty members who had signed the call and a few Scotsmen drawn by curiosity or friendship. Among these were artists like Wilkie and Robertson. They in turn brought their friends, e.g., Sir Thomas Lawrence and Mr. John de Fleury. Andrew Robertson had once taken Mr. De Fleury to the Caledonian Chapel during Mr. Boyd's ministry. Later, he asked, "Well, how are you getting on at the Caledonian?" "Oh," came the reply, "there's an extraordinary man coming up from Scotland to be our minister who will astonish all London.' Shortly after this, the Anglican church where Mr. De Fleury worshipped was closed for repairs, so he said to his wife, "I think I will go and see if Andrew Robertson's extraordinary man has arrived yet." He sat in one of the side pews and was much struck by the resemblance of Irving's profile to representations of our Lord. He was deeply moved by prayer and preaching; it was the new minister's first sermon in Cross Street. He went back for several Sundays. Then his wife said, "My dear, it will never do for you to go to one church and me to another. I will go and hear Andrew Robertson's extraordinary man too." She did so. That very week they became seatholders and afterwards faithful members. There was something in Irving that appealed to one who was an artist and the proud descendant of a Huguenot.

Letters give us glimpses of the young minister after his settlement in London. From his lodgings in Bloomsbury he writes to Mr. Graham, of Burnswark:—

"You cannot conceive how happy I am here in the possession of my own thoughts, in the liberty of my own conduct and in the favour of the Lord. The people have received me with open arms; the church is already regularly filled; my preaching, though on the average of one hour and a quarter, listened to with the most serious attention, my mind plentifully endowed with thought and feeling, my life ordered as God enables me after His holy Word, my store supplied out of His abundant liberality. These are the elements of my happiness, for which I am bound to render unmeasured thanks."

To a Glasgow friend, David Hope, he writes that he has no time for vain speculation, being engrossed with things strictly professional.

"You are not more regular at the counting-house, nor, I am sure, sooner, neither do you labour more industriously, till four chaps from the Ram's Horn Kirk, than I sit in this my study, and occupy my mind for the benefit of my flock. The evening brings more engagements with it than I can overtake, and so I am kept incessantly active. My engagements have been increased, of late, by looking out for a house to dwell in. I am resolved to be this Ishmaelite no longer, and to have a station of my own upon the face of the earth."

Dr. Chalmers, in the course of one of his rapid journeys through England collecting statistics of pauperism, found time to preach in the Caledonian Chapel, and was able to give a favourable report to his wife:—

"I found Irving in good taking with his charge. He speculates as much as before on modes of preaching; is quite independent with his people, and has most favourably impressed such men as Zachary Macaulay and Mr. Cunningham (of Lainshaw). . . . He is happy and free, and withal making his way to a very good congregation."

In another letter he added:

"I hope he will not hurt his usefulness by any kind of eccentricity or impudence."

A series of unpublished letters from Irving in his early London days to Carlyle has recently come into the possession of the National Library of Scotland. Several of these are reproduced in an illuminating article by Mr. W. Forbes Gray (*The Scotsman*, 7th December, 1934). Irving gives unrestrained expression to his feelings; tells how he goes out of his way to deal adequately and cogently with the subjects he handled in his sermons so that they might convince "the young and thoughtful audience" before him; tells how critics have already complained of his "new method of preaching", his preference for Scotch hearers and his aloofness from the Evangelicals. He concludes: "I take my place here slowly but I think securely." This state of quiet progress did not last more than a year.

One Sunday in 1823 the little chapel was invaded by a host of distinguished strangers; no one connected with the congregation was prepared for it. The cause of this amazing influx was a reference made by George Canning in the House of Commons. Church revenues were being discussed and the connection between high talent and high *pay* was emphasised by speaker after speaker. Canning told the house that, so far from this being universal, he had himself recently heard the most eloquent sermon he had ever listened to, preached by a Scotch minister trained in one of the most poorly endowed Churches and now officiating in one of her outlying dependencies. How did Canning find his way to the Caledonian Chapel? In a conversation with his friend Sir James Mackintosh, he heard of a touching expression the new Scottish preacher had used in prayer for a family who had lost their parents: "We pray for these orphans who are now thrown upon the Fatherhood of God." Canning started at the expression and asked Mackintosh to take him to the Caledonian Chapel the very next Sunday (*Life of Sir James Mackintosh*, by his son, Vol. II, p. 478).

The crowds came to hear Irving—and not merely on one occasion. According to a contemporary account:—

"Sunday after Sunday the mean-looking, dingy chapel was thronged with statesmen, philosophers, poets, painters, and literary men; peers, merchants and fashionable ladies were mingled with shopkeepers and mechanics, while many hundreds were unable to obtain admission."

The Duke of Sussex, the Earl of Aberdeen, Sir James Graham—even the Tory Premier, Lord Liverpool—were among Irving's frequent hearers. Mr. Gillespie, one of the embarrassed office-bearers, tells that on one Sunday not less than thirty-five carriages with coronets were counted, beside those of commoners; the line of carriages often extending down Hatton Garden almost to Holborn. People had to be admitted by ticket; ladies were glad to sit on the pulpit stairs; every available inch of standing-room was occupied in a building seated for six hundred. On one occasion W. E. Gladstone, then a schoolboy, was taken by his father to hear Irving and from a comfortable seat in the front gallery, secured beforehand, surveyed at ease and leisure the struggling crowds below.

"The crush was everywhere great, but greatest of all in the centre aisle. Here the mass of human beings, mercilessly compressed, swayed continuously backwards and forwards. . . . What was my emotion, my joy, my exultation, when I espied among this humiliated mass, struggling and buffeted—whom but Keate! Keate, the master of our existence, the tyrant of our days! . . . Such a reversal of human conditions of being, as that now exhibited between the Eton lower boy uplifted to the luxurious gallery pew, and the headmaster, whom I was accustomed to see in the roomy desk of the upper school with vacant space and terror all around him, it must be hard for anyone to conceive, except the two who were the subjects of it. Never, never, have I forgotten that moment" (Morley's *Life of Gladstone*, Vol. I).

"What went" the people "out for to see?" With George Gilfillan as guide, let us pay a morning visit to the Caledonian Chapel:—

"You go a full hour before eleven, and find that you are not too early. Having forced your way in with difficulty, you find yourself in a nest of celebrities—almost every person of note or notoriety in London. There shines the fine open glossy brow and speaking face of Canning. There you see the small shrimp-like form of Wilberforce, the high Roman nose of Peel, and the stern forehead of Plunket. There Brougham sits coiled up in his critical might, his whole bearing denoting eager but somewhat sinister expectation. Yonder you see a venerable man with mild placid face and long grey hair; it is Jeremy Bentham coming to hear his own system abused as with the tongue of thunder. Near him, note that thin spiritual-looking little old individual, with philosophic countenance and large brow; it is Godwin, the author of 'Caleb Williams'. In a seat behind him sits a yet more meagre skeleton of man, with a pale face, eager eyes and nervous aspect; it is the first of living critics, William Hazlitt, who had 'forgot what the inside of a church was like', but who has been fairly dragged out of his den by the attraction of Irving's eloquence. At the door, and standing, you see a young, short, stout person, carrying his head high with careless schoolboy bearing; it is Macaulay, on vacation from Cambridge. And in a corner, Coleridge—the mighty wizard, with more genius under that white head than is to be found in the whole bright assembly—looks with nebulous eyes upon the scene, which seems to him rather a swimming vision than a solid reality.

"Eleven o'clock strikes, and the beadle appears, bearing the Bible . . . the forerunner of the coming man. There is a rustle, instantly succeeded by deep silence. Edward Irving mounts the pulpit with a measured and dignified pace, as if to some solemn music heard by his ear alone, and, lifting the Psalm-book, calmly confronts that splendid multitude. His expression is very peculiar; it is not that of fear, deference, still less impertinence, anger or contempt. It is simply the look of a man who says internally, 'I am equal to this occasion, in the dignity and power of my own intellect and nature, and MORE than equal to it in the might of my Master, and in the grandeur and truth of my message'. He is a son of Anak in height, and his symmetry is worthy of his stature. His whole aspect is spiritual, earnest, Titanic; yea, that of a Titan among Titans—

a Boanerges among the sons of thunder. He gives out the psalm—perhaps it is his favourite, the twenty-ninth—and as he reads it, his voice seems the echo of the 'Lord's voice upon the waters', so deep and far-rolling are the crashes of its sound. It sinks, too, ever and anon into soft and solemn cadences, so that you hear in it alike the moan and the roar, and feel both the pathos and the majesty of the thunderstorm. Then he reads a portion of Scripture, selecting probably, from a fine instinctive sense of contrast, the twenty-third psalm, to give relief to the grandeurs that have passed or that are at hand. Then he says, 'Let us pray', not as a mere formal preliminary, but because he really wishes to gather up all the devotional feeling of his hearers along with his own, and to present it as a whole burnt-offering to Heaven. Then his voice, 'Like a steam of rich distilled perfumes', rises to God, and you feel as if God had blotted out the church around, and the universe above, that that voice might obtain immediate entrance to His ear.

"The prayer over, he announces his text. The sermon is upon the days of the Puritans' and Covenanters, and his blood boils as he fights over again the battles of Drumclog and Bothwell; he paints the dark muirlands, whither the Woman of the Church retired for a season to be nourished with blood, and you seem to be listening to that wild eloquence which pealed through the wilderness and shook the throne of Charles II. Then he turns to contrast that earnest period and 'our light, empty and profane era', and opens with fearless hand the vials of apocalyptic vengeance against it. He speaks of our 'godless systems of ethics and economics', and Bentham and Godwin shrug their shoulders in unison. He attacks the poetry and criticism of the age, inserting a fierce diatribe against the patrician Byron in the heart of an apology for the hapless ploughman Burns; knocking Southey down into the same kennel into which he had plunged Byron; and striking next at the very heart of Cobbett; and Hazlitt bends his brow into a frown, and you see a sarcasm (to be inserted in the next *Liberal*) crossing the dusky disk of his face. Waxing bolder, and eyeing the peers and peeresses, the orator denounces 'wickedness in high places', and his voice swells into its deepest thunder, and his eye assumes its most portentous glare, as he characterises the falsehood of courtiers, the hypocrisy of statesmen, the hollowness, licentiousness and levity of fashionable life. It is Isaiah or Ezekiel over again, uttering their stern yet musical and poetical burdens. The language is worthy of the message it conveys, not polished indeed, rather rough and diffuse withal, but vehement, figurative, and bedropt with terrible or tender extracts from the Bible. The manner is as graceful as may well co-exist with deep impetuous force, and as solemn as may evade the charge of cant. The voice seems meant for an 'orator of the human race', and fitted to fill vaster buildings than earth contains, and to plead in mightier causes than can even be conceived of in our degenerate days. It is the 'many-folded shell' of Prometheus, including in its compass 'soft and soul-like sounds', as well as loud and victorious peals. The audience feel in contact, not with a mere orator, but with a demoniac force."

Anyone who has read Gilfillan's *Literary Portraits* may be inclined to think that he is merely taking Irving as an excuse for over-indulging in the rich rhetoric so dear to the "Spasmodic School". But the evidence of Irving's contemporaries is as striking. Canning repeatedly declared that he was the most powerful orator, in or out of the pulpit, he ever heard. De Quincey called him "a very demon of power"; there was an untamed energy which ran in his blood and spoke in his private talk and public oratory ("the only man of our times who realised one's idea of Paul preaching at Athens or defending himself before King Agrippa"). Dorothy Wordsworth had not been much impressed by a copy of Irving's *Orations* read at Rydal. But when she actually visited London in 1823, she found the preacher far more attractive than "the Swiss giantess" or "the Mexican Exhibition."

"His person is very fine in my opinion and his action often graceful—though often far otherwise—his voice fine—reading excellent, and, while he keeps his feelings under, nothing can be finer than his manner of preaching—but it is grievous to see him wasting his powers—as he does in the latter part (especially) of his discourses—the more grievous as it is plain he must sink under such exertion while yet a young man. When I say *wasting* his powers . . . I mean that with less effort the effect on his hearers would be more beneficial. He wholly wants taste and judgment—but one essential I give him full credit for—*sincerity*—without which no preaching that would address the feelings can be efficacious" (E. de Sélincourt's *Dorothy Wordsworth*, 1933, p. 364).

Hazlitt gives a shrewd if journalistic estimate of Irving in *The Spirit of the Age* (1825). In the perspective of a century one feels that he was right in setting Irving side by side with such different personalities as Coleridge, Bentham, Southey, Malthus, Jeffrey, Cobbett, Leigh Hunt, and Charles Lamb. For Irving was far more sensitive than most ministers of that time to literary and political currents.

A few years after Hazlitt's book appeared, Irving had withdrawn from the main stream of national life, making his way up an obscure tributary which to him appeared a veritable Jordan. But in his early London ministry he appealed tremendously because he was essentially the Romantic in the pulpit at a time when Evangelicalism was losing influence because it was unimaginative and prosaic.

He is cautiously characterised by Hazlitt as "a burning and a shining light, though perhaps not 'one of the fixed'". The critic thinks that the secret of his success has escaped observation; it is the *transposition of ideas*. If he had kept within the proper bounds of pulpit oratory, he might have been quoted among the godly as a powerful preacher of the Word, but would never have become the cynosure of the metropolis. If he had been a mere author his affectation of an obsolete style would soon have palled. As an actor, he would have had many rivals.

"But he has contrived to jumble these characters together in an unheard-of and unwarranted manner, and the fascination is altogether irresistible. . . . He has converted the meeting-house into a play-house. Without leave asked or licence granted, he has converted the Caledonian Chapel into a Westminster Forum or Debating Society, with the sanction of religion added to it. . . . Instead of drawling out the doctrine of eternal punishment so as to lull men to sleep, he has kindled the expiring flames with the very sweepings of sceptical and infidel libraries so as to excite a pleasing horror in the female part of the congregation."

Hazlitt is a good psychologist in attributing Irving's success to the fact that "he has found out the secret of attracting by repelling".

"Those whom he is likely to attack are curious to hear what he says of them; they go again, to show they do not mind it. . . . He keeps the public in awe by insulting all their favourite idols. He does not spare their politicians, moralists, poets, critics, magazine-writers; he levels their resorts of business, their places of amusement at a blow—their cities, churches, palaces, ranks and professions, refinements and elegances—and leaves nothing standing but himself, a mighty landmark in a degenerate age, overlooking the wide havoc he has made!"

Hazlitt, like most other critics of Irving, finds it difficult to account for his popularity apart from his appearance.

"Conceive a rough, ugly, shock-headed Scotchman, standing up in the Caledonian Chapel, and dealing 'damnation round the land' in a broad northern dialect, what ear polite, what smile serene would have hailed the barbarous prodigy, or not consigned him to utter neglect and derision? But the Rev. Edward Irving, with all his native wildness, 'hath a smooth aspect framed to make women' saints; his very unusual size and height are carried off and moulded into elegance by the most admirable symmetry of form and ease of gesture; his sable locks, his clear iron-grey complexion, and firm-set features, turn the raw uncouth Scotchman into the likeness of a noble Italian picture; and even his distortion of sight only redeems the otherwise 'faultless monster' within the bounds of humanity. . . . His controversial daring is *backed* by his bodily prowess; and by bringing his intellectual pretensions boldly into a line with his physical accomplishments, he, indeed, presents a very formidable front to the sceptic or the scoffer. Take a cubit from his stature, and his whole manner resolves itself into an impertinence."

Hazlitt goes on to compare Irving and Chalmers—the latter being "a monkey-preacher" so far as appearance was concerned, but possessing continuity of thought and matter, while the former shone only by patches and in bursts.

"These two celebrated preachers are in almost all respects an antithesis to each other. If Mr. Irving is an example of what can be done by the help of external advantages Dr. Chalmers is a proof of what can be done without them. The one is most indebted to his mind, the other to his body. If Mr. Irving inclines one to suspect fashionable or popular religion of a little *anthropomorphitism*, Dr. Chalmers effectually redeems it from that scandal."

In this connection, it is interesting to recall Carlyle's comparison of Irving and Chalmers:—

"Irving's discourses were far more opulent in ingenious thought than Chalmers', which, indeed, were usually the triumphant on-rush of *one* idea with its satellites and supporters. But Irving's wanted in definite *head* and *backbone*, so that on arriving you might see clearly where and how. He had 'grand forest-avenues with outlooks to right and left', but not a broadly defined and clearly marked course right through; 'more thoughts than Chalmers, but took less pains in setting them forth'. The uniform custom was, he shut himself up all Saturday; became invisible all that day. Sermon an hour long or more. . . . He always *read*, but not in the least slavishly and made abundant gesticulation in the *right* places. 'Originality and truth of purpose; but withal, both in the manner and matter, a something which might be suspected of affectation—a noticeable preference and search for striking and ancient locutions'. Voice one of the finest —but not a power quite on the heart, as Chalmer's was . . ." (*C.R.*, p. 216f.).

If one asks why Irving subsequently failed so disastrously and Chalmers became the greatest Scottish Churchman of the nineteenth century, one must bear in mind their very different characters. Chalmers, with his feet planted on the solid earth, was sometimes too intent on what was clearly *practical;* he was impatient of idealism that soared too high. But Irving, with his head in the clouds, had the more dangerous fault of waving aside all human impediments and disregarding the considered judgment of mature Christian leaders, besides the advice of friends on whom he could safely rely. Chalmers passed through a definite experience of conversion that set his feet on the rock. Irving claimed to advance in the apprehension of truth, but it was neither a clear rational development nor a simple religious experience. It was a confused, subjective development affected by his peculiar temperament and set a-moving by happenings to which he reacted in a certain morbid way. Chalmers conceived of grace, like Paul, as an emancipation of the heart and conscience from the bondage of self; the crisis of conversion over, his soul became free and his mind "healthy". Unfortunately for Irving, he was disposed to regard grace as flowing to the faithful rather through the ordinances and ministers of the Church. Far from being consciously self-centred, he was apt to overemphasise his own ministry and to imagine that *he* had a special mission to set the world right, as the Lord's prophet. He gradually identified himself so closely with the Lord's purposes that he either ignored opposition or denounced it as the work of knaves or fools. Mr. John Hair, who spent many years in patient, scholarly thought on Irving and his environment, came to this conclusion:—

"If Irvingism is to be traced to its original germ, so far as any system can be traced to an individual, it may be found in Irving's religious experience, and in his consequent mode of apprehending divine truth not by open spiritual vision, but through a human medium" (*Regent Square*, p. 42).

There might be exaggeration and strain in Irving's early ministry in London, but there was little abnormality and much sanctified sense in his preaching. Theologically, we feel he is emancipated and is trying to emancipate his hearers. He teaches faith without fear.

"All schemes of doctrine which uphold God in character of a sovereign—some men advancing, some reprobating—from the pleasure of his will . . . however expedient, are essentially Jewish and out of place in the Christian temple where the gate is open to all. I do not wish to leave one soul, believer or unbeliever, without a witness in his breast of God's good title to the name of 'Father'. It is to no chartered few, but to all mankind that he makes the overtures" (Sermon on Matthew, vi., 9).

We read with surprise, in view of subsequent developments, of:—

"The foolish notion of ignorant men, that the further they move things from the ordinary into the extraordinary, the more they remove them into the hands of God; as if a common thing was by its commonness separated from the divine Providence—which is to destroy providence, and to make religion a succession of novelties. Among the fruits of the Spirit I find peace, joy, gentleness, truth, and a *sound mind* . . . neither trembling, nor quaking, nor entrancements" (same sermon).

Irving claimed "liberty of prophesying". He discoursed of duty rather than belief, appealed to the better nature of his hearers rather than their fear of punishment and refused to exclude from the pulpit anything that touched the mind and heart of humanity.

He appeals "to imaginative men, and political men, and legal men, who bear the world in hand". The time-serving of politicians, the errors of intellectuals and the shams of the religious are all passed in stern review. The sins of the upper classes are condemned far more severely than the sins of "the lower orders", and there is no patronising of "the pious poor". He reminds the landed gentry that their armorial bearings and family mottoes do all declare that they hold nothing in their own right, but are God's stewards —where is the public spirit that their ancestors exhibited in feudal times? What are they doing to prevent the peasantry of England from degenerating into parish paupers? He is fully aware of the materialism that is infecting business men with ambition to pile up profits at all costs and the readiness of the public to invest in joint-stock companies irrespective of industrial conditions. He is also conscious of the indifference of employers to the welfare of their workers, blind to the fact that beneficent employers like David Dale could command the love and loyalty of their workers. "But *competency* satisfies no man. The merchant must dwell beside the lord, and the tradesman must have his villa beside the squire." The age has its own answer to the first question in the Catechism, "What is man's chief end?"—"Man's chief end is to glorify Mammon, and to enjoy him while he can."

When one thinks of the monotonous preaching common in Irving's time, the convention that ruled out concrete discussion of contemporary problems and prescribed a set doctrinal treatment whatever the text, one is not surprised that his preaching broke with a specially startling crash upon the decorous slumbers of "the religious world."

The social and ethical range of Irving's preaching during his first three years in London can be grasped by turning to the *Thirty Sermons* taken down by Mr. T. Oxford, shorthand writer, and published after his death in 1835. His critics were not all "hard-shell conservatives" who objected to him on the grounds that he did not confine himself to dividing the doctrines of election, reprobation and predestination into fourteenth, fifteenth and sixteenth heads. On the contrary, in that day of prudential individualistic pietism, many must have welcomed his social vision, his presentation of Christianity as a faith "more heroic, more magnanimous than this age affects". Irving, unfortunately, was too much of a rhetorician. As social censor, he was too lurid, too personal in his onslaughts. His disparagement of his own age was too dramatic to ring true. His style was too affected and archaic to persuade. He was a preacher for those who loved a good sermon rather than for those who needed a good religion. The effect of his preaching was to leave men dazzled and stupefied rather than convinced or converted; they went home wondering at the power of the orator, rather than mourning over their besetting sins and striving after amendment.[1]

---

[1] "His expression was usually very mild," reported Rev. A. D. Campbell, Pittsburgh, U.S.A; but in preaching "his sarcasm was caustic in the extreme, his sneer withering, his gesticulation strange—like a being of another age."

CHAPTER IV

THE ORATOR FOR GOD

" Books of devotion are no longer read (if we read Irving's *Orations*, it is merely that we may go . . . to see the man)."
—Hazlitt, "On reading New Books."

" He felt he had a Divine mission to Babylon the Great. Beyond Luther, beyond Knox, he seemed to regard himself as 'servant of the Lord,' and, with earnestness unparalleled in modern times, he delivered his burden before the nation of England."
—Dr. Stoughton, Church Historian.

HAZLITT was partly right in saying:—"We believe that the fairest and fondest of Mr. Irving's admirers would rather see and hear him than read him. The reason is, that the groundwork of his compositions is trashy and hackneyed, though set off by extravagant metaphors and an affected phraseology; that without the turn of his head and the wave of his hand, his periods have nothing in them; and that he himself is the only *idea* with which he has yet enriched the public mind!" F. D. Maurice, on the other hand, thought Irving was much more than a popular preacher. In the Introduction to his *Doctrine of Sacrifice* he acknowledged his debt:—

"I had no personal intercourse with the late Mr. Irving, and I heard him preach rarely. . . . But I learnt lessons from some of Mr. Irving's books, which I hope I shall never forget. . . . What he taught me was to reverence the education he had received in the John Knox School, and the fathers who had imparted it to him. I had not that reverence before; I had shrunk from what I believed to be hard, narrow and unhuman. He showed me that the old patriarchs of Scotland had a belief in God as a Living Being, as the Ruler of the earth, as the Standard of Righteousness, as the Orderer of men's acts in all the common relations of life. He made me perceive how entirely different their godliness was from the sentimental religion which consists in feelings about God; or from the systematic religion which consists of notions about Him. He led me to see that unless we begin from God—unless we start from the conviction that the thing which is done upon earth He doeth it Himself—the belief in Christ will pass into a belief in the mere Saviour for us,—the belief in a Spirit will be at first a mere recognition of certain influences acting upon us, and will evaporate at last into pantheism. I perceived clearly that Mr. Irving had not acquired these convictions in England. . . . *That* he brought with him; it was part of his covenanting, Calvinistic culture. . . . I have learnt since to honour the teaching of the English Church. I have to bless God for teaching what belongs to what calls itself the Catholic Church. But I have found nothing in either to supersede *this*. I reverence it as Protestant theology in the highest, purest meaning of the word, and as the very ground of all theology."

Irving's first book consisted of two parts entitled *For the Oracles of God : Four Orations. For Judgement to Come : An Argument. In Nine Parts* (1823).

The object of these discourses was to appeal to a wider circle than could assemble to hear him in the Caledonian Chapel; they were to be specimens of what he conceived to be the right manner of presenting divine truth. *The Oracles of God*, dedicated to Dr. Chalmers, claimed to follow the model of "the Ancient Oration—the best vehicle far beyond the sermon, of which the very name hath learnt to inspire drowsiness and tedium". The Press and every other new means must be used to reach the people. *The Oracles* deal with the neglect of the Bible and suggest the remedy.

"The Oracles of God have ceased. No burning bush draws the footsteps to His presence chamber; no invisible voice holds the ear awake; no hand cometh forth from the obscure to write his purpose in letters of fire. The vision is short, and the testimony is sealed, and the solitary volume is the sum total."

Irving is craving for a religion of the heart. He is reacting against the Bibliolatry of his age that honoured the letter rather than the spirit of Scripture. His romanticism rebels against the dull Catechism, so often used in preference to the Bible in religious instruction.

"In the Catechism, religion is presented to the intellect, chiefly; in the Bible it is presented more frequently to the heart, to the fancy, to all the faculties of the soul. In early youth, an association takes place between religion and intellect. . . .

The solemn stillness so favourable to rapt communion, is destroyed at every turn by suggestion of what is *orthodox* and *evangelical*; the spirit of the reader becomes lean, being fed with abstract truths; his temper ungenial; his prayers undevout recital of opinions. Intellect, cold intellect hath the sway.

"The Bible had been used too much as 'as a sort of elbow-monitor, rather than as a universal law to *impregnate* all the sources of action. . . . Doctrines should be like mighty rivers which fertilise our island. . . . Pour ye out your whole undivided heart before the oracles of God. Be free to catch all its moods and all its inspiration. Then shall you be thoroughly furnished for every good work'."

Professor C. H. Herford has said:—

"The *Orations* at times come as near to the rolling majesty of Milton's impassioned prose as rhetoric that rarely rings quite true well can. But the intellectual substance is of a meagreness which ill corresponds to its sumptuous clothing" (*Age of Wordsworth*, p. 33).

If only Irving had been himself! Unfortunately he "played the sedulous ape" to Milton to such an extent that the cumbrous seventeenth century style, laden with obsolete auxiliaries and a superfluity of conjunctions, ultimately became his own, and he would use it even for urgent business. Coleridge and other literary contemporaries of Irving were right in drawing attention to the forgotten charm of old English writers like Hooker and Sir Thomas Browne. But for an individual to affect the diction of a bygone age revealed both lack of historic sense and lack of taste.

The *Argument of Judgement to Come* was dedicated to his friend Dr. Gordon, of Edinburgh (Moderator of the Church of Scotland in 1841). It was "after the manner of the ancient Apologies," and the author claimed the right to argue "like a man, not like a theologian—like a Christian, not like a churchman".

"Like the botanist, we should give up the *artificial* method of treating religion—and bear down at once upon the occupation of the hearts and life of men. They care not for our controversial warfare, they laugh at our antiquated method—and so they perish, because of the unintelligible signals which we hang out."

Irving seems to have realised the weakness of the Presbyterian appeal to the intellect, the Methodist appeal to the emotions and the (contemporary) Anglican appeal to the moral sense:—

"The tribunal before which we plead is the *whole* understanding of man. Not his intellect merely, but his affection, his interests, his hopes, his wishes—his whole undivided soul."

And his sanctified common sense rejected current popular conceptions of the Future Life:—

"Of how many lightwitted men is the constant psalm singing of heaven a theme of scorn; the fire and brimstone a theme of derision. And by how many zealous but injudicious ministers are they the themes of rhapsodies, which end in nothing but tedium and disgust of all who hear them. . . . They shun activity and shut all in rest and contemplation. I cannot think of heaven otherwise than as the perfection of every activity of body, soul and spirit."

Discussing the "tests of judgement", he stands for Life rather than Doctrine:—

"'Upon whatsoever future destiny is made to turn, it is not upon a refined and finical creed.' Those who are obsessed with 'fretted arches and longdrawn aisles' seek not 'Christ dismantled but Christ invested, not his members but his goodly raiment.' If the test were 'evanescent feelings . . . I know not what a rabble of devotees and *self-deluded enthusiasts* would have rushed forward in the greatness of their self-confidence.'"

The Argument was a protest against "two most nauseous and ill-formed abortions", the respective *Visions of Judgement* of Southey and Byron—the one a panegyric of George III, the other a parody of that panegyric. To Irving, both appeared equally profane. To the writer of the article on Irving in the *Dictionary of National Biography*, his performance appears "incredibly silly". Carlyle's opinion was fairer:—

"There is strong talent in it, true eloquence and vigorous thought, but the foundation is rotten, and the building itself a kind of monster in architecture, beautiful in parts, vast in dimensions, but on the whole decidedly a monster" (Froude, I, 193).

Carlyle went on to remark that even Irving's great admirer, Mrs. Buller, very nearly stuck in the middle of it;

Mr. Buller did so and remarked, "Can't fall in with your friend at all, Mr. C." Carlyle himself confessed, "Sometimes I burst right out laughing when reading it. At other times I admired it sincerely."

A book so unequal might have passed unnoticed except by the religious Press. Yet from 2nd July, 1823, the daily papers were full of the *Oracles* and *Argument*. These were days when *The Times* was but "a folio of four pages", with little space for material not of strong public interest. It was not a dull season for journalists either. There were night-long debates in Parliament, for Canning had just returned to office and Brougham was taunting him with political infidelity. Lord Byron was publishing his last poem. Abroad, the Duc d'Angoulême was marching into Spain to bolster up the Bourbons; the Spanish "patriots" were raising men and money in London. The Greeks were fighting for Independence; Mackintosh was making eloquent speeches on their behalf at the Freemason's Tavern. But "The Celebrated Irving" must be found room, and for many days an extract from *The Orations* might be seen side by side with dispatches from the seat of war or a canto of *Don Juan*. *The Times* fell upon Irving in its capacity of guardian of the public taste, and deplored the "poor thought wrapped up in tinsel . . . of this turgid and shallow declaimer". "Surely, surely it cannot be long before this bubble bursts!" rumbled the Thunderer. The conservative papers generally were hostile. Radical papers, like Leigh Hunt's *Examiner*, were liberal in applause. The religious papers were most severe, especially the orthodox ones that scented heresy in some of the progressive ideas that the author struck off, sparks from his anvil. Of the reviews, *The Quarterly* was bitterly hostile (as might be expected). *The Westminster* recognises his latent genius and implores him not to waste his powers by hankering after premature fame. He seeks to win for Christianity literary, political and scientific men.

"But instead of stealthily and gradually sealing up the hive —patiently stopping each particular chink—and carrying off his enemies while wrapt in darkness and sleep—he has chosen to break in upon the honeycombs at mid-day, deranging the whole economy of the cells, and rousing the very drones to resent his unceremonious invasion. The knife and the cautery are only to be used in desperate cases: and our complaint against

THE ORATOR FOR GOD

Mr. Irving is, that he uses these when other specifics would be preferable. He is a Quixote, who holds all parley in scorn; and rides, with lance couched, not only against ravishers and giants, but also against fulling-mills and flocks of sheep."

In the preface to the third edition of *The Orations* (two large impressions had sold off in five months), Irving replies at considerable length, to the strictures of the Press. His attitude was like that of Milton in his second sonnet *On the Detraction which followed my writing certain Treatises*:—

> "I did but prompt the age to quit their clogs,
> By the known rules of ancient liberty,
> When straight a barbarous noise environs me
> Of owls and cuckoos, asses, apes, and dogs;
>
> * * * * *
>
> But this is got by casting pearl to hogs."

But when an author speaks of his critics as "all the insect tribe that fly around", and, "the reptile tribe that bow the knee", is he not, plainly, "asking for it"? What can he expect but contempt when he puts into print expressions that might be excused in the heat of speech? e.g., "Look abroad over the world and what do you behold? Noiseless nature putting forth her buds, and drinking the milk of her existence from the distant sun". The experience of authorship and the intercourse that he was fortunate enough to enjoy with men of letters might have induced him to correct his faults. But Irving was not made that way. He could gain new thoughts from others when communication was voluntary on his part. But he could not brook criticism.

That was unfortunate. For Irving had the opportunity of restoring to religious literature the high place it had held in the seventeenth century. He fully realised that Theology was no longer read by educated men as a branch of Literature, —the theology of his own generation anyhow. The Romantic Revival had brought forth great poets, novelists and essayists. It had been sterile theologically. Technical theology was produced for the clergy and tracts and sermons for the laity, but it was "non-literary" for the most part. Irving thought of the seventeenth century and of divines who were men of letters—Lancelot Andrewes, John Donne, George Herbert, Jeremy Taylor, Richard Baxter:—

"The writers of these times are too much forgotten, I lament; and their style of writing hath fallen much out of use; but the time is fast approaching when this stigma shall be wiped away from our prose, as it is fast departing from our poetry. I fear not to confess that Hooker and Taylor and Baxter have been my companions in theology . . . as Shakespeare, and Spenser, and Milton, in poetry. . . . They are my models. They were the fountains of my English idiom; they showed me the construction of sentences, and the majestic flow of continuous discourse . . . and through the whole there ran a strain of melodious feeling, which ravished the soul as a vocal melody ravisheth the ear. Their books were to me like a concert of every sweet instrument of the soul, and heart, and strength, and mind. *They seemed to think, and feel, and imagine, and reason, all at once*; and the result is, to take the whole man captive in the chains of sweetest persuasion. They are not always in taste. But who is Taste, and where are his works, that we may try what right he hath to lift his voice against such gifted men? This Taste . . . his troops are like King David's —'every one that is in distress, every one that is in debt, every one that is discontented'. And what are his manifestoes? Paragraphs in the daily papers, articles in magazines, critiques in reviews. And how long do they last? A day, a week, a month, or some fraction of a year—aye, and until the next words of the oracle are uttered. And what becometh of these oracles of the dread power? They die faster than they are born: they die, and no man regardeth them" (Preface to *Orations*, 3rd edition).

This is all very well. But there is one seventeenth century writer whose style Irving might have studied to advantage—John Bunyan. And he might have learned clarity from the eighteenth century writers he professed to despise. William Law, Bishop Butler, John Wesley and William Cowper would all have taught him something that he could have fused by his own personality. It was his misfortune to choose seventeenth century writers as his models, for he was only too ready to copy their confused redundancies and flowery imagery. There was more in the eighteenth century than the formal elegance of Dr. Hugh Blair and the sulphureous declamation of Whitefield. One turns to a historical survey like Dr. McAdam Muir's *Religious Writers of England* and notices how the record tails to a close with the rather obscurantist Evangelical authors of the early nineteenth century. Had Irving been less of a rhetorician, and had he survived into the middle of his century, he might well have conveyed to the public the

THE ORATOR FOR GOD

results of newer developments in religious thought. His influence would have done much to "mediate" German theology before the impact of modernism on evangelical traditionalism later in the century. If you point to the fate of McLeod Campbell, the innovator, one can always reply that Irving's position was most advantageous. He was of the Church of Scotland but not in it. He had been ordained in Scotland, but was out of the reach of heresy-hunters, and the little Scots Presbytery of London had no official status. The publicity Irving obtained had set the ball at his feet. The educated laity would have listened to him as to none else, Anglican or Nonconformist.

This was not to be. If Dr. Alexander Whyte acclaimed Irving as "The Scottish Hooker", I fear this is true only in the sense that Allan Ramsay was "The Scottish Theocritus'" and Klopstock "The German Milton". Even the heart of his message, contained in *Miscellanies* extracted from his collected works (Strahan, 1866) is readable only in purple patches, here and there. Irving's works sold surprisingly well, when first published. But it is doubtful if they were *read*, like Dr. Chalmers' *Astronomical Discourses* which were then running like wildfire through England and could be seen everywhere, in inns and places of resort. Dr. Chalmers "adapted" orthodoxy (as best he could) to the new astronomy and geology of his age. Irving took the thorns and briars of scholastic divinity and garlanded them with the flowers of modern literature. True, his mind teemed with ideas and was ever susceptible to new impressions; but it had already been organised around a hereditary Calvinistic centre. His boyish pilgrimages to the Secession meeting-house had prepared the way for entering into the spirit of the rejuvenated Church of Scotland, then reacting from prudential "Moderatism" to the absolute claims of "high-flying Presbyterianism"; that meant hide-bound Calvinism in doctrine and the Church's demand for spiritual independence from the State.

Rays of spiritual enlightenment illumined the background of Irving's austere Calvinism. But soon the clouds gathered, only to break in stormy flashes of lightning. Bright sunshine flooded his teaching during his early years in London. Soon after his arrival, he was introduced to Coleridge by his friend Basil Montagu. (See p. 84). Few young preachers have had his unique opportunity of receiving the best thought of the age at first-hand. At Coleridge's he had the further advantage of meeting fellow-disciples like R. C. Trench and John Sterling.

"We can easily imagine the handsome Caledonian," said Washington Wilks, "loitering beside the shrunken crooked form that shuffles from side to side of Mr. Gilman's garden walks, talking for two hours and three quarters at a time, in nasal dialect, of diseased humanity, dead churches, the all-expressive Logos, 'Om-ject' and 'sum-ject', *vernunft* and *verstand*" (*Edward Irving*, 2nd ed., 1860, p. 151).

Coleridge loved to impart: Irving loved to receive. Each recorded his high impression of the other, the former in *Aids to Reflection*, the latter in the "dedication" of a published sermon preached for the London Missionary Society in 1824. Irving would leave Highgate feeling "a new impulse towards truth, a new insight into its depths". It has sometimes been suggested that the Sage received from the Caledonian divine as much as he imparted. The fact is, that far from anticipating Coleridge's teaching, Irving embraced it with the enthusiasm and imperfect apprehension of a late learner.

"Coleridge's conversational style, 'proceeding from no premise, and advancing to no conclusion,' was better qualified to inflate than to concatenate the mind of a sympathetic hearer; and to a born rhapsodist like Irving it was a perilous experience" (C. H. Herford, *Age of Wordsworth*, p. 33).

Mr. L'Anson Fausset reminds us in his penetrating biography, that Coleridge was ill-fitted to be the moral and spiritual guide of anyone. But he dismisses too summarily "the chief" of his disciples "poor, eloquent, effeminate Irving."

Not everyone felt drawn to Coleridge. Mr. and Mrs. Montagu drove Chalmers as well as Carlyle up to Highgate. Chalmers described the interview in a letter to his wife (May, 1826):—

"We spent three hours with the great Coleridge. His conversation flowed in a mighty unremitting stream. You know Irving drinks in the inspiration of every syllable that falls from him. There is a secret and, to me, unintelligible communion of spirit between them, on the ground of a certain German mysticism, and transcendental lake poetry which I am not yet up to."

On returning to Irving's, Chalmers remarked on the obscurity of the sage and said that for his part he liked to see all sides of an idea before taking it in. "Ha!" said Irving. "You Scotchmen would handle an idea as a butcher handles an ox. For my part, I love to see an idea *looming through the mist.*"

Carlyle's impression of the Sage was:—

"A puffy, anxious, obstructed-looking, fattish old man hobbled about with us, talking with a kind of solemn emphasis on matters which were of no interest (and even *reading* pieces in *proof* of his opinions thereon); I had him to myself once or twice, in narrow parts of the garden-walks; and tried hard to get something about *Kant* and Co. from him, about 'reason' *versus* 'understanding', and the like; but in vain: nothing came from him that was of use to me, that day, or in fact any day" (Cp. Carlyle's *John Sterling*, Ch. VIII).

Carlyle tried hard to revere the Sage, and resorted to the shrine again and again, but without success; the Sage appeared to be "sunk in putrescent indolence", like "a steam engine of a hundred horses' power with the boiler burst", and morally an awful warning instead of an example.

If his ideas appeared to Carlyle a mere hocus-pocus to disguise an orthodoxy no longer tenable, to Irving they represented a Gospel for the Age. To begin with, Irving found a pessimistic strain that pointed to facts and an optimistic strain that shimmered through the darkness. The world was in a sunk condition, given over to atheistic philosophy, materialistic science, the very Churches mere cases of articles, like the dried carcases of once-swift camels. "Let this young man know that the world is not to be converted, but judged", said the Highgate Oracle. The world was in a bad way, but the Divine life could quicken even a fallen world—by *transcendental* methods. Perhaps God might even quicken the world through the Church, a divine spiritual organism (which eighteenth century individualism had forgotten). If this emphasis on the Church was prophetic of the coming Oxford Movement the idea of Salvation as something *internal* rather than superadded was reflective of Schleiermacher's theology. Coleridge taught that man was essentially a religious being and the appeal of Christianity was primarily to the heart.

(Would that Irving had studied Schleiermacher, then flourishing in Germany —his conceptions of "the religious consciousness" would have been infinitely more satisfying than Coleridge's misty notions!) Further, there was Coleridge's recognition of the significance and power of the Holy Spirit. The following diagram appears in his *Notes on English Divines* (Vol. I, p. 66, 1853 ed.).

```
——————————  CHRIST = Prothesis  ——————————
                HOLY SPIRIT = Mesothesis
SCRIPTURE                                CHURCH
 = Thesis                               = Antithesis
                THE PREACHER
                = Synthesis of
             CHURCH AND SCRIPTURE
             —"the sensible voice of the
——————————         Holy Spirit."    ——————————
```

This equation of the Preacher with "the sensible voice of the Holy Spirit" was distinctly bold. It was precisely the kind of speculative proposition that would appeal to Irving, and as taught by Coleridge in personal converse, cannot have failed to turn his thoughts towards the Holy Spirit. The way was thus gradually prepared for the restoration of "apostolic gifts".

Bryan Procter ("Barry Cornwall") thought that Coleridge's influence was particularly evident in Irving's course of sermons on the Trinity, "which produced on multitudes an effect which has abided to the present day" (*Fraser's Magazine*, Jan. 1835). But the sage himself was sadly disappointed in his pupil's later development. He devotes a chapter to him in his second volume of *English Divines*, but can only reproach him sadly for his lurid, apocalyptic longings. And he might have been able to acclaim Irving as the worthy successor of those "old divines" at whose shrine the pupil had worshipped! To think that Coleridge had helped his young friend to break the chains of hard dogmatism, only to see him forge the fantastic fetters of millenarian prophecy! Had Irving been less "ductile", Coleridge's influence would have reinvigorated his thought. Dr. R. H. Story, son and biographer of his friend Robert Story of Rosneath, believed that "his stores of theologic learning were not weighty enough to ballast his mind" (*Scottish Divines*, 1883, p. 245). No doubt a regular Divinity course would have given him a far more satisfactory grounding in systematic theology than was possible for a "partial student", reading theology in his spare time. But Irving escaped the dislike of theology that the discipline of perpetual note-taking is known to cause. He enjoyed striking out on his own, and his erudition was certainly above the average of his time in Scotland though he had little "exact scholarship". No, there was something in Irving's personality that was strained and inflated, and set on an erratic course despite all salutary, restraining influences.

It is amazing to turn from the garden walks of Highgate Hill and thread the crowded streets of London and find "the Caledonian divine" a public figure. Few divines till the day of Dean Inge were as familiar to the public. And few preachers have had the "presence" of Irving. Look and voice, tone and gesture, all combined to give the world "assurance of a Man".

The publication of his *Orations* led to a flood of pamphlets. The comments and ferment of the time are preserved in a curious and amusing form in *The Trial of the Rev. Edward Irving, M.A., a Cento of Criticism* (1823). Six months after the appearance of Irving's book, this pamphlet had run into five editions. It is the report of a prosecution of the new preacher, before "The Court of Common Sense", by "Jacob Oldstyle, Clerk". All the editors of the leading papers are examined, cross-examined and covered with comic confusion. The editor of *The Times* is asked:—

"Did you find that your exposure of the defendant's pretensions had the effect of putting an end to the public delusion?"

"Quite the reverse. The crowds which thronged to the Caledonian Chapel instantly doubled. The scene which Cross St. presented on the following Sunday beggared all description. It was quite a Vanity Fair. Not one half of the assembled multitude could force their way into the *sanctum sanctorum*. Even we ourselves were shut out among the vulgar herd. For the entertainment of the excluded, however, there was Mr. Basil Montagu preaching peace and resignation from a window; and the once celebrated Romeo Coates acting the part of trumpeter from the steps of the church, extolling Mr. Irving as the prodigy of prodigies, and abusing the *Times* for declaring that Mr. Irving was not the god of their idolatry".

The critical teeth of all kinds of periodicals then fell upon him; it was not hard to press the indictment of poor taste and arrogance. He was then indicted: "For being ugly; for being a Merry-Andrew; for being a common quack; for being a common brawler; for being a common swearer; for being of very common understanding; for following divisive courses, subversive of the discipline of the order to which he belongs, and contrary to the principles of Christian fellowship and charity." It says much for "The Court of Common Sense" that he was found guilty only of the last charge; and his chief assailant, *The Times*, was by its own confession convicted of having condemned Sir Walter Scott as "a writer of no imagination", and Lord Byron as "destitute of all poetic talent".

Another pamphlet of note was *An Examination and Defence of the Writings and Preaching of the Rev. Edward Irving, M.A.* It gave a lively picture of the man and his church. Like all other accounts of "the Caledonian divine", the description is largely personal;

". . . as he goes on preaching, his countenance, which is surrounded by a dark apostolic wave of hair towards his shoulders, becomes strongly expressive and lighted up, and his gesture marked and vehement."

Publicity of this kind was distinctly harmful to the best in Irving, and one can only say he laid himself open to Cockney caricature as "Doctor Squintum". He seemed to be looking at the same time in opposite directions. No eyes were more bright and penetrating, but he saw with distracted vision. A discerning American, the Rev. W. W. Andrews, admitted that "obliquity of vision" was a symbol of the man.

There was a true dignity in Edward Irving, despite a tendency to the bizarre and grandiose. (He was sometimes mistaken for Paganini, the one-stringed fiddler, owing to his broad hat and flowing black hair.) He emphasised, not so much himself as the ministry to which he had been called.

"And in his opinion," says Dr. R. H. Story, "no bishop inherited a more undoubted episcopate than he. He, minister of the Scots Kirk in Hatton Garden, was the bishop of that 'ecclesia'; his kirk-session the presbyters; his deacons as truly deacons as Stephen and Philip of old. The whole 'three-fold ministry' was fully represented, and worked in perfect harmony, and, as he believed, in unbroken order, within the circle of his own congregation. With the consciousness of all this apostolic and episcopal dignity and authority, he preached from the ungainly puplit, which his kingly imagination sublimed into a throne as grand as that of Athanasius; and he moved on the week-days through the streets and lanes of London, on his ceaseless errands of charity, not the poor minister of a struggling Presbyterian chapel, but a brother of bishops, and heir of the Apostles" (*Scottish Divines*, p. 234f).

If you would know Irving's Churchmanship, read his *Ordination Charge* delivered to the Rev. Hugh Baillie McLean at the Scots Church, London Wall (March 15th, 1827). Of all Irving's works, it is perhaps the best worth reading and is reprinted in his *Miscellanies* (1866). It is without a peer in theological literature. Here and there it is marred by peculiarities that had become accentuated since his own induction in 1822. But, taken as a whole and in the perspective of over a century, it is a lofty, inspiring address. He opens by appealing to the candidate's sense of adventure:—

"Of all the offices in this world . . . you have been set apart to the most burdensome and responsible: of all the churches called Christian, you have this day chosen to take upon you vows the most severe and uncompromising: and, I may add, that you have accepted a call, and are now ordained to labour, in the most difficult portion of the vineyard of the Lord. Therefore gird up your loins like a man; and hear me while I set forth at length what the Church of Scotland expecteth at your hands in this city. And that I may keep order in my charge, I shall present it to you under these five heads:—first, the student; secondly, the preacher; thirdly, the pastor; fourthly, the churchman; and fifthly, the man."

From his treasury, Irving brought forth things new and old. As there were no fellowship endowments in the Scottish Universities to preserve a separate order of learned men, a great responsibility rested on the ministry to cultivate the Greek and Hebrew and the critical study of Scripture. Further, "I invite thee to physiology, which is the science of life in all its forms and conditions, and of philology, which is the science of words, the forms of human thoughts.

... Make not thyself a mere sermon-maker, or clerk, or committee-man, or a drudge of any kind". As steward of the mysteries of Christ, the young minister is to prepare himself by filling the fountain of his spirit by secret prayer and meditation (this interest in public prayer was uncommon in the early nineteenth century, the recognition that lack of liturgy called for all the greater care). In preaching, there is a lively sense of the need for "personality":—

"Here put forth all thy knowledge, all thy wisdom, all thy strength of manhood, with all the gifts and graces of the Divine nature. Take thy liberty; occupy thy commission; wound and heal; break down and build up again. Be of no school, be fettered by no times, accommodate no man's conveniency, spare no man's prejudice, yield to no man's inclinations, though thou should scatter all thy friends, and rejoice all thine enemies. Preach the Gospel: not the gospel of the last age, or of this age, but the everlasting gospel; not Christ crucified merely, but Christ risen: not Christ risen merely, but Christ present in the Spirit, and Christ to be again present in person. Dost thou take heed to what I say? Preach thy Lord in humiliation, and thy Lord in exaltation: and not Christ only, but the Father, the will of the Father. Keep not thy people banqueting, but bring them out to do battle for the glory of God and of His Church: to which end thou shalt need to preach them the Holy Ghost, who is the strength of battle."

On the sacraments, the young minister is to study "any author older than a century" but none later; "these clear-headed times" were barren.

"Brother, to my certain knowledge the atmosphere of theology hath been so long clear and cloudless, that there hath been neither mist nor rain these many years: and even to talk of a mystery is out of date. But thou must preach Christ in a mystery. Get thee out of this bright sunshine of the intellect, and meditate the deep mysteries of the Spirit, which the natural man perceiveth not. When they talk of plainness and perspicuity, to thy text, my brother: to thy warfare of prayer and meditation; try the depths; sound with thy deepest line, my brother. Oh, I charge thee to enter into the mysteries of these two sacraments: if I should hear of thee setting them forth as bare and naked signs, I will be the first to charge thee with a most dangerous error. Fill these vessels with spiritual water; awaken the faith of the people . . . let them come in mysterious expectation and assurance of God's spiritual blessing; not in a clear-headed belief that nothing is to be expected or received."

Dealing with the pastoral office, Irving says he has met with more insolence from Scottish lads treating him as a mere Scottish lad, and Scottish men of substance treating him as a mere Scottish adventurer, than from the peers of England. "I will not call thee brother if thou force not thy people to regard thee as their pastor . . . be thou the pastor always, less than the pastor never. Go thus or go not at all." As minister of the most apostolic Church under heaven, he is to remember the spirit of the Reformers and Covenanters, "looking through the cloud of the Papal Apostasy into the Presbyterian discipline and primitive worship of the Culdees."

"As a churchman thou owest brotherly love to the Church of England, such as the church of Philippi did to the church of Ephesus; but thou owest also rebuke for her backslidings in doctrine and discipline; which also she oweth to us; and both debts of love must be discharged. To the Nonconformists also, who hold sound doctrine, thou owest brotherly love; and reproof also for their uncharitable spirit towards us and all Establishments. To the Papacy and to the Socinian, thou owest no mercy. Superstition on the one hand, liberality on the other (for the sign of the prophet is accomplishing now when the churl is called liberal) . . . these thou must fight against with the two-edged sword of the faith."

We see here the growth of that fanaticism which was ultimately to darken his life by driving out entirely the spirit of enlightenment. No doubt his warnings against "the prudential maxims of this metallic age" were seasonable —the first half of the nineteenth century *was* an age of utilitarianism and materialism, despite external religiosity. But his warning was exaggerated: "Thou knowest, brother, thou well dost know the serpent cunning of this liberal spirit . . . it is deadly poison against Christ."

Irving concludes this remarkable Ordination Charge by reminding him of his duties as a Man:—

"Thy cloak and thy parchments, brother,—be these thy riches and then thou canst speak out against Mammon. . . . Show thou to lordly prelates what the word bishop meaneth. Show thou to substantial citizens what hospitality meaneth.

Show thou to rich men what charity meaneth; and to all, what faith meaneth. Go thou out as poor as thou came in. And if God should bless thee with a wife and children, put no money in the bank for them, but write prayers in the record of the book of life: be this thy bank of faith and let the lords of the treasury be the prophets and apostles who went before thee. O brother, be zealous for the good primitive customs of the Church."

We may smile at poor Irving sometimes, but we are not surprised that he won London by gallantry. He certainly voiced a demand for a faith "more heroic, more magnanimous" than his age ever expected or desired. In his Ordination Charge at London Wall he was surely at his best as "Orator for God".

CHAPTER V

"TWO STRINGS?"

"Mr. Irving feels more than he reasons."—
(Mrs. Basil Montagu to Carlyle.)

IRVING'S call to London brought to a head the question of his engagement with Isabella Martin. His successful settlement as a city minister called for a definite decision. After leaving Kirkcaldy he had turned to Haddington with the hope that the Martins would release him from what was, after all, only a half-engagement. D. A. Wilson, in *Carlyle till Marriage* (1923), is less than fair to Irving, who is represented as a man interested in Jane Welsh because she obviously belonged to the upper middle class and would bring with her a dowry.

"The chance of 'a lass with a tocher'—was one of the standing attractions of the Church, and to miss an opportunity like this was unprofessional; but he was trustworthy, and as soon as he had made sure in some way that his Bella held him to his word, he agreed to abide by it and broke it off with Jane" (p. 171).

Nothing could be more unlike what we know of Irving's character. It seems likely that the more he saw of Jane the more he realised that their temperaments were widely different. He would have been even surer he was right in breaking with her if he could have lived to read her *Early Letters*, edited by D. G. Ritchie! Jane had many suitors and such expressions as "passionately returning his love" must not be read in the modern sense; it was the fashion then for young ladies to use the language of romanticism. Irving realised that Jane would never make a suitable "manse-wife", and "Bella" certainly would . . . had she not encouraged him in his Kirkcaldy days to persevere in getting a parish and not get too settled in school routine? Had she not shown she loved him by her jealous attitude when at Kirkcaldy he became too interested in his fairest pupil, Margaret Gordon? He introduced Margaret to Carlyle, as he afterwards introduced Jane to him. "It is not lost what a friend gets." (See *C.R.*, p. 205f.)

While Irving sincerely believed that Isabella Martin was the kind of life-partner best suited to him, there is no doubt that from time to time his heart went back to Haddington. Between his settlement in London in 1822 and his marriage in the autumn of 1823, he was undoubtedly unhappy at times. This is obvious from his letters. On 29th April, 1822 he wrote to Carlyle, describing his Call to the Caledonian Chapel and referring to "other things" besides partings which "oppress" his spirit—"an independence about my character, a want of resemblance especially with others of my profession, that will cause me to be apprehended ill of. I hope to come through honestly and creditably. God grant it!" Several letters then passed between Irving and Jane Welsh. The dates are vague. On the scrap of paper not destroyed is a sonnet that she cut out:—

"Thou raven lock! On which mine eyes do rest
    Unwearied. Thou dear emblem of my Jane
    Whose hand did crop thee from her head, fit test
    Of her affection ever to remain . . ."
                    (and so on for fourteen lines).

On the back of this may be read: " . . . I have resolved neither to see Isabella nor her father before I . . . cannot brook the sight of either until this be explained". (*Love Letters of T.C. and J.W.* II, pp. 49 and 404f.). He then informed Mr. Martin of his attitude. "That precise, innocent, didactic man" (Carlyle's phrase) stubbornly refused to release him from an engagement on the grounds that his daughter had remained true to him. Whereupon, Irving wrote to Jane and expressed to her his "most affectionate and tender regard" which would:

"long ago have taken the form of the most devoted attachment but for one intervening circumstance. . . . When I am in your company my whole soul would rush to serve you, and my tongue trembles to speak my heart's fullness. Heaven grant me its grace to restrain myself. . . . But I feel within me the power to prevail, and at once to satisfy *duty to another* and *affection to you*. . . . It is very extraordinary that this weak nature of mine can bear two affections, *both of so intense a kind*, and yet I feel it can. It shall feed the one with faith, and duty, and chaste affection; the other with paternal and friendly love, no less pure, no less assiduous, no less constant—in return seeking nothing but permission and indulgence" (Froude, I, 157).

Froude, with his usual readiness to jump at conclusions, made the most of the Irving-Welsh case. During the year between the confirmation of his engagement to Isabella Martin and his marriage, "he flung himself into religious excitement as grosser natures take to drink" (Froude, I, 158). Carlyle's unfair biographer would fasten eagerly on a certain passage in the letter just quoted:—

"I have to find other avenues than the natural ones for the overflowing of an affection which would hardly have been able to confine itself within the avenues of nature if they had all been opened."

In other words, Froude is certain that Irving eagerly quaffed the heady wine of popularity when he took London by storm and in these long and unexpected draughts found some compensation for the enforced loss of intimacy with Jane Welsh. It would be truer to say that he frankly enjoyed his pulpit popularity because it had been so long denied him, and because he felt that at last he had scope for his tremendous energy. There was a certain strained self-conscious note in his rhetoric, but that had always been his failing, even as a boy-student; at the age of ten, his attendance at Seceder preachings was already moulding him into the type of character who believes he had a "special mission" to "lift up his testimony and rebuke the backslidings of the age". Apart altogether from the question of "thwarted love", Irving's bias was towards a striking, metropolitan ministry that would make its mark on the age. From the beginning his ambition far outstripped that of the average youth proceeding to the ministry. Loss of publicity led to an accentuation of the abnormal element, obsession in prophecy and "the gift of tongues"—but that came seven years after his marriage.

When he first settled as a young bachelor in Bloomsbury lodgings, he would feel lonely and dispirited at times; even *he* would feel the pressure of work and the glare of publicity rather trying at times; and as a stranger furth of Scotland his heart would yearn for well-kent faces. He would write and tell Mrs. Welsh that her house had been a haven of peace to him; that nowhere had thoughts of piety and virtue come to him so little sought as with her and his dear pupil. Every day he passed a window where there was a portrait of Miss Kelly as Juliet. "It had the cast of Miss Welsh's eye in one of its most piercing moods which he could never stand to meet, the roundness of her forehead, and somewhat of the archness of her smile."

Extracts from the following letter reveal Edward striving to control his feelings and adapt himself to circumstances. They reveal, also, the fact that his temperament was singularly different from that of the sprightly Miss Welsh, so far as we can judge from her correspondence:—

"London: September 9, 1822.

"My dearest Friend,—I said in the last walk which we enjoyed together on a Sabbath evening—when by the solemn stillness of the scene, no less than the pathetic character of our discourse, my mind was in that solemn frame which is my delight—that in future I was to take upon me in my letters the subject of your moral and religious improvement, leaving to other correspondents matters of literature, taste and entertainment. But I have not forgot that you discharged me from preaching to you in my letters, and I fear that what you humorously call preaching is the very thing which I shall have to do if I fulfil my resolution. Now I can chat, though somewhat awkwardly, I confess; and ten years agone I had a little humour, which has now nearly deceased from neglect.

"My mind was then light and airy, and loved to utter its conceptions, and to look at them and laugh at them when uttered. Then I could have written letters trippingly, and poured out whatever was uppermost in my mind; but I can do that no longer. I am aiming from morning till night to be a serious and wise man, though God knows how little I succeed. The shortness of life is evermore in my eye, the wasting of it before my conscience; the responsibility of it overwhelms me. . . . I cannot make a mock heroic of these things, or laugh them away. I was never so far lost to good sense and good feeling as to try. So they hang over me, and I must either sink down into a melancholy forlorn creature, weeping and sighing and talking over the difficulties of living well, or I must rise up in the strength of Him who made me, and endeavour to work my passage through in the best and surest way I can. This last I have chosen . . . and by God's help I will fulfil it."

Then follows about seven hundred words, urging a greater care for the nurture of her soul and less anxiety for "elegant learning", with the hope that his pupil may not be "alienated from men of genius by their being men of religion".

He continues:—

"Of my own condition, I can speak with great satisfaction, in as far as favour and friendship are concerned, and the outward prosperity of my calling. I have no evidence to judge by farther than that my Chapel is filled, and that their patient hearing of discourses, each an hour and a quarter long, testifies they are not dissatisfied with the stuff they are made of.

"In another respect I have reason to be thankful that God has revealed to me of late the largeness of my own vanity and the worthlessness of my own services, which, if He follows up with further light upon the best way for me to act in future, and with strength to act as He teaches me, I have no doubt of a great increase both of happiness and fruit.

"I have made no acquaintance in London of any literary eminence, but I shall, I doubt not, in good time. The next moment I have unemployed I devote to my friend Carlyle, to whom I have not yet found time to write. Oh that God would give rest to his mind, and instruct him in his truth. I meditate a work upon the alienation of clever men from their Maker. . . . My love to your mother. Oh, how I would like to see you both, to live with you in the quietness and love I have so often —— [word omitted]" (Froude, I, 159–63).

This letter shows Irving very much the tutor persisting mildly obstinate in his rôle of spiritual mentor. He starts preaching before he comes to the problem of his own life, and then returns to preaching. No doubt Jane thought him tiresome and found much more stimulating that other correspondent who discussed "literature, taste and entertainment". It is true that Mrs. Welsh thought this other young man boorish, and preferred the former tutor with his courtly old-world manners. Even if Irving had been free from the Martin bond it is doubtful if Jane would have accepted him from the time that he introduced her to Carlyle. Well might Carlyle consider that introduction "Irving's crowning kindness."

"Irving is in Scotland," writes Dr. Gordon from Edinburgh to Robert Story. "I have seen him twice for a little. The same noble fellow—and in spite of his *alleged* egotism, a man of very great simplicity and straightforwardness. He is to be married to-day, I believe, to Miss Martin, of Kirkcaldy" (Ol. I, 178).

The ceremony took place in Kirkcaldy Manse, on 13th October, 1823. They were married by the bride's grandfather, brother of the well-known Scottish painter, David Martin. Most of the honeymoon was spent in the Highlands, then becoming popular through the influence of Scott. Irving determined to pass near Kinnaird, where Carlyle was tutoring the Bullers.

"On this his Wedding-Jaunt, he seemed superlatively happy; as was natural to the occasion, or more than natural; as if at the top of Fortune's wheel, and in a (generous) sense striking the stars with his sublime head. Mrs. Irving was demure and quiet, though doubtless not *less* happy at heart; really comely in her behaviour . . . Irving had loyally taken her as the consummate flower of all his victory in the world,—poor, good tragic woman; better probably than the fortune she had, after all!" (*C.R.*, p. 238).

The friends had not met for two years—since their parting at the Black Bull Inn, when the Caledonian minister-elect had left for his new field of labour *in partibus infidelium*. Irving had much news of London. His talk was of that Sage, Coleridge; of Hazlitt, talented too, but tending towards scamphood; of the Fonthill-Abbey Sale ("hired to attend as a *White-bonnet*[1] there", said he with a laugh!) One can imagine how Beckford's amazing "Gothick" castle appealed to his romanticism and what his "homiletic mind" would make of the fall of the great tower, owing to rotten foundations, two years later. Irving was in high good humour and in reply to his friend's criticism of *The Orations*, remarked: "Well, Carlyle, I am glad to hear you say that; it gives me the opinion of another mind on the thing." His friend's "surly and dyspeptic utterances" only produced jovial bursts of laughter. The only occasion when this jocose mood changed to solemnity was when they were all three standing at the Falls of Aberfeldy. It was an October dusk. The moon was rising and they had still ten miles to walk to Taymouth. "Doesn't this subdue you, Carlyle?" "Subdue me?" came the reply, "I should hope not. I have quite other things to front with defiance, in this world, than a gush of bog-water tumbling over crags as here!" (which produced "a joyous and really kind laugh from him as sole answer"). Carlyle mentions this incident

---

[1] "Annandale," for a false bidder, paid 5s. to raise prices at a "roup".

of the waterfall "subduing" him, as an instance of *falsetto*. To anyone with a spark of imagination, a remark like this would seem perfectly natural among the *Birks*, haunted by the memories of song. I feel that when Carlyle wrote this about his friend in 1866, he tended to read back into Irving's life "abnormality" the whole time, though it was only in his later ministry that this became pronounced. On this occasion it was Carlyle who was ill and depressed.

Irving was preaching in Taymouth Kirk. As he came out into the broad village street, Carlyle had a vivid recollection of him pulling off his big broad hat as he walked.

"Looking mostly to the sky, with his fleece of copious coal-black hair flowing in the wind, and in some spittings of rain that were beginning; how thereupon, in a minute or two, a Livery Servant ran up, 'Please, Sir, aren't you the Rev. Edward Irving?' 'Yes.' 'Then my Lord Breadalbane begs you to stop for him one moment. Whereupon *exit Flunkey*; Irving turned to me, with what look of sorrow he could, and 'Again found out!' upon which the old Lord came up (father of the 'Free-Kirk' one) and civilly invited him to dinner. Him and party, I suppose; but to me there was no temptation, or on those terms less than none; so I had Bardolph saddled; and rode for Aberfeldy. Home, sunk in manifold murky reflections, now lost to me. . . ." (*C.R.*, p. 240).

After visits to Rosneath and Annan, the couple moved south, Irving making his wife alight at the Border and walk over the bridge of Sark into England ("a pleasant bridegroom fancy", as Mrs. Oliphant remarks). We next hear of them installed at 4 Myddelton Terrace, Pentonville, then on the outskirts of London and favoured with faint breaths of country air. Those who still think that he lived on the approbation of the West End need to be reminded that he went far further from a fashionable neighbourhood than he need have done with his adequate stipend. And when he removed from Pentonville after the building of the new church in 1827, it was to 13 Judd Place East—a dingy scorched street in Bloomsbury.

If he received some of the distinguished friends who had found their way to the Caledonian Chapel, he was equally hospitable to humble members of his own flock, and even to dubious strangers who wasted his time. The following account of his daily routine was given by one of his nearest relatives, who often stayed with him:—

"Mr. Irving's rule was to see any of his friends who wished to visit him without ceremony at breakfast. Eight o'clock was the hour. Family worship first, and then breakfast. At ten he rose, bade every one good-bye, and retired to his study. He gave no audience again till after three. Two o'clock was the dinner hour; and, after that, should no one come to prevent him, he generally walked out, Mrs. Irving accompanying him."

This lady tells us that he almost always carried little Edward in his arms (born 24th July, 1824). "Some people laughed at this, but that he did not care for in the very least."

If he shared the burden of taking out the baby, he committed money matters entirely to his wife. This primitive custom sometimes landed him in awkward situations. He would find himself penniless in a public conveyance. On one such occasion, he told his amused family circle, he looked round the coach for the most benevolent-looking face. "I told him that I was a clergyman, and that since I had obtained a wife from the Lord I had given up all concern with the things of this world, leaving my purse in my wife's hands; and that to-day I had set out to visit some of my flock at a distance, without recollecting to put a shilling in my purse." The good man paid the fare and had the satisfaction of learning that he had just helped "the celebrated Irving".

Irving seemed to Carlyle to *mount* far away from him during his early London ministry; and he was a poor correspondent. But he mounted to some purpose and to Carlyle's advantage. Mrs. Strachey, wife of a distinguished East Indian Company director, had been one of his most enthusiastic hearers; she was a devout Evangelical wholly given over to things sacred and serious—a *Schöne Seele*. To her sister, Mrs. Buller, she pleaded: "Come and dine with us, come and see this uncommon man!" Mrs. Buller was not so enthusiastic but came. Both she and her husband took to Irving and after several meetings asked his advice about their son, Charles, who had left Harrow but was too young for the University. This lively youth was far more interested in the annals of boxing than those of the Peloponnesian War and his parents scarcely knew what to do with him. Irving's considered advice was: "Send this gifted unguided youth to Edinburgh College; I know a young man who could lead him into richer spiritual pasture, and take effective charge of him." This young man of course was Carlyle, who found himself tutor to Charles and Arthur Buller, attending daily at George Square, Edinburgh. The salary of £200 per annum came in most opportunely and for the time being ended his hand-to-mouth existence. During the vacations he would stay with his charges at Kinnaird.

In June, 1824, he sailed from Leith to London, at the request of Mrs. Buller, who was changing her plans (as she frequently did—to Carlyle's annoyance). Irving had persuaded him that London would welcome him as a new genius from the North. Carlyle knew better than that. "He would never go to bed unknown and wake to find himself famous." He was warmly received by the Irvings at Pentonville and saw much of them, off and on, for the next ten months. He had never cared much for any of the Martins except the Rev. John—"altogether honest, wholesome as Scotch oatmeal". But he came to like Bella better and recognised her as a hospitable hostess and a good wife. His first afternoon in Myddelton Terrace he never forgot—the dash of a fine carriage driving up and the entry of

"A strangely-complexioned young lady, with soft brown eyes and floods of *bronze*-red hair,—Kitty Kirkpatrick, Mrs. Strachey's cousin, with whom she lived; her birth, an Indian *Romance*, mother a sublime Begum, father a ditto English official. . . . A very singular 'dear Kitty'; who seemed bashful withal, and soon went away,—twitching off the loose label sticking to my trunk still in the lobby as she tripped past. . . . With what imaginable object then, in Heaven's name? To show it to Mrs. Strachey I afterwards guessed; to whom, privately, poor I had been prophesied of, in the usual grandiloquent terms. . . . Then after dinner, in the drawing-room, which was prettily furnished, the *Romance* of said furnishing,—which had all been done, as if by beneficent fairies, in some temporary absence of the owners: 'We had decided on not furnishing it,' Irving told me; 'not till we had more money ready; and, on our return, this was how we found it. The people here are of a nobleness you have never before seen!'—'And don't you guess yet at all who can have done it?' 'H'm, perhaps we guess vaguely; but it is their secret, and we should not break it against their will.' It turned out to have been Mrs. Strachey and dear Kitty that had done this fine stroke of art-magic. Perhaps the 'Noble Lady' had, at first been suspected; but how innocently she,—not flush in that way at all, though notably so in others!" (*C.R.*, p. 243f.).

The "Noble Lady" was Irving's pet-name for Mrs. Basil Montagu, the wife of a successful Chancery Barrister. Her house in Bedford Square was "a most singular social and spiritual ménagerie" according to Carlyle, her drawing-room the best London equivalent of a Paris salon. Basil Montague (1770–1851) was the son of the notorious Earl of Sandwich by the singer, Miss Ray, but was in every way the opposite of his father. He was a man of letters—one of Macaulay's famous *Essays* reviewed his edition of Bacon's Works (1829–34). But Montagu's forte was public life. His talk was of benevolence, health, peace and happiness; "he wished all the world well, could wishing have done it", said Carlyle. To-day, we would speak of him as "a professional uplifter". He was the gentleman described by *The Times* as "preaching peace and resignation from a window" to the disappointed multitude unable to gain admission to the Caledonian Church. Most people thought him rather a bore and some rather a humbug. But Irving found him a good friend, accepted some seasonable advice about the "seduction of fashion" when he received invitations from high quarters as "lion of the season", and dedicated a volume of sermons to him later.

At 25 Bedford Square Irving was a welcome caller and was fully appreciative of that subtle atmosphere of refinement and good breeding, of which he had hitherto seen so little in Scotland. Carlyle was soon introduced to Montagu, who was delighted with the new-comer from the North; Montagu's sons "admired neither his dress, his uncouth manners, nor his dialect". He also met the poet and lawyer Bryan Procter ("Barry Cornwall") whose "airy friendly ways" were rather attractive. He was steeped in the Jacobean dramatists and as a friend of Irving's unconsciously influenced his old-world style, though he had little sympathy with his theology, and as a "Commissioner in Lunacy" must have watched the later "tongues" manifestations sadly. He paid his tribute to Irving in *Fraser's Magazine* (January, 1835) Other people introduced to Carlyle by Irving were Crabb Robinson (one of the first "Special Correspondents" of the Press) and Badams (an Edinburgh medical student who established a chemical factory in Birmingham). All sorts of ill-assorted people could be seen at the Montagus. There was much talk of "the grand old English writers"—Fuller, Sir Thomas

Browne, etc., then in vogue. But there was also a physician, Sir Anthony Carlile (a native of Durham and a hard-headed Utilitarian) who defined poetry to Irving once as "the prod*oo*ction of a rude *Aage!*"

The presiding genius of the circle was Mrs. Basil Montagu, Irving's "Noble Lady". As a young widow she came to take charge of Montagu's motherless family as governess, becoming in due time his third wife. Her position was rather difficult but she was equal to it; her diplomatic genius won her mild authority. Irving once spoke of her as "one in command of a mutinous ship which is ready to take fire!" Carlyle described her as a "consummate *Artist*, about fifty, with the remains of a certain queenly beauty which she still took strict care of, a nose decidedly Roman, a pair of sharp black eyes, with a cold smile as of inquiry". Irvin gradually discovered she was rather a flatterer, though he continued to be friendly. Perhaps her "soft ministrations" did him some good, for she taught him to rest and relax. She was much too interested in his private life, however, as we shall see in the next chapter.

Of the people whom Irving introduced, Carlyle liked Mrs. Strachey best—"a singular pearl of a woman, incapable of unveracity to herself or others". They lived in Fitzroy Square and had a pleasant country house at Shooter's Hill. Mrs. Strachey took to Carlyle at once. She would have been a good friend to Irving had he taken her into his confidence more, when tempted, after his loss of popularity, to associate with "prophetical" visionaries. She was a woman of ripe Christian experience and sound judgment. Her husband Edward Strachey, an "Examiner" at the India House, was a straightforward, genially abrupt man, who cheerful scorned "the general humbug of the world." He was a Utilitarian and a democrat but far from unimaginative; he dearly loved his Chaucer. He had no definite religious convictions, but respected his wife's. Had Irving kept such friends as the Stracheys near him as the years passed by, they would have been a salutary corrective for "overbelief"; and he would have had to modify his sweeping generalisations about the undogmatic tendencies of the age resulting in materialism and demoralisation. Mrs. Strachey once spoke to Carlyle with affectionate sorrow about their mutual friend's inability to readjust himself to reality, when his hope faded "that the Christian religion was to be a truth again, not a paltry form, and to rule the world,—he, unworthy, even he the chosen instrument!" (she had heard him speak like this in her own house).

Carlyle attended Irving's preaching regularly while his guest. It did not strike him as at all superior to his "Scotch performances"; neither the manner not the matter appealed to him; "there was a want of spontaneity and simplicity, a something of strained and aggravated, of elaborately intentional, which kept jarring on the mind".

I think that Carlyle's criticism of his friend's "too sanguine and too trustful spirit" is borne out by the fact that he allowed himself no peace even in his own house. Preachers like Dr. Joseph Parker have retired every Sunday evening from the blaze of publicity to the quiet of the home. But Irving kept "open house" and welcomed crowds of visitors, week in, week out. He professed that "he loved their love", and refused to listen to Carlyle's contention that whereas love was like a river flowing within its appointed banks, calm, clear and rejoicing in its course (when centred on a few objects or one)—when diffused, it was like that river spread abroad upon a province, stagnant, shallow and unprofitable.

Not many of Irving's visitors were people of fashion; most of them were of the well-dressed, decorous middle-class. There were rich aldermen, like Sir Peter Laurie; polished poets like Thomas Campbell; vernacular poets like Allan Cunningham; Scottish adventurers, hoping to get help from Irving—some of them Glasgow youths who had taken him at his word, when he issued an open invitation in his assistant days. A good many tiresome, ignorant and weak-minded persons took advantage of Irving's good-nature. Carlyle recalls several "disastrous or unpleasant figures—a Danish fanatic of Calvinistic species (?), one insolent 'Bishop of Toronto' triumphantly Canadian, but *Aberdeen* by dialect". [This was Dr. John Strachan (1778–1867), whose life was devoted to the "Establishment" of Episcopacy in Canada—in which he was ultimately thwarted by the secularisation of the "Clergy Reserves"]. There were office-bearers from the Caledonian Chapel, zealous simple men like old Mr. Dinwiddie (who would call on the minister on a Sabbath morning to pray for a blessing on the services of the day); shrewd and successful men like William Hamilton, merchant in Cheapside ("who, in the inglorious but profitable toils of business, concealed from the world an amount of practical sagacity . . . which might have honoured a higher place"—Oe. I, 64n.). William Hamilton married Isabella Martin's sister and indeed had been urged to do so by Irving himself ("directed by the Lord to one of those sisters who are in my mind always represented as one"). This warm-hearted couple were his faithful counsellors to the last, but even their advice he would not follow when "the Tongues" captured his imagination.

Carlyle had many pleasant memories of his visit to Pentonville. He remembered those walks before breakfast with his friend along the high embankment by the "New River", watching the traffic of the "New Road" twenty feet or so below. He remembered in particular a walk one bright summer evening in the outskirts of Islington. Jerry-builders had been busy (then as now!) defacing the fields with "human dog-hutches of the period". In a hollow however, where the grass was still smooth and green, they suddenly came across a

"Considerable company of altogether fine-looking girls, who had set themselves to dance; all in airy bonnets, silks and flounces; merrily alert, nimble as young fawns; tripping it, to their own measure: with the bright beams of the setting sun gilding them, and the hum and smoke of huge London shoved aside as foil or background, nothing could be prettier. At sight of us they suddenly stopped, all looking round; and one of the prettiest, a dainty little thing, stept radiantly out to Irving,

'Oh, oh, Mr. Irving!' and, blushing and smiling, offered her pretty lips to be kissed, which Irving gallantly stooped down to accept, as well worth while. Whereupon, after some benedictory or Pastoral words, we went on our way" (*C.R.*, p. 244f.).

CHAPTER VI

HOME AND FRIENDS

> "The Angel, Islington! It was there that I was set down on my first arrival in London; and Mr. C. with Edward Irving was waiting to receive me. 'The past is past and gone is gone!'"
> (Jane Welsh Carlyle, Journal 21 April, 1856).

IN the summer of 1824 Carlyle terminated his engagement with the Bullers, finding tutorship irksome. After two months with his friend Badams at Birmingham, he again descended on Irving, to find him alone in town. To his brother John he wrote on 27th September:—

"I found the orator at Pentonville sitting sparrowlike, companionless, in—not on—the housetop alone. His wife had left him, and had taken all the crockery and bedding and other household gear along with her. He extended to me the right hand of fellowship notwithstanding, and even succeeded in procuring me some genial tea with an egg, only half rotten, which, for a London egg, is saying much. By-and-by, one Hamilton, a worthy and accomplished merchant from Sanquhar, came in and took me to his lodgings . . . and there on a splendid bed, I contrived, in spite of agitation from within, and noise and bugs from without, to get six hours of deep slumber. Next morning I was fitter to do business."

This picture of a husband left to shift for himself does not suggest that the good Bella deserved all the credit she received for being a good housekeeper; she was in Scotland with baby Edward, born 22nd July, 1824. Carlyle had suggested boarding with Irving, but there was now the further obstacle of "a squeaking brat, who indeed brings us many 'blessings'—but rather interrupts our rest at night!" Besides, Irving had already engaged to board a medical youth from Glasgow (at a very high rate). So his friend bade him consider the proposal unmade.

On reflection, Carlyle realised that Myddelton Terrace would be favourable for study—only of religion in general and the Caledonian Chapel in particular. However, the two friends agreed to go together for an October holiday at Dover. Carlyle was to lodge with the Irvings; Mrs. Strachey and Kitty Kirkpatrick took a more expensive house near them. "Dear Kitty" laughed at the awkward extravagances of "the Orator", but liked him tremendously for all that, and busied herself in the duties of hospitality. She joined Carlyle in "little spices of laughter and quiz", while Irving tried to be solemn as he read aloud Phineas Fletcher's *Purple Island*, a seventeenth century poem in the Spenserian manner (the rivers of the island are the veins of the human body, the mountains are bones, and so on by analogy). One evening on the beach, they noticed bricklayers finishing a house; they were crowding noisily round the gable. Irving was quite excited and grasped Carlyle's arm, as he quoted Scripture: "See—they are going to bring out their topstone with shouting!" "What is it?" Carlyle enquired of a bystander. "You see, sir, they gets allowance of beer," was the reply. Poor Irving!

The arrival of Mr. Strachey brought this pleasant holiday to a different conclusion. He had no use for humbug and was one of the "logical", argumentative people whom Irving was always denouncing from the pulpit. The atmosphere was different at once. Mrs. Strachey and "dear Kitty" good-naturedly intervened. The French coast lay invitingly opposite. The weather was lovely. A trip to Paris was proposed. Carlyle was to accompany Mr. Strachey and Kitty. Mrs. Strachey and the Irvings were to remain at Dover.

Carlyle thought Irving had "much improved since last winter" and that the effects of the holiday were wholesome. Those walks on Dover beach brought back old times at Kirkcaldy, and nowadays there were choice cigars to smoke as well. On October 4th he wrote to his father at Mainhill:—

" . . . Of Irving, I have much kindness towards me to record. I like the man, as I did of old, without respecting him much less or more. He has a considerable turn for displays, which in reality are sheer vanity, though he sincerely thinks them the perfection of Christian elevation. But in these things he indulges very sparingly before me, and any little glimpses of them that do occur I find it easy without the slightest ill-nature arising between us to repress. . . . The fashionable people have totally left him, yielding like feathers and flying chaff to some new 'centre of attraction'. The newspapers also are silent, and he begins to see that there was really nothing supernatural in the former hurly-burly, but that he must content himself with patient well-doing, and liberal, though not immoderate success; not taking the world by one fierce onslaught, but by patient and continual sapping and mining as others do.

"I for one am sincerely glad that matters have taken this change. I consider him a man of splendid gifts and good intentions, and likely to be of much benefit to the people among whom he labours. His Isabella also is a good, honest-hearted person, and an excellent wife. She is very kind to me, and though without any notable gifts of mind or manners or appearance, contrives to be in general extremely agreeable. Their son . . . a quiet *wersh gorb* of a thing, as all children of six weeks are, but looked upon as if it were a cherub from on high. Kitty Kirkpatrick smiles covertly, and I laugh aloud at the devotedness of the good orator. 'Isabella,' said he the other night, 'I would wash him, I think, with *warm* water to-night,' a counsel received with approving consent by the mother, but somewhat objected to by others. I declared the washing and dressing of *him* to be the wife's concern alone; and that, were I in her place, I would wash him with oil of vitriol if I pleased, and take no one's counsel in it."

To Jane Welsh, Carlyle wrote (5th October) in a manner that makes clear his ignorance of the relations between her and Irving. One can imagine her expression as she read the letter:—

"The Orator is busy writing and bathing, persuading himself that he is scaling the very pinnacles of Christian sentiment, which in truth, with him, are little more than the very pinnacles of human vanity rising through an atmosphere of great native warmth and generosity. I find him much as he was before, and I suppose always will be, overspread with secret affectations, secret to himself, but kind and friendly and speculative and discursive as ever. It would do your heart good to look at him in the character of dry nurse to his first-born, Edward. Oh that you saw the Giant with his broad-brimmed hat, his sallow visage, and his sable, matted fleece of hair, carrying the little pepper-box of a creature folded in his monstrous palms along the beach, tick ticking to it, and dangling it, and every time it stirs an eyelid grinning horribly a ghastly smile, heedless of the petrified spectators that turn round, gazing in silent terror at the fatherly leviathan; you would laugh for twelve months after, every time you thought of it. And yet it is very wrong to laugh if one could help it. Nature is very lovely; pity she should ever be absurd. On the whole I am pleased with Irving, and hope to love him and admire him and laugh at him as long as I live. There is a fund of sincerity in his life and character which in these heartless, aimless days is doubly precious. The cant of religion, conscious or unconscious, is a pitiable thing, but not the most pitiable. It often rests upon a groundwork of genuine, earnest feeling, and is, I think, in all except its very worst phases, preferable to that poor and arid spirit of contemptuous *persiflage* which forms the staple of fashionable accomplishment so far as I can discern it, and spreads like a narcotic over all the better faculties of the soul."

After this October holiday Carlyle settled in lodgings at 25 Southampton Street; it was near the Irvings who would be able to have Jane as their guest.

When Irving had been preaching at Haddington a few days before his marriage and staying with the Welshes, he discovered that Mrs. Welsh was opposed to any intimacy between his old pupil and his (boorish?) friend Carlyle. On that occasion he said to Jane: "Come to London and be my guest all next summer along with him —you'll have his company all the time." Jane had never seen Mrs. Irving, but Carlyle had spoken of her quite favourably. Her flirtation with Irving was a distant memory of four years ago. She took for granted at first that Mrs. Irving did not know it was for her sake that Irving had wanted then to cancel his engagement. But Irving's trade was utterance; the very Christ he adored lived openly and bade His followers do likewise; and Irving had lived so cleanly that he was heedless of appearances. He had no false shame about him, and less than the usual share of the other kind. So it soon appeared that Mrs. Irving knew who her rival had been, and steadily tabooed Jane Welsh, and the invitation to London did not come. Carlyle, a friend of her father as well as of her husband, and an old acquaintance of her own, was always a welcome guest, and in expensive summer quarters a paying guest; but Jane Welsh indeed! She had always sufficient reasons for not asking her, and left Irving to make his excuses as best he could. He wrote to Carlyle about May (1824), reiterating the invitation to himself and explaining that their house was "not in a condition to receive a lady". This was repeated to Jane, but she would not take the hint, and persisted in hoping against hope, till Irving wrote to her direct at last (10th May, 1824) more than enough. He had abundance of excuses; house not all furnished, wife to be confined, her sister coming, and so on; but he was also, as she said, "nonsensical":—

"One thing more, my dear Jane, into your own ear. My dear Isabella has succeeded in healing the wounds of my heart, but I am hardly yet in a condition to expose them. My former calmness and piety are returning. I feel growing in grace and in holiness; and before another year I shall be worthy in the eye of my own conscience to receive you into my house and under my care, which till then I should hardly be. Be assured, my dear Jane, the child of my intellect, of the same affection from me as ever, and as I have said, pure and more pure."

His wife did not even send "her regards" till the risk of a visit was past for the year. Would she or anyone give Carlyle a hint of the old flirtation? No wonder Jane was anxious.

"Pity she did not tell it to him at once, is easy to say when one knows the other man was blabbing; but she was not sure of that as yet, and would feel it wrong to blab—it might sunder the best of friends. Give the woman her due!" (D. A. Wilson, *Carlyle till Marriage*, p. 329f.).

Carlyle was thinking more about Irving—his novelties in doctrine, his eccentricities in practice. He felt that though his friend was as yet some way from the rocks he was heading for them steadily. A clever wife might save him. Isabella not being that kind of wife, the next best thing was to bring her into closer friendship with Mrs. Basil Montagu. That did not achieve much. The thought then occurred to him, why not introduce Jane to Mrs. Montagu? An intellectual correspondence on books and ideas would be a stimulus to both. Jane approved of the suggestion. So on 5th May, 1825, he wrote to Mrs. Montagu accordingly. After confessing his failure to bring Mrs. Irving into her circle, he continues:—

"Ill-success in this attempt does not deter me from a new one. You know Miss Welsh of Haddington, if not in name, at least in character and from her friends. . . . She asked would you not write to *her*. I engaged to try, and now will you? Can you? This young lady is a person whom you will love . . . ardent, generous, gifted . . . but without models. It was Mr. Irving's wish, and mine, and, most of all her own, to have you

HOME AND FRIENDS

for her friend, that she might have at least one model to study. Separated by space, could you draw near to one another by the imperfect medium of letters? Jane thinks it would abate the 'awe' which she must necessarily feel on first meeting with you personally. She wishes it; I also if it were attainable; is it not?" (*v.* Moncure Conway's *Thomas Carlyle*, p. 231f.).

Little did Carlyle realise that the "Noble Lady" believed that she had been commissioned as a confidant. He had not told her the secrets of his heart—but then Irving had! Mrs. Montagu imagined herself a *dea ex machina*, called on to unravel the skeins of a pathetic romance. She pictured Jane Welsh as a young and plastic girl still pining in secret for her lost lover: she had no idea that she was writing to a mature woman of twenty-four, with experience far beyond her years. Irving she regarded as a martyr to duty, who had given up his true love through pressure. But in her letter to Miss Welsh she thought it best to disparage him somewhat as a person whose inconstancy did not deserve prolonged and hopeless affection; she too had tried to find in him a close friend, but he had other interests and ambitions. The motive was, reconcile the damsel to her disappointment. Mrs. Montagu then wrote to Carlyle that he was "doubtless aware of the circumstance". She thought of him in perfect innocence as simply an intimate friend of Miss Welsh and Edward Irving. She spoke of the love of these two as unextinguished on both sides, and hoped that something might be done to put an end to vain regrets. "If Miss Welsh were to pass one week with me, she might be satisfied that to be Mr. Irving's wife would—to a spirit of her tone—be entire and unmixed misery: they are not the least fitted to each other" (30th May, 1825). Jane did not like this effusive, interfering correspondent and was alarmed by a reference in Carlyle's last letter; he must keep Mrs. Montagu's curious epistle and take care not to light his pipe with it. She adds: (Mrs. M.) "will surely be satisfied *now* that there is no worm of disappointment preying on my 'damask cheek'; for I have told her in luminous English that my heart is *not* in England, but in Annandale" (3rd July, 1825). On 19th July she noted in a postscript to Carlyle: "I had *two* sheets from Mrs. Montagu, the other day, trying to prove that I knew nothing at all of my own heart! Mercy! How romantic she is!" Several days later she received the following amazing letter:—

"My dear Miss Welsh,—

"There is now before me on my table a beautiful green Mandarin basin. It is to me *valueless*; it will not hold water. Notwithstanding its elegance, *it has a flaw in it*. And this illustrates my feeling of the truth, entireness, and integrity of friendship. Shall such a flaw be found in my dear Jane Welsh? No, my dear young lady, the past as well as the present must be laid open; there must be no Bluebeard's closet in which the skeleton may one day be discovered. You have received a new and dear guest to occupy your heart, not a tenant at will, but as tenant for life; and if, with a noble show of friendship, you have still only a show of it, what conclusion will that 'soul of fire' arrive at? The wisdom that was before all time hath said, 'Perfect love casteth out fear'; and till your fears are all cast out, your love is still imperfect and your cure incomplete. . . . I could say much to you of the policy of a perfect integrity, but I scorn that base and grovelling word. You will think how easy it is to sit and dictate? Believe me, my love, I owe many peaceful days and nights to a similar disclosure poured into the ear of a passionate and jealous man; a disclosure most painful, most humiliating. If this confession had not been made . . . how could I have hoped to regain confidence? *Pride* is a paltry thing.

"You see, my dear friend, what a terrible monitor you will find in me. The poor monk who puts on voluntarily a hair shirt will be but the type and shadow of your patient endurance, —if you do endure me—and you must learn to do so; for your wit will not overawe me, or your loveliness bribe me. I shall be the only friend you have out of the circle of your spells.

"Mr. Irving is here again; his Wife and Child are with her friends. He is now staying under our roof, where I have so often entreated Mr. Carlyle to stay. We would have exorcised the bitter spirit that rends him, and have it cast out for ever. You will do this much more readily. . . . Will you come to Bolton Abbey, near Harrogate? And when you are safe under my protection, will Mr. Carlyle come too? 'He hears me not, he minds me not'; but he will answer and mind you.

"Your attached friend,

"D. B. Montagu."

In utter misery, Jane informed Carlyle that she had deceived him in asserting that she disliked Irving. It was false. She had once loved him passionately (the term used by young ladies who read *Werther* meant little more than Dominie Samson's "Prodigious!") "If she had shown weakness in loving a man whom she knew to be engaged to another, she had made amends in persuading him to marry the other, and save his honour from reproach." For two years, she confessed, she had never mentioned Irving's name except with bitterness and contempt. On 12th January, 1823, Carlyle had to protest in a letter: "What a wicked creature you are to make me laugh at poor Irving! Do I not know him for one of the best men breathing, and that he loves both of us as if he were our brother? . . . Let us like him the better, the more freely we laugh." Carlyle thought that Jane was only criticising Irving's "radically dull organ of taste" and "floundering awkward ostentatious way"; he hoped that his friend would "give up all attempts at superfineness and be a son of Anak honestly at once, in mind as in body", but doubted whether he would ever be entirely free of these absurdities. Many men might have had their suspicions aroused by a tone so marked and acid as Jane's. But Carlyle was not as other men. For a long time he thought the whole affair was "a strange delusion" of Mrs. Montagu's. However, "All's well that ends well". Everything was cleared up. Jane decided to see Carlyle in his own home and among his own folk in Dumfriesshire. Their marriage was hastened and took place on 17th October, 1826. Strangely enough the Mrs. Montagu correspondence was kept up. But in December, 1831, we find Jane writing to her sister-in-law:—

"With the 'noble lady' my intercourse seems to be dying an easy natural death. Now that we *know* each other, the 'fine enthu-si-asm' cannot be kept alive without more hypocrisy than one of us at least can bring to bear on it. Mrs. Montagu is an actress. I admire her to a certain extent, but friendship for such a person is out of the question."

One can imagine Carlyle's reaction to a letter which he received from Mrs. Montagu on 12th December, 1825:

"Mr. Irving says, 'No person keeps her friends at such a distance as Mrs. Montagu.' And yet I have told him again and again that I love him as much as if he were ten times my son."

As for Edward Irving, the reader may have already concluded that Jane Welsh would not have suited him. We shall refer to that later (p. 274ff). I cannot find any evidence that Irving continued to pine for Jane or that he was unhappy with Isabella. On the contrary, there is much to show that his married life was distinctly happy and peaceful. The only criticism is that Isabella fell in with her husband's abnormal courses too readily, though her father was watching his career uneasily at Kirkcaldy. The death of their first child, Edward, at Kirkcaldy (11th October, 1825) and the birth of Margaret on October 2nd—undoubtedly drew them closer than they had ever been. On his return to London Irving wrote to Isabella :—

"I do now sit down with true spiritual delight to commune with my soul's sweet mate. Yea, hath not the Lord made us for one another, and by his providence united us, against many fiery trials and terrible delusions of Satan? And as you yourself observed, has he not over again wedded us, far more closely than in any joy, by our late tribulation, and the burial of our lovely Edward, our holy first-born who gave up the ghost in order to make his father and mother one, and expiate the discords and divisions of their souls? Dear spirit, thou dearest spirit which doth tenant heaven, this is the mystery of thy burial on the wedding-day of thy parents, to make them one for ever. . . . My wife, this is not poetry, this is not imagination which I write; it is truth, rely upon it, it is truth that lovely Edward hath been the sweet offering of peace between us for ever; and so, when we meet in heaven, he shall be as the priest who joined us—the child of months being one hundred years old."

This passage comes from Irving's Letter-Journal, in which he describes his daily life during Isabella's absence at Kirkcaldy between 18th October and 2nd December, 1825. No one could be busier than "the Caledonian divine", but he always found time to make graphic to his wife his studies, his preaching and his visiting. In spite of much moralising and a tiresome pietistic manner, this is a remarkably revealing document, and Mrs. Oliphant was right in printing it (Vol. I, pp. 249–375). During his wife's absence he led an austere life, alone in the study often for hours with just a slice of bread and a glass of water, and sometimes only soup for dinner. He refuses the hospitable invitation of Sir Peter Laurie. He mentions a gift of figs from a friend in Constantinople, but only to have the opportunity of "exhorting him to stand fast among the alien". In reading an old book of tracts about the Revolution of 1688 he records his sentiments in proper "Orange" fashion and enthusiastically takes up Bishop Overall's *Convocation Book*, a High Church seventeenth century work much prized by the Nonjurors. He comes across the denunciation of Locke's contract theory that power is derived from the people. "Passive obedience" to throne and altar was at the other pole from Irving's heroic Calvinism, yet he accepts Overall's book as a new revelation. A little later he notices that a new copy of *The Edinburgh Review* has come in from the library. He glances at a remarkable article on Milton. "I take it to be young Macaulay's. It is clever—oh, it is full of genius!—but little grace. Theology of this day—politics of this day—neither sound." He decides to call at Bedford Square and see Zachary Macaulay, hearing he is poorly:—

"With a view, if opportunity offered, of saying a word to their son concerning Milton's true character, if so be that he is the author of that critique. For I held with him once, but am now assured that Milton, in his character, was the archangel of Radicalism, of which I reckon Henry Brougham to be the arch-fiend. But I found they had gone to Hannah More's for retirement and discourse."

Irving's pastoral experiences had something to do with his views. He visits an old couple for whom he has procured a pension and finds they are sadly tried with their sons, one of whom has fits of madness and the other "has caught the fever of the day" (according to the father) and become infidel, "which is amazingly spread among the tradesmen".

He had some strange cases to deal with. There was a widow who had been a prodigal for twenty-one years in the West Indies,

"Having followed into dissipation a dissipated husband, buried ten children, and now returned *in forma pauperis*—left upon the shore by the good Samaritan, who provided her a fortnight's lodging, expecting that in that time her brother, to whom he wrote, would be eager to relieve her."

Her brother, a Scottish minister, wanted Irving to get her into some institution. He told the minister it was his duty to make room for her at his fireside. He had seen the poor paralysed woman, now humble and penitent; how she wept when he read aloud her brother's unforgiving letter! He was doubtful if the prodigal sister would be received in the Scottish manse; he at least had proved a second Good Samaritan.

The story of his visit to a London "sponging house" is worth telling.

"When I went to Mr. P——'s shop his sister took me to her mother's sick-room, saying little or nothing by the way. Her mother took me by the hand and said, 'The Lord hath sent you this day, for my Andrew is cast into prison.' . . . Andrew, you must know, is betrothed to a young lady whom he has been the instrument of converting to the Lord, and when he left S——'s, being unresolved what to do with his little capital, which could not meet his present business, his betrothed's uncle said, 'Get your bills discounted, and you shall not want for money; for they had always said that he was to have £500 on the wedding-day, and £500 afterwards. To this the servant of the Lord trusting, sunk his money in his lease, trusting to have floating bills met by his friend, who, growing cool because Andrew did not instantly succeed, withdraws his promises, and leaves our friend in deep waters; and deals with his niece to send poor Andrew all his letters, and to request hers in return. This took place on Friday, and this day, at breakfast, two of the officers of justice, at the instance of a creditor, came, and he went with them. Thus was his mother left and thus I found her all but overcome. I comforted her as I could and prayed with her as I could, and saw that something was to be done as well as said. So coming down, I sat down to write in the back shop, while his sister sought some clue to the creditor's address, that I might find the prison.

"So I proceeded and after diligent search, found Andrew in a house of which the door is kept always locked, seated with three men who seemed doleful enough—one resting his forehead on his hands, another reclining on a sofa, and the third, contemplating, half sottishly, a pint of porter. We communed together, and he was as calm and cheerful as Joseph, having Joseph's trust. . . . And he had tasted my evening discourse upon the minister's wayfaring, raven-brood life to be very good. While I talked with dear Andrew, not knowing but the others were the watchful officers of justice, he upon the sofa struck his forehead and started to his feet with a maniac air, crying, 'Oh, God, the horrors are coming upon me!' and wildly, very wildly, strode through the room. . . . And he with his hand upon his head wept, and the other man would comfort with 'patience'—'philosophy'. But the wounded man continued to burst out, and stride on, and beat his forehead. We gathered that he had been there for a whole month, daily expecting releasement, but none came, every message worse than another; and ever and anon he spoke of his wife. . . . I addressed words of comfort to him, and prevailed to sooth him; so that, when I came away, he said, 'It were well for us to receive many such visits, Sir.'

"*Tuesday, 15th*.—Andrew, who realised to me the idea of

Joseph in prison, has come away in great haste, and omitted to take his Bible with him, which I supplied with my far-travelled and dear companion, now firmly bound as at the first" (Ol. I, 320 ff.).

Irving told his wife that he had been able to help two Spaniards, the brothers Sottomayor. The elder had been abbot of a monastery. Enlightened by a copy of the Bible, he fled to England, and found a refuge with Irving. There he learnt English and the Caledonian divine learnt Spanish. The abbé married a lady whose confessor he had been; Irving had much difficulty in persuading her to give up her "idolatry" of the Virgin. It was not long before her husband died, but she found a chivalrous protector in the younger Sottomayor, who had been a soldier. Irving enjoyed reading with these brothers the Spanish Bible and *Don Quixote*—was he not somewhat of a *Quixote* himself? He was particularly interested in young men. His own observation taught him the deteriorating effect of the city on physique and character. "Men really dwindle as if they were plants." Family ties seemed to count for little. He describes a visit to two sisters and a brother in Fleet Market:—

"Their father dead, their mother in Essex, and two married brothers in town, so estranged from her by selfishness and worldliness, that 'If five shillings would save me from death, I hardly think I could muster it among all my relations.' Oh, what a blessing to Scotland are her family ties!"

Throughout his London ministry Irving spared neither time nor trouble in trying to help Scottish adventurers in London, being always careful to warn them of the dangers of "rising in the world" ("however approved by our ambitious countrymen"). Carlyle tells of his kindness to Macbeth, a probationer who had failed to get a parish, and had come to London,

"With no outlooks that were not bog meteors, and a steadily increasing tendency to strong drink. He knew Town well, and its babble, and bits of temporary cynosures and frequented haunts, good and perhaps bad. Macbeth had a sharp, sarcastic, clever kind of tongue. Like him I did not; there was nothing of wisdom, generosity or worth in him; but in secret, evidently discernable, a great deal of bankrupt vanity. Undeniable envy, spite and bitterness, looked through every part of him. A tall slouching lean figure; face sorrowful, malignant, black; not unlike the picture of a devil. . . . This broken Macbeth had been hanging a good while about Irving, who had taken much earnest pains to rescue and arrest him on the edge of the precipice; but latterly had begun to see that it was hopeless. One evening, it was dirty Winter weather, and I was present, there came to Irving, dated from some dark Tavern in Holborn, a piteous little Note: 'Ruined again (tempted, O how cunningly, to my old sin); been drinking these three weeks, and now have a chalk-score and no money, and can't get out. Oh help a perishing sinner!' The majority were of opinion, 'Pshaw, it is totally hopeless!' but Irving, after some minutes of serious consideration, decided, 'No, not *totally*,'—and directly got into a Hackney-coach, wife and he, proper moneys in pocket; paid the poor devil's tavern score (some £2 10s. or so), and brought him groaning home. I remember to have been taken up to see him, one evening, in his bedroom (comfortable airy place) a week or two after: he was in clean dressing-gown and night-cap, walking about the floor; affected to turn away his face, and be quite 'ashamed,' etc. etc. Comment I made none, here or downstairs. . . . Another time, which could *not* now be distant, when he lay again under chalk score and bodily sickness in his drinking-shop, there would be no deliverance but to the hospital; and there I suppose the poor creature tragically ended. He was not without talent; had written a 'Book *on the Sabbath*', better or worse; and, I almost think, was understood to have real love for his old Scotch mother" (*C.R.*, p. 255f.).

At a later period in his ministry, Irving undertook the care of two Greek youths, sent to him by Wolff the eccentric Jewish Christian missionary. "These two Greeks has Joseph Wolff wholly entrusted to me—so that I am to them as father, and guardian, and provider, and everything, which also I am right happy to be . . . till they return to their native Cyprus again." They were sent to Rosneath, to be educated at the parish school and to be under the care of the Rev. Robert Story. Irving afterwards realised that he had been rather rash to undertake this charge. But as he introduced Wolff to his friend Lady Georgina Walpole in 1826 (whom he married in 1827) it is probable that her ladyship gave financial assistance.

The Kirkcaldy Manse was not without its troubles. Mr. Martin had been unfortunate enough to own shares in a Fife Bank which suddenly collapsed owing to the misconduct of certain directors. He received a letter from Irving (21st January, 1826), reminding him that:

"We are but promised to live by the altar, and the rest is so much burdensome stewardry to which we submit in accommodation to the weakness of the people. . . . Therefore, be not cast down. Though the worst come to the worst, what mattereth it? The Kingdom of Heaven is still ours, unto which all things shall be added. . . ."

The letter concludes:—

"If we have been able to say, 'The will of the Lord be done,' [after the death of little Edward] . . . I trust you will be enabled to take well the spoiling of your goods."

But the Irvings did not forget to make this counsel more palatable by sending a good contribution to the Manse folk in their distress. The minister of Kirkcaldy had had to bring up a family of nine on a moderate stipend. He was gratified by receiving a St. Andrews D.D., in 1834, but died three years later from the effects of a carriage accident, leaving behind him a volume of *Remains ; Sermons ; Essays and Letters* (Edinburgh, 1838).

CHAPTER VII

"CLOUDCAPT TOWERS"

> " A Gothic fane, twin-towered, impressive, bold,
>   Looming majestic in the murky air;
> A home of hearts—a shrine—a house of prayer—
> Dear now as to the fathers who of old
> Heard IRVING the prophetic page unfold,
>   And wept that lying signs could him ensnare."

EVEN before Irving descended on London, the question had been raised whether it might not be practical to erect a kind of national "Cathedral" to represent the Church of Scotland in the metropolis. There were a hundred thousand Scotsmen with their descendants living in London, yet there was only accommodation for five thousand in the various churches connected with the Scottish Establishment and its seceding offshoots. The sanguine and energetic artist, Andrew Robertson, had written on 27th March, 1822, to the Rt. Hon. Charles Grant, M.P., urging him to secure the co-operation of other influential Scotsmen in promoting this object. Mr. Robertson further suggested to Edward Irving after his first visit to London, that a second visit might furnish the motive-power for launching the new movement. From Glasgow, Irving (still Dr. Chalmers' assistant) wrote declining the invitation. The reply shows how little his character was tinged with ignoble self-seeking:

"I could not ask from Dr. Chalmers the liberty of a second visit, because I do not myself see the fitness of it. It would be an act in the face of all my better sentiments, which truly are my whole wealth, and which, therefore, I am the less disposed to trifle with. If I were to come to London a second time, then indeed I were seeking and hunting after a settlement, and that by the stepping-stone of notoriety, the least evangelical of all approaches to the ministry. You all know what I am. I am making great improvement in my own opinion and in the opinion of others, which I date from the hearty reception of my London friends, under God. I have shown you to what lengths my compliance will go, the cause being worthy. . . ."

REGENT SQUARE CHURCH
Exterior in 1829

[To face page 102

The plan for a National Scots Kirk was then abandoned as visionary, but fifteen months later the Caledonian congregation, in urgent need of expansion, decided to appeal to the Scottish public for subscriptions; Irving was in the chair and fully approved of the project. (19th May, 1823). The appeal closed with a call to action:—

"that the religious spirit of many souls may be fostered, the dearest institutions of our fathers preserved in the reverence of their sons, the higher ranks retained in the communion of the Church, the emigrant children of Scotland comforted and established in the faith, and an accession of able and industrious ministers brought to sustain the religious state of this great Metropolis".

Through the patriotic spirit of the Highland Society of London, the accepted design (£12,000) was set aside in favour of a grander one by Mr. Tite (afterwards Sir William Tite, F.S.A.), a rising young architect. The cost, including the site in Regent Square, came to £21,000. The style was to be Gothic (then coming into favour) though the architect was a Greek protagonist in "the battle of the styles". The two "noble towers" were copied from York Minster and even now the façade is impressive in its way. Ecclesiastical architecture was at a low ebb in the early nineteenth century and the combination of Gothic architecture with provision for a maximum number of "sittings" has always presented a difficult problem. The new "National Scotch Church" compared creditably with the numerous Anglican churches built during the 'twenties, before Gothic was really understood. It was by far the finest place of worship outside the Establishment in London. It was even set up as a model in an important American publication (Lafever's *Modern Builder's Guide*, 2nd ed., 1841). The foundation-stone was laid on 1st, July 1824, by the Earl of Breadalbane, in the absence of the Duke of Clarence (afterwards William IV). The occasion passed off with éclat. *The Times* gave a full account of the proceedings, graced by "a number of the Scottish nobility and gentry". Among the seventeen hundred within the enclosure was Thomas Carlyle:—

"I well remember Irving's glowing face, streaming hair, and deeply-moved tones, as he spoke. . . . Twenty years after, riding discursively towards Tottenham, one summer evening, with London hanging to my right hand, like a grim and vast sierra, I saw among the peaks, easily ascertainable, the high minarets of that Chapel; and thought within myself, 'Ah, you fatal *tombstone* of my lost friend; and did a soul so strong and high avail only to build YOU!'" (C.R., P258 F.).

Some of the seventeen hundred spectators were doubtless less concerned with Irving's address than with the prospect of the sumptuous banquet that was afterwards to be served at the Freemason's Tavern, Great Queen Street.

Irving watched the yellow stones rising steadily against a background of green fields and gently undulating hills—no environment *then* of busy thoroughfares and teeming tenements. "When it is finished I doubt not it will be a seemly sanctuary." It suggested peace and quiet, in contrast to the confused bustle of the Caledonian Chapel. To his congregation he remarked:—

"We have had a most difficult and tedious way to make, through every misrepresentation of vanity and ambition: we have stood in eminent peril from the visits of rank and dignity which have been paid to us. There was much good to be expected from it; therefore we paid willingly the price, *being desirous that they who heard the truth but seldom should hear it when they were disposed.* But these, you know, are bad conditions to our being cemented together as a Church; they withdraw us from ourselves to those conspicuous people by whom we were visited; from which I have not ceased to warn you, and against which I have not ceased to be upon my own guard."

Before the new church was opened in May, 1827, four new elders and seven deacons were ordained. The question arose whether this should take place at Cross Street or Regent Square. "I think, brethren," said the minister in the kirk session, "that our hands will be strengthened if we number these men with us before we go up to take possession." Of the three existing elders, Mr. Dinwiddie had taken the lead in the building of the new church (d. 1830); Mr. Horn resigned when the "tongues" broke out; Mr. Blyth survived into a new era (d. 1875). Of the new elders, Mr. Hamilton and Mr. Nisbet were devoted to their minister but could not conscientiously follow him when it came to "tongues"; Mr. Mackenzie supported him throughout that controversy and left the church with him. The institution of the diaconate (almost extinct in Scotland at that time) appealed to Irving's love of the "apostolic" and made also for practical efficiency, as the deacons were entrusted with finance and church business generally; 867 sittings were let in the new church, giving a revenue of nearly £1,300.

The sanctuary with its proud inscription "ECCLESIA SCOTICA" was opened on Friday, 11th May, 1827. The special preacher was Dr. Chalmers, now Professor of Moral Philosophy in St. Andrews University. Years later, he described his experience to a friend:—"The congregation, in their eagerness to obtain seats, had already been assembled three hours. Irving said he would assist me by reading a chapter for me. *He chose the longest in the Bible*, and went on for an hour and a half. On another occasion he offered me the same aid, adding, 'I can be short.' I said, 'How long will it take you?' 'Only an hour and forty minutes'." No wonder Chalmers was doubtful and anxious, and thought it advisable to say "a word in season". His text was a pointed one (Jer. 6, 16): "Thus saith the Lord, Stand ye in the ways, and see, and ask for the old paths, where is the good way, and walk therein, and ye shall find rest for your souls." On Sunday (May 13th) Dr. Chalmers again preached and recorded in his journal:—

"Walked with Mr. Vertue, in whose house I am staying, to the church. The crowd gathered and grew, and the church was filled to an overflow. Lord Bexley still in the place where he was on Friday; Mr. Peel beside him on Friday. Lord Farnham, Lord Mandeville, Mr. Coleridge, and many other notables whom I cannot recollect, among my hearers. Coleridge I saw in the vestry, both before and after the service; he was very complimentary."

On May 20th the special preacher was the minister's friend, Dr. Gordon of Edinburgh. On the following Sabbath Irving conducted both services himself for the first time and shared in the general spirit of hope and satisfaction. Speaking of his countrymen, for whom the church had been built, he exclaimed: "Let us go in quest of them; let us search them out and bring them to the house of God." Then he proceeded to suggest how the church could be of use to the neighbourhood in which it was planted. In honour of the opening he presented to the congregation two silver salvers, which had been given to him by friends in Liverpool several years before at the dedication of the Scots Church, Rodney Street. These plates are now carefully treasured as a memorial of Irving himself and the inscription is very characteristic of his old-world piety:—

"These two plates I send to the National Scotch Church, London, on the 11th of May, 1827, the day of its opening, that they may stand on each side of the door to receive the offerings for the poor, and all other gifts of the congregation of the Lord in all time coming while He permits. And if at any time, which God forbid, the fountain of the people's charity should be dried up, and the Poor of the Lord's house be in want of bread, or His house itself under any constraint of debt, I appoint that they shall be melted into shillings and sixpences, for the relief of the same, as far as they will go.

"EDWARD IRVING, A.M., V.D.M.
"Minister of the National Scotch Church, London."

The opening of the new church was a turning-point for minister and congregation. The office-bearers were relieved to find the building well filled but no longer crowded, and settled down to the routine of congregational life and the task of lessening the debt. "The wide popular current ebbed away from the contracted ways of Hatton Garden, and subsided into a recognisable congregation in Regent Square" (Ol. I. 409). Had Irving been wise, he would have accepted the fact that he was no longer addressing the metropolis or "the age", but a clearly defined congregation. The effect was Irving's wounded vanity, said Carlyle:—

"Fashion went on her idle way, to gaze on Egyptian crocodiles, Iroquois hunters, or whatever else there might be; forgot this man, who unhappily could not in his turn forget. The intoxicating draught had been swallowed; no force of natural health could cast it out. Unconsciously, for the most part in deep unconsciousness, there was now the impossibility to live neglected; to walk on the quiet paths, where alone it is well with us. Singularity must henceforth succeed singularity. . . . For the last seven years Irving . . . shut himself up in a lesser world of ideas and persons, and lived isolated there". (*Fraser's Magazine*, No. 61).

No doubt Carlyle exaggerated—like Irving he was a rhetorician, though a more successful rhetorician. He could not resist the much-quoted sentence:—

"Siren songs, as of a new moral reformation (sons of Mammon, and high sons of Belial and Beelzebub, to become sons of God, and the gumflowers of Almack's to be made living roses in a new Eden), sound in the inexperienced ear and heart. Most seductive, most delusive!"

Allowing for over-colourful language, I feel Carlyle was in the main right; Irving was his greatest friend and had recognised his worth long before he was appreciated by the public. Had "the Caledonian Divine" been more of a realist, he would have realised that those who had been drawn to him to be "titillated by his picturesque originality" would tire of it after four years. He had specially trained himself for "teaching imaginative men, and political men and legal men, who bear the world in hand". But these thoughtful people could not be expected to attend regularly a service that "extendeth to three hours in the morning and two and a half in the afternoon". His practice of enlarging on the meaning of the psalms sung, besides expounding the Scripture lesson, must have been tedious. The deacons complained that people *would* enter and leave during public worship, "unless the duration of the services be made conformable to that of other churches." Had Irving ministered in the sixteenth or seventeenth century, his congregation would probably have rejoiced in getting "full measure running over". He refused to recognise changed times. To the embarrassed Kirk Session he declared, "I am resolved that two hours and a half I will have the privilege of".

But it was not merely the lengthiness of the services that kept away his more intelligent admirers. The ethical and social basis of his preaching had grown into something more doctrinal, interwoven with a dry strain of "unfulfilled prophecy". While the walls of the new church were rising under the hand of the builder, gradually indicating in concrete form the design of the architect, a like process of "edification" was going on in the mind of the preacher. On Moral and Doctrinal foundations there was rising a strange temple, sustained by Millenarian buttresses and reaching ever higher into the soaring pinnacles of the Miraculous. To change the metaphor—Coleridge used to say that Irving had "a growing mind". The trouble was that the growth was unnatural. Carlyle knew that "his once immeasurable quasi-celestial hope remained cruelly blasted, refusing the least *bud* farther. . . . Fallacious semblances of bud it did shoot out, again and again, under his continual fostering and forcing; but real bud never more" (*C.R.*, p. 254f.).

Even as early as 1824 his overwrought imagination and lack of historic sense found dramatic expression in a special sermon before the London Missionary Society at Tottenham Court Chapel. Instead of appealing for funds, as he was expected to, he tore off the veil of nineteen centuries and held up the example of the Apostles preaching without staff or scrip as "a standing order for the church, of continual obligation." "Though a missionary should go stocked like a trader and accredited like a royal envoy, when he cometh into close communication with the Spirit of God and the spirit of the people, he will be taught the utter helplessness of all these helps." Irving had heard an Evangelical orator proclaiming that "the first requisite of the modern Missionary is *prudence*, and the second *prudence*, and the third *prudence*." Quite rightly he pointed his hearers to Jesus, Who "took men of no name or reputation, by science untaught, by philosophy unschooled; fishermen, Galileans; a people despised of the Jews, who were themselves a despised people." But Irving overshot the mark. Mr. Orme, secretary of the London Missionary Society, cannot be blamed for addressing to him "An Expostulatory Letter", deploring his "ill-timed rhetorical display" (*three and a half hours in length*). The dedication of this sermon to Coleridge in printed form further alienated many people who would readily have forgiven a lapse in a spoken speech; further, it gave Irving a reputation for unsound doctrine in "the religious world". Charles Lamb refers to the Dedication in a letter to Leigh Hunt:—

"I have got acquainted with Mr. Irving, the Scotch preacher, whose fame must have reached you. Judge how his own sectarists must stare when I tell you he has dedicated a book to S.T.C., acknowledging to have learnt more from him than from all the men he ever conversed with. He is a most amiable, sincere, modest man in a room, this Boanerges in the temple. Mrs. Montagu told him the dedication would do him no good. 'That shall be a reason for doing it,' was his answer." The kind Elia adds, "Judge, now, whether this man be a quack" (*Works*, Methuen ed., vol. VII, 661).

On 5th July, 1824, Crabb Robinson was taking tea at Lamb's, and met Irving "and his friend, Mr. Carlyle." To his surprise—"an agreeable evening enough." For between Irving and Lamb, "with his incurable levity", there was room for "so little sympathy" that they "ought not to be intimate."

Irving unfortunately gained a reputation for notoriety from which he found it difficult to escape. There was a dispute in the Bible Society during the 'twenties owing to the circulation of the Apocrypha along with the canonical Scriptures.

Dr. Waugh, of Wells Street Secession Church, one of the most outstanding Scottish ministers in London, assured the Society that "all Scotland would rise as one man against the Apocrypha". After several years of controversy, the Edinburgh committee refused to accept "the adulterated Word." Irving sided with his countrymen but went to the London society's anniversary meeting, with the express object of preventing a schism. When he entered the Freemasons' Tavern on 2nd May, 1827, and ascended the platform after the meeting had started, he was greeted with mingled hisses and applause, and cries of "Chair, chair, support the chair!" "How is this, my Lord?" he demanded of Lord Teignmouth, who was presiding. "Do you know in what spirit I speak that you thus dare to put me down?" After much confusion and cries of "Irving, Irving!" he spoke in a loud, emphatic voice:—

"My lord, I rise to support the motion, and not to oppose it. . . . I left my sick bed in order to perform that duty to the Christian Church, and I will perform it, although for so doing I were to be hissed out of this assembly; aye, even if force were applied to thrust me out." (Cries of "No, no!"). "Your society has its arms on the two pillars of human superstition, and I believe that it will pull them down. But why should this mighty Samson commit a suicidal act, if by your wisdom and moderation you can attain the same end, and complete the same work? . . . If you will pour no oil into the wound which has been inflicted, it may prove to be incurable."

He pointed out that in Scotland the Apocrypha was not at all known or recognised, and suggested that the Society should bear this in mind and give a preference to agencies which distributed the canonical Scriptures. He then left the meeting as abruptly as he had entered, amid some cries of deprecation but with much applause. At the present day one is surprised at the heat provoked by this "Apocrypha controversy". The modern mind appreciates the books of *Wisdom* and *Ecclesiasticus*, and is well aware of arid tracts in *Leviticus* and *Ezekiel*, "canonical" though they be. But a century ago the idea of what was "inspired" was hard-and-fast. Irving would have been surprised to know that, at the service held in his memory at Annan on 7th December, 1934, the first lesson was taken from a book which he pronounced "shrewd rather than divine" with "little heavenward drift in it to the soul". That reading was from Ecclesiasticus 44: "Let us now praise famous men."

The two main influences in the development of Irving's later theology were: (1) inferences drawn from the sixteenth century standards of the Scottish Church; (2) his identification with the "Prophetic Movement", influential in his day.

He preferred the *Confession of Faith* drawn up immediately after the Reformation in 1560 to the *Westminster Confession* of 1646. Twice a year he read the *Scottish Confession* to his congregation—it was "the banner of the Church in all her wrestlings and conflicts", while the *Westminster Confession* was "but the camp colours which she hath used during her days of peace". He liked "the honest style of the 1560 Confession . . . without affectation of logical precision". He liked the vivid contrast of faith and expediency; providence and judgment were brought into the immediate foreground. He found that the Evangelicalism of his own day was preaching less than the full truth in making the Lord's Supper only "subjective in the believer and not elective in God". He liked the uncompromising statement: "We utterly condemn the vanity of those who affirm the sacraments to be nothing but bare and naked signs." "Conversion," so much stressed in Evangelical preaching, was merely the ripening of the germ implanted by baptism. Did he believe in the mechanical theory of "Baptismal Regeneration", soon to be pressed by the zealots of the Oxford Movement? Hardly—for baptism was inoperative in the case of "the non-Elect". But as Dr. R. H. Story pointed out:—

"This lingering belief in Calvinistic 'Election' by and by became extinct. Its extinction, like most of Irving's mental advances or retrogressions, was less the result of a logical development of his own thought, or a rigid study of the question, than of a personal influence. Walking down the shores of the Gairloch in the summer of 1828, after long discussion with A. J. Scott, and McLeod Campbell, Irving exclaimed, 'I see what you mean, Sir,' and then stated, satisfactorily, the doctrine of the universal love of God. On that very day, in preaching at Rosneath, he proclaimed it for the first time. Speaking afterwards of this to a friend, he said: 'Till I came to acknowledge the unlimited love of God, I was always finding myself striking against something or other, like a fish in a tub; but now I am in the ocean" (*Scottish Divines*, p. 242f.).

Only a few weeks earlier had McLeod Campbell called on Irving, who was staying with friends in Great King Street, Edinburgh. He afterwards corrected Mrs. Oliphant's interpretation of the interview (*Life*, II, 23ff.). He did not go to consult Irving as a diffident youth "warm in Celtic fervour" but harassed by intellectual difficulties. He came as one seeking a *sharer* in his own life-giving convictions.

"I found Irving sitting alone; at least there was no one with him but a child of his host playing on the drawing-room rug. I told him that I had come to see him, to state to him what my experience in personal dealing with my people had brought me to see on the subject of Assurance. He said that Assurance was a subject on which he needed more light, and that God might teach him by me; and turning to the child he added, 'He might teach me by that child.' . . . I mentioned it to Mrs. Oliphant simply as illustrative of what was very characteristic of him—viz., his practical expectation of Divine teaching through others; in cherishing which he had no feeling of giving place to others—either exalting them or lowering himself. . . . To understand him thus is to have the key to what seems to puzzle people—viz., the seeming weak yielding to the influence of others in his receiving anything—the seeming strong self-reliance in which he stood to what he had once received. But his ideal was to put himself and others out of account, and exalt God alone" (McLeod Campbell's *Memorials*, I, p. 51ff.).

Thus two kindred souls were brought together. "Dear Campbell, may your bosom be a pillow for me to rest upon, and my arm a staff for you to lean upon." Campbell had to visit London to meet his sister returning from India. He officiated in Regent Square the last three Sundays of June, 1828. He preached in Gaelic to the "Caledonian Society"—how Irving envied him that gift! It was eight years since he nearly accepted a call to the Caledonian Church; Principal Baird of Edinburgh had recommended him, but his father dissuaded him. Would Regent Square have been built *without* Irving's magnetism? Would Irving have "come into his kingdom" if he had never left Scotland?

The *Homilies on Baptism* (1828) were dedicated to "my wife, and the mother of my two departed children" (Edward and Mary). He avowed his belief that the true doctrine of baptism had been revealed to him "to prepare the parents for the loss of their children." "It remained in my mind," he said, "like an unsprung seed till watered by our common tears." This revelation was for others besides himself. "I resolved at every risk to open to all the fathers and mothers of the Christian Church the thoughts which had ministered to us so much consolation."

During this period Irving "enlarged" on the doctrines of the Trinity and the Incarnation. The mysteries of the faith had for him a special attraction. His attitude was that of a receiver waiting for a revelation rather than of a patient seeker after truth. He always spoke of "opening" a subject, as one who is in possession of a secret and has the privilege of unfolding it to others. No one can ignore the personal element in Irving's views—not even laborious, unimaginative German professors intent on reconciling the conflicting aspects of his theology! His doctrine of the Person of Christ puzzled his contemporaries. Actually he went behind the usual Evangelical emphasis on the Saviour's Atoning Death to the more Catholic doctrine of His Incarnation. He discovered it in the sixteenth century *Scottish Confession*, which theologians had almost forgotten. This doctrine he "opened" in the pulpit in such a one-sided, unguarded way as to give some people the impression that he believed Christ's body to be a mortal, corruptible body like that of all mankind, and His human nature to be identical with all human nature. He thus attracted the attention of a skulking spy of orthodoxy, the Rev. H. Cole. Mr. Cole heard Irving preach on one occasion and what he heard "made him tremble from head to foot". He saw the preacher afterwards in the vestry and asked: "Do you then, sir, really believe that the body of the Son of God was a mortal, corrupt and corruptible body like that of all mankind—the same body as yours and mine?" "Yes," was the reply, "just so; certainly, that is what I believe." Instead of availing himself of the preacher's courteous invitation to meet him during the week, the stranger rushed into print and in a pamphlet accused him of holding and teaching "the sinfulness of Christ's human nature". Nothing could have been further from Irving's intention than such gross heresy. He gloried in the Divinity of Christ. A clear refutation of the charge in his vestry would have silenced Mr. Cole—and how Irving *could* have silenced him! But Mr. Cole was an unscrupulous type of controversialist. He was a clergyman of the Anglican Church (of Clare College, Cambridge, and later a D.D.). He was the author of an obscurantist pamphlet attacking the Rev. Adam Sedgwick, Professor of Geology at Cambridge, whose teaching was "a Scripture-prostrating and Revelation-subverting philosophy". The learned ignoramus was sure his tract would settle for ever the relations of Scripture and Geology! One wonders if this pamphlet hurt Professor Sedgwick as much as the other pamphlet hurt Irving.

There was a regular hue and cry in the "religious world". The pious J. A. Haldane wrote a *Refutation of Mr. Irving's Heretical Doctrine* (1828). Irving replied in *The Orthodox and Catholic Doctrine of Our Lord's Human Nature* (1830) and *Christ's Holiness in the Flesh* (1831). The following passage illustrates his occasional clarity in setting his position:—

"The great point between us is, *not whether* Christ's flesh (human nature) was holy—for surely the man who saith we deny this blasphemeth against the manifest truth—*but whether* during His life it was one with us in all its infirmities and liabilities to temptation, *or whether*, by the miraculous generation, it underwent a change so as to make it a different body from the rest of the brethren. They argue for an identity of origin merely; we argue for an identity of life also. They argue for an inherent holiness; we argue for a holiness maintained by the person of the Son, through the operation of the Holy Ghost" (Preface, *On the Human Nature of Christ*, Works, vol. V, Appendix).

Irving derived Christ's sinlessness indirectly from God through the Holy Ghost, while his critics derived it directly from God. This stress on the Holy Ghost is significant; over-emphasis afterwards laid him open to the charge of holding that its working in Christ and in men was similar in nature and different only in degree. In practice it led to "Perfectionism" in the Irvingite circle, and ultimately to the belief that "Gifted" persons were mouthpieces of the Holy Ghost when "in the power".

The Reformation Standards of the Scottish Church also directed Irving's attention to the ideals of the Apostolic Church. In his discourse on the Parable of the Sower (1828) we find him comparing the Apostolic, Reformed, Nonconformist and Methodist eras to gold, silver, brass and lead Ages.

"Depend upon it, there will be no fifth. Ours is to gather together the crew, and warn them of a shipwreck, undergird the ship, and keep her afloat for a while. . . . We have experienced the Revival of a much inferior evangelical spirit, which I long hoped against hope to see perfected into the *Apostolic* spirit, but now behold drooping, a temporary and ineffectual shoot. . . . Verily the soil is growing thinner and thinner amongst us."

In his Notes on the Reformed *First Book of Discipline* he complains that

"To-day the gifts of the Spirit are not looked for by the Presbyters, but certificates of professors and petty attainments in literature and science; and floods of such unspiritual, *ungifted* persons are poured upon the Churches. I am one who feels the bondage of this system, and wait on Divine Providence for a call and the work of the Spirit for a warrant to restore to the Church its ancient liberty. And I believe I shall not wait long, when it shall please the Holy Ghost to furnish men with *gifts* to fit them for apostles, prophets, evangelists, discerners of spirits, *speakers with tongues* and interpreters of tongues. I am prepared for my part, and will seek to shew my brethren their duty to concur with me."

The earlier Scottish Reformers had their "Weekly Exercise." The object was:—

"That the kirk have judgement and knowledge of the graces, gifts, and utterances of every man; the simple, and such as have somewhat profited, shall be encouraged daily to study and prove in knowledge, . . . and every man shall have liberty to utter and declare his mind."

Irving asks:—

"Where is this ordinance now? I have no hesitation in saying, that, for want of this ordinance the Holy Ghost hath been more grieved and quenched than by almost anything else; and our church-meetings, from being for edification of the brethren by the *Holy Ghost showing himself in the variously gifted persons*, have become merely places for preaching."

Further, he thinks

"that the office of reader ought to be revived that the Spirit might have liberty to *draw out* the gifts of his servants and *show Himself in His Church*, which he is entirely prevented from doing. Not a man may open his lips of a thousand persons, save one only. What a divergence from the primitive Church, and from the platform of our Reformed Church!

"But to revive it, as our Churches are now constituted, would cause great confusion, and perhaps do more harm than good."

Commenting on the *Second Book of Discipline*, Irving notes that

"while it is stated that three out of five orders (Apostles, Evangelists, Prophets) were extraordinary and temporary, it is not declared they were done away with; but, contrariwise, that God 'Extraordinarily for a time may stir some of them up again'."

He adds:—

"There is no hint in Scripture of the withdrawal of the gifts. . . . I do not mean to place them by the side of the Twelve

Apostles. Gifts are now in the Church and not in any order of men.

"But we may not say the Apostolic office hath ceased; and I believe the prophetic office to be in the Church at this day.

"To the doctrine that they have been withdrawn by any act of God, I can never subscribe.

"To the fact that they have not been apparent, I confess with shame and confusion.

"To the hope that they are all reviving and will soon be manifested, I cleave with strong assurance.

"I hope to see the day when *not* ecclesiastical *courts*, of which we hear nothing in Scripture except for emergencies, but *persons* apostolical, evangelical, prophetical . . . shall rule over the Word of God."

It may be asked, if Irving was so devoted to Scotland and its Church, why did he continue to remain in London after he realised his popularity was on the wane? As a matter of fact he was approached in 1825 by a deputation from St. Cuthbert's, Edinburgh, with a view to succeeding his friend, Dr. Gordon. To his wife he wrote on 8th July: "I fear it would disperse the flock and smite down the proposed National Church." But during the Assembly week, May, 1828, he addressed crowded congregations day after day in St. Cuthbert's, the largest church in Edinburgh; St. Andrew's Church had proved too small. Six a.m. was the hour and the Apocalypse was the subject of his lectures! "I have no hesitation in saying it is quite woeful," notes Chalmers (Monday, 26th May). "There is power and richness, and gleams of exquisite beauty, but withal, a mysterious and extreme allegorization." Later in the summer he addressed a great audience at Perth. The Kirkcaldy catastrophe was fresh in people's thoughts (p. 28f) but the East Church was filled. As he unfolded his subject (the coming of the Son of Man, Matthew 24)—from a dark cloud which obscured the building, there came a flash of lightning and a crash of thunder. There was deep stillness in the congregation. The preacher paused; then from the stillness and the gloom his powerful voice rang out: "For as the lightning cometh out of the east, and shineth even unto the west, so shall the coming of the Son of Man be." One can imagine the effect!

In 1829 he was at the Assembly again. Dr. Dickson refusing him the use of St. Cuthbert's "upon very reasonable grounds of damage and danger", he thought of the grassy slopes of the King's Park as a place of gathering; however,

Hope Park Chapel was granted him (now Newington Parish Church). Business took him to the General Assembly, for he had received a commission from the Burgh of Annan to represent them as an elder. Living as he did, furth of Scotland and without the bounds of its National Church, he was not entitled to sit in the Assembly as a minister. The commission was challenged as illegal and rejected in spite of the championship of Dr. Andrew Thomson (who soon after entered the lists against him in matters of doctrine). He received, however, not only an invitation from the Moderator to sit on the floor of the House, but also one from the Lord High Commissioner to dine; Sir Walter Scott sat opposite him at table—was impressed but thought him unctuous and afterwards declared his squint "diabolical"! At Dumfries he preached in the Academy grounds to about 10,000 people, the same afternoon at Holywood to 6,000. The surveyor at Annan had the curiosity to measure the ground and estimate the people; he made it as many as 13,000.

"My voice easily reached over them all. At Holywood I was nearly four hours, and at Dumfries three hours; and yet I am no worse. Next day I went to Dunscore . . . I visited Lag the persecutor's grave and found it desolate; though surrounded with walls and doors, it was waste, weedy and foul. There is not a martyr's grave that is not clean and beautiful. At Dunscore, Thomas Carlyle came down to meet me. It is his parish church, and I rode up with him to Craigenputtock, where I was received with much kindness by him and his wife."

Irving suggested six weeks of rest on the Continent— he would take Carlyle with him as *dragoman!* Unfortunately nothing came of this; what he needed was not a holiday of preaching, but a holiday in some place where it was impossible for him to gather a congregation. Irving went on to Glasgow, the only town where he failed to gain the ear or heart of the community. He preached to a crowded but restless, unsympathetic audience, and found a hostile throng outside the church, ready with vernacular taunts, such as: "Ye're an awfu' man, Mr. Irving: they say you preach a Roman Catholic baptism, and a Mohammedan heaven." Irving faced the crowd calmly, took off his hat, bowed and with the words, "Fare ye well," strode forward. The crowd swung back, "like a door on its hinges", said an observer.

CHAPTER VIII

GATHERING CLOUDS

"Through the stained window of his rich-coloured fancy
every landscape wove its luxurious gaiety or its purple gloom."
(Dr. James Hamilton).

IN 1830 Irving wrote to his father-in-law, Mr. Martin, about a young minister who had asked his advice:—

"Tell him from me that it is a great advantage to be out of Scotland for a while; Knox and Melville, and almost all the reformers, were so; and there is rising in your quarters a commotion which will give forth, if I err not, fearful issues."

The hide-bound orthodoxy of Scotland was being roused to a heresy-hunt by the "new views" of John McLeod Campbell, minister of Rhu. His doctrine of God's universal love (not confined to the Elect) stirred up the hatred of ecclesiastics and secured his deposition from the ministry. He preached independently and studied quietly, giving to the world his epoch-making *Nature of the Atonement* in 1856.

Irving had met McLeod Campbell at Rosneath manse and learnt from him the "freeness of the Gospel". But for the awakening of controversy through the alleged heresy of McLeod Campbell and the layman, Erskine of Linlathen, it is possible that the General Assembly might not have paid much attention to the hue and cry that had been raised in London, owing to Irving's unfamiliar doctrine of the Person of Christ. But the presentation of the Rev. Hugh Maclean to the parish of Dreghorn, Ayrshire, was challenged by the orthodox, for he had imbibed Irving's views since hearing his noble Ordination Charge at London Wall in 1827. The fact that he was a protégé of Irving drew attention to the heresy of his teacher. Dr. Andrew Thomson and the *Christian Instructor* attacked him vigorously. Irving himself could be fiercely controversial when he liked, but his attitude to one of the principal contributors to the *Instructor* reveals remarkable candour and magnanimity. His chief orthodox assailant was the Rev. Marcus Dods, of the Presbyterian Church, Belford, Northumberland (father of the famous Professor Marcus Dods, destined to bring heresy-hunting into disrepute). Irving writes to him in the most brotherly way, greets him as a fellow-labourer in the Lord's vineyard and invites him to come and talk theology whenever he is in London. "I write this without the knowledge of any one, my wife asleep on the sofa beside me and my porritch cooling before me." (This letter is printed in full by Mrs. Oliphant, II, 113ff).

On 2nd June, 1830, Irving appealed to Chalmers, as his "dear master", to intervene and vindicate his orthodoxy; "Mind my words when I say, 'The Evangelical party in the Church of Scotland will lay all flat if they be not prevented'". Mrs. Oliphant speaks of "Chalmers' timid silence" (II, p. 119). I feel that the doctor, *par excellence* of the Scottish Church, ought to have stood up for fairplay when McLeod Campbell was hounded out of the Church by the obscurantists. But Irving was himself fast becoming an obscurantist in his tirades against freedom of thought in Church and State. And in any case, not holding a parish in Scotland put him out of their reach to a large extent. Chalmers knew Irving's character; he probably felt that there was a strain of fanaticism so potent that it would in course of time prove his undoing and there was no use shielding him temporarily.

Irving's views on the doctrine of our Lord's human nature came up in the Presbytery of London in 1830 in connection with the ordination of his assistant, A. J. Scott, who had received a call to the kirk at Woolwich. Scott held the same views as Irving. The Presbytery purposely appointed Irving as member of a committee that was to confer with the minister-elect; the former acquiesced in a statement that was to settle the dispute, but this warning did not lead to any change in the doctrine preached at Regent Square. On 20th July a proposal to examine Irving's writings was only set aside out of courtesy to his objection that Christ's rule as to offences (Matt. 18, 15) had not been complied with. This private interview having failed, the Presbytery on 19th October decided to examine *The Orthodox and Catholic Doctrine of our Lord's Human Nature*, the author alone dissenting. He who had so often exalted

Presbyterian polity then withdrew from the jurisdiction of the Presbytery. The Presbytery on 30th November accepted its committee's report that the said book contained "errors subversive of the great doctrines of Christianity". The court thrice summoned Irving to return to its jurisdiction, and finding him contumacious, declared him no longer a member of Presbytery till he should openly renounce his errors. On 15th December, the minister, assistant, elders and deacons of the National Scotch Church, without actually referring to the decision of Presbytery, issued a solemn statement denying the charges brought against them, "whether from ignorance, misapprehension, or wilful perversion of the truth", affirming in the most definite manner their adhesion to the orthodox Christian doctrine of the Person of Christ. A copy of this declaration was published in the newspapers. The Presbytery retaliated by publishing their proceedings.

A. J. Scott, Irving's protégé, was a young minister whose broad culture, keen intellect and profound spirituality were fully recognised only in a later generation, by the *Dictionary of National Biography* and by Dr. John Hunter (*Expositor*, 8th Series, Nos. 125-6). After the withdrawal of his licence, Scott continued preaching at Woolwich, but his supreme gift was lecturing. He was Professor of English Literature at Owens College, Manchester, from 1851 till his death in 1866.

Irving had no great respect for the three ministers and two elders who then composed the minute "Presbytery of London". No doubt several of them were envious of his gifts and influence. In the eyes of the law, the Presbytery in England was a voluntary association with no power to bind any congregation that refused to be associated. Irving's position was roughly analogous to that of a few English (Evangelical) clergy in Scotland who profess to be Episcopalians and yet reject the jurisdiction of the Scottish bishops. The time was not far distant, however, when the office-bearers of Regent Square Church would find it necessary to approach the Presbytery again, with a view to removing their minister. Irving still looked proudly to the mother-Church, his National Zion. But the General Assembly of 1831, the Assembly that deposed McLeod Campbell, withdrew A. J. Scott's licence to preach, remitted the case of H. B. Maclean to his Presbytery; and on the occasion of a *Report upon Books and Pamphlets containing Erroneous Opinions*, urged that it was the duty of any Presbytery within whose bounds the Rev. Edward Irving might be, to inquire whether he was the author of certain works, and to proceed thereafter as they should see fit. This censure was passed by the Assembly, though there were two other motions, one more severe, the other a contemptuous appeal for toleration (on the ground that these works were not calculated to influence any well-informed mind). Irving felt deeply wounded, but the censure made little difference to his actual position. He was still an ordained minister of the Church of Scotland, though now a "congregationalist" in practice. In the normal course of events, his future was secure—unless he was foolish enough to put his head in a hornet's nest by seeking a parish in Scotland and thus coming under the jurisdiction of a Presbytery.

Irving was now isolated. He might have used his isolation to good purpose had he devoted himself, a lonely pioneer, to the hard task of emancipating contemporary theology from the bondage of traditionalism. But in these later years he voluntarily associated with obscurantists of the narrowest type in Church and State. Political reform was abhorrent to him. He opposed Catholic Emancipation and the repeal of the "Test Acts" which in England still made partaking of the sacrament in the Anglican Church a necessary qualification for taking public office. He talked of the old Puritan divines, but failed to realise that the galling disabilities of the Nonconformists of his own time were the real cause of "Voluntaryism". London University, then being founded by progressives anxious to escape from the dead ecclesiasticism of Oxford and Cambridge, was to him "the Synagogue of Satan" (p. 11*n*). This descendant of Covenanters and Whigs announced himself a believer in the Divine Right of Kings! In the midst of all his theological and ecclesiastical troubles, he waited on Lord Melbourne and presented a petition calling on the new king, William IV, to proclaim a national fast. While awaiting the Premier's leisure in the busy ante-room, Irving called on his three accompanying elders to kneel down with him and pray aloud "that they might find favour in the sight of the king's minister". Admitted to Lord Melbourne's presence, he read his address at length, sonorously denouncing the revolutionary principle that power is from the people, the lack of true doctrine and discipline in the Church, the luxury and selfishness of the noble and rich, the avarice of the traders, the disaffection of the poor. What did he recommend? He urged the appointment in the royal household of "grave and godly chaplains", the strict observance of the "Sabbath" at Court and elsewhere; the "entertainment" by the nobility of "men of piety within their houses for morning and evening worship"; finally, the injunction of a day of fasting and humiliation for the national shortcomings. Then Mr. Mackenzie, Irving's right-hand elder, solemnly addressed the Premier. Lord Melbourne was much impressed, we are told, by Irving's simple-hearted earnestness, and cordially shook hands on parting with the Caledonian divine, who, "holding him in his gigantic grasp implored the blessing and guidance of God on his administration". On the one hand was the bland and politic man of the world, whose favourite motto was "Why not leave it alone?" On the other was the man of God, to whom all truth was absolute and hesitation or compromise unknown.

In the autumn of 1830 the Irvings accepted an invitation to stay with Lady Powerscourt in Ireland. It was not much of a holiday, day after day was occupied with public meetings and private conferences. Mrs. Irving does not seem to have taken much care of his health. "You know well from my feeling and acting with regard to dear Edward, that I am not one who am continually in fear about health, when a man is doing the Lord's work." One of the Irish papers gives us a glimpse of his preaching at the Scots' chapel, Dublin:—

"This place was not only crowded to suffocation, but several hundreds assembled outside on benches placed in the yard. The reverend preacher was placed at the south-west window, the frame of which had previously been removed, from which he was audibly heard. . . . We observed many highly respectable Roman Catholic gentlemen present." (*Saunders' News-Letter*, 18th September, 1830).

In a letter to his sister-in-law Elizabeth, Irving describes how Lady Powerscourt drove them to Kingstown and waited with them for the boat, which had been delayed. As Isabella was resting on a sofa in the inn, five-year-old "Maggie", sitting on Lady Powerscourt's knee, broke the silence and offered to sing her ladyship a song. This was what she sang:

"Come, my little lambs,
　And feed by my side,
And I will give you to eat of my body,
And to drink of the blood of my flesh,
And ye shall be filled with the Holy Ghost,
And whosoever believeth not on me
　　Shall be cast out;
But he that believeth on me
　　Shall feed with me
Beside my Father."

"Then said I to Isabella, 'Where did Maggie learn that song?' She said: 'Nowhere, and no one taught her.' I called the child and said: 'Maggie, my dear, who taught you that song?' She said: 'Nobody. I made it one day after bathing;' and so I thought upon the words, 'Out of the mouths of babes and sucklings I have ordained praise,' and I was comforted."

His infant Samuel had died a few months before: the day after his death he preached from the words of David: "I shall go to him, but he will not return to me." Martin was born early in 1831; this was the son who lived to be Principal of Melbourne University—Melbourne, named in honour of the statesman with whom his father had that singular interview. Maggie (or Meggy) was the only child who lived long enough to be a companion to her father, who well knew how to write to a child. Here is a letter he wrote from Birmingham, where he was to preach at the Scots' church:—

"My own Meggy,—Papa got down from the coach, and his large book, and his bag, and his cane with the gold head. And a little ragged boy and his little sister, with ballads to sell . . . trotted by papa's side. The boy said, 'I will carry your bag, sir.' Papa said, 'I have no pennies, little boy; so go away.' But he would follow papa, he and his little sister, poor children! So papa walked on with his bag under his cloak in one hand, and his book and his staff under his cloak in the other. It was dark and the lamps were lighted, and it was raining, but still (they) followed papa—and the boy said, 'I will find you where Mr. Macdonald lives.' So we asked, and walked through very many streets, and came to a house. And the door was open, and I said to the woman, 'Is Mr. Macdonald in?' The woman said, 'No, sir, he is dining out.' Papa said, 'What shall I do? I am come to preach for him to-morrow.' She said, 'There is no sermon till Saturday.' Papa said, 'Are you sure?' She said, 'There is mass in the morning.' Now, my dear Meggy, the mass is a very wicked thing, and is not in our religion, but in a religion which they call Papacy. So papa knew by that word Mass that this was not the Mr. Macdonald's, but another one. So away trudged papa, his bag, his book, and his staff under his cloak, and the little ragged boy, and his sister with the ballads. Papa was angry at them because they would not go away, and had brought him to a wrong place. But papa had pity upon them, and asked them about their papa and mamma. Their papa was dead, and their mamma was in bed sick at home. So papa took pity upon them, and gave them a silver sixpence—and they went away so glad. I heard them singing as they ran away home to their poor mother. Now papa took his bag and put his cane through it, and swung it over his shoulder upon his back, as he does when he carries Meggy downstairs. . . ."

In his letters to his wife, Irving could see the lighter side of life, even when the shadows were closing in upon him. We find, amid passages of barren controversy and morbid pietism, the relating of some incident that has tickled his fancy, e.g.

"Dr. Sumner, now Bishop of Chester, was in Hatchard's, and said to a clergyman whom he met there, 'I have a note here to wait upon the Duke of Wellington. Tell me where he lives.' He went, was back in about ten minutes, and the clergyman was still there. 'You have soon got your business over.' 'Yes, and in so short a time I am promoted to the see of Chester. I was shown into a room—in came the Duke: Are you Dr. Sumner? I am commanded to offer you the bishopric of Chester. Do you accept it or not? Yes? Then put down your name here. Good morning'."

For all his belief in the national recognition of religion, Irving had little in common with the worldly Erastianism of the Church of England as he saw it. When he died in 1834 the Oxford Movement was but a year old. No doubt he would have had hard things to say about "Puseyism". But he would have acknowledged in a man like Newman a lofty unworldly soul, akin to his own.

In the midst of his many-sided activities, Irving found time in 1828 to write *A Tale of the Times of the Martyrs* for his friend, Allan Cunningham, editor of the *Anniversary* (an "Annual" which only appeared once). For *Fraser's Magazine* he wrote a short narrative, *The Loss of the Abeona* (reprinted in Jones' *Biographical Sketch of the Rev. Edward*

Irving, 1835, p. 14–p. 26). This is a dialogue between a Glasgow minister and a young man who was wrecked on his way to the Cape of Good Hope, one of the few survivors from the burning ship, rescued in an open boat by a Portuguese ship. It is detailed, graphic and true to life—no doubt based on a pastoral experience of his own in Glasgow. A story like this would draw heavily on the melodramatic resources of any author. Yet Irving's manner is simple and straightforward. Written in 1828, it shows that Irving's "inflated style" had not entirely become his own and he *could* write unaffectedly when he chose to.

The Glasgow publisher Collins would sometimes call on him when in London. Carlyle tells how on one occasion he discoursed on the villany of common publishers;

"How, for example, on their '*Half-profits* System', they would show the poor Author a Printer's Account pretending to be paid in full, Printer's signature visibly appended—Printer having really touched a sum *less* by 25 per cent. . . . Irving could not believe it; denied stoutly on behalf of his own Printer, one Bensley, a noted man in his craft; and getting nothing but negatory smiles, and kindly but inexorable contradiction, said he would go next morning and see. We walked along, somewhere Holborn-wards; found Bensley and Wife in a bright, comfortable room; just finishing breakfast; a fattish, solid, rational and really amiable-looking pair . . . by both of whom we were warmly and honourably welcomed. Irving with grave courtesy laid the case before Bensley (perhaps showing him his old signature and account), and asked, If that was or was not really the sum he had received? Bensley, with body and face, writhed uneasily, evidently loth to lie, but evidently obliged by the laws of trade to do it. 'Yes, on the whole, that was the sum!' Upon which we directly went our ways—both of us convinced, I believe, though only one of us said so" (*C.R.*, p. 276f.).

Irving was always mortified when his high opinion of men was shaken, that is, where character was concerned. He was not always ready to accept literary reputations at face value—"I think not of them so highly as I was wont", he remarked after his first interview with Wordsworth. He had seen in his friend Carlyle a genius who would one day startle London, and right proud would he have been if spared to see him as author of *Sartor, The French Revolution* and *Past and Present*.

Irving was not such a "simple siren" after all! His

testimonial failed to procure for Carlyle the Chair of Moral Philosophy at St. Andrews (on the transference of Dr. Chalmers to Edinburgh in 1828). But his other supporters were Goethe, Jeffrey, Brewster and Leslie; and even these names did not dazzle Principal Nichol who wanted a respectable, manageable parish minister for his vacant Chair. Irving himself was interested enough in academic distinctions to write to Dr. Chalmers (December, 1828), inquiring whether it was not possible for him to earn the D.D. degree by examination, defending his "theses" in the Latin tongue, according to the ancient discipline. Sir John Sinclair had volunteered to obtain for him the D.D. five years earlier, but he objected to degrees being "honorary". This Sir John Sinclair, first President of the Board of Agriculture, was the compiler of the *Statistical Account of Scotland* which has been appraised at its true worth in our own day as a Scottish *Domesday Book*. Carlyle met him in the street in 1825, "a lean old man, tall but stooping, in tartan cloak; face very wrinkly, nose blue; he spoke to Irving with benignant respect; whether to me at all I don't recollect".

Unfortunately, it was someone of a very different type whom Irving went to see on one occasion. Near the Admiralty, they mounted narrow wooden stairs and entered a comfortless little office where an elderly official was seated within rails, "busy in the red tape line".

"This was the Honourable Something or other," explains Carlyle, "great in Scripture Prophecy, in which he had started some sublime new idea, well worth prosecuting, as Irving had assured me. Their mutual greetings were cordial and respectful; and a lively dialogue (ensued) on Prophetic matters. . . . I strictly unparticipant, sitting silently apart till it were done. The Honourable Something had a look of perfect politeness, perfect silliness; his face, heavily wrinkled, went smiling and shuttling about, at a wonderful rate, and in the smile there seemed to me to be lodged a frozen sorrow, as if bordering on craze. On coming out, I asked Irving, perhaps too markedly, 'Do you really think that gentleman can throw any light to you on anything whatever?' To which he answered, good-naturedly, but in a grave tone, 'Yes, I do.' Of which the fruits were seen before long" (*C.R.*, p. 279).

This person was Hatley Frere, brother of J. H. Frere, British envoy in Spain during the Napoleonic wars. But it was Henry Drummond, banker and landowner, who was to prove the driving power of the "Prophetic Movement". Carlyle describes a dinner party at his house in Belgrave Square, August, 1831.

"This Drummond proved to be a very striking man. Taller and leaner than I, but erect as a plummet, with a high-carried, quick, penetrating head, some five-and-forty years of age, a singular mixture of all things—of the saint, the wit, the philosopher—swimming, if I mistake not, in an element of dandyism. His dinner was dandiacal in the extreme: a meagre series of pretentious kickshaws, on which no hungry jaw could satisfactorily bite, flunkies on all hands, yet I had to ask four times before I could get a morsel of bread." (The guests were Spencer Perceval, M.P.; Tudor, a Welshman; Irving and Carlyle.) "They were all prophetical, Toryish, ultra-religious. I emitted, notwithstanding, floods of Teufeldröckhist Radicalism, which seemed to fill them with *weender* and amazement, but was not ill received. We parted with friendliest indifference, and shall all be glad to meet again, and to part again" (To Mrs. Carlyle, 22nd August, 1831).

This Henry Drummond (1786-1860) was of an old Scottish family on his father's side, since 1717 bankers at Charing Cross; his mother was a daughter of the first Viscount Melville, whose monument in St. Andrew Square is an Edinburgh landmark. After Harrow and Christ Church, Oxford, he entered the banking business and became an M.P. in 1810. He was responsible for the passage of an Act protecting the public against fraudulent bankers. Later in life he sat for West Surrey (1847-60) and became noted for learned, sarcastic and witty speeches. He was inclined to be crotchety and was at his best when dealing with such subjects as tithes, Jewish disabilities or the inspection of convents. Tory in tendency, he was usually very independent in his attitude to the Government. But it was as Churchman that he was most notable. In 1817 he came under strongly religious influences and, "satiated with the empty frivolities of the fashionable world", broke up his hunting establishment and was on his way to the Holy Land, when he was stopped by circumstances that he regarded as providential. He came to Geneva just as Robert Haldane was leaving it. Haldane had sold his paternal estate of Airthrie to devote himself to evangelistic work, and at Geneva inveighed against the Socinian tendencies of the Church authorities. Drummond threw his whole energy into the task of restoring to Evangelical purity the city of Calvin, refused to be silenced by the Council of State, encouraged the separatist ministers to organise a new Church, and helped to found the Continental Society which for many years he largely maintained.

On his return to England he became interested in Irving, particularly when in 1825 he started preaching on the "Second Advent". His association with Irving (in spite of his "heresy" as to the Person of Christ) led to a fast and furious pamphlet controversy with the Haldanes, but long after it had spent itself, Drummond and James Haldane met accidentally and "shook hands with mutual goodwill, like Christians and gentlemen, as if nothing had occurred to interrupt their cordiality".

Henry Drummond was "a singular mixture of all things". Banker, politician, evangelist, controversialist, prophet, philanthropist, economist and historian of "Noble British Families"—he played many parts in his time. With all his gifts, he was a dangerous friend for Irving. "He, without unkindness of intention, did my poor Irving a great deal of ill," said Carlyle in retrospect. Only two years after Irving's death, Drummond, far from disheartened at the fiasco of *prophesying* and *tongues*, actually hastened to Nuneham to inform the Archbishop of York that the end of the world was imminent! Shortly before his death in 1860, he invited the Carlyles to Albury—a mistaken date. "In a few months more Henry himself was dead; and no more mistake possible again", remarks Carlyle grimly.

Drummond had a favourite saying: "In proportion as the Bible is known, the Church is sound and the people moral; in proportion as the Bible is concealed, the Church is corrupt and its members perverted." That is true, but it depends upon how the Bible is interpreted. Drummond shared with the Haldanes and other evangelistic people an interpretation of Scripture that was painfully literal. "Simple Bible teaching" was sometimes ingeniously complicated in laborious attempts to settle difficulties in the Old Testament and extract the Gospel from Leviticus, Ezekiel, and Daniel. There was no real excuse for educated people persisting in what we would now call an arid and acrid "Fundamentalism". The old eighteenth century rationalism had been swept aside by the new insight and passion that arose in romantic poetry and in prose expressed itself in a larger and closer study of nature and humanity.

There were constructive as well as destructive German critics; the startling theory of Strauss did not appear till 1835, nor did Feuerbach start writing till 1833. "The Oriel School" at Oxford was interpreting the new German criticism in the terms of Christian experience during the 'twenties. Thirlwall translated Schleiermacher's essay on Luke's Gospel in 1825. Coleridge and Erskine of Linlathen were drawing attention to the spirit of Scripture rather than its letter, and showing the folly of building theology on either a catena of Scripture texts or Patristic citations.

This new light was generally disregarded. In a theological public opinion so unenlightened it was not surprising that there would soon arise the un-historical claims of the Oxford movement. The German hypothesis as to the composition of the Gospels was deemed by T. H. Horne:—

"Not only detrimental to the character of the sacred writings, but also as diminishing the value and importance of their testimony, and further, as tending to sap the *inspiration* of the N.T." (*Introduction to critical study of Scripture*, 1818.)

"The mere fact," said Principal Tulloch, "that the Biblical studies of the age were mainly pursued under the guidance of this book, entirely uncritical in its spirit and method—is the best evidence of how low these studies had sunk, and how little the theological mind of the time was prepared to welcome such an essay as Thirlwall's *St. Luke*."

Irving himself wrote an Introduction to Bishop (George) Horne's *Commentary on the Psalms* which appeared as far back as 1771.

If such was the clerical level, we can well understand that to a theologian like Whately the majority of people seemed to live in an atmosphere of delusion, making New Testament writers responsible for notions that, to a just and intelligent criticism, had no existence there, and indeed were contrary to its spirit and teaching rightly interpreted. "Criticism" was merely a signal for such people to retire within the shell of strict Verbal Inspiration, and to be constantly on the defensive.

This granted, the "insight" of the O.T. prophets and of the writers of Daniel and Revelation was entirely overlooked in favour of their "foresight". The prevailing "mass psychology" was one of alarm, fear, and expectation of the "end of the age". The fury and violence of the French Revolution was succeeded by the meteor-like passage

GATHERING CLOUDS

of Napoleon. If the prelude was so striking, what would be the consummation? Nor was the Apocalyptic Spirit entirely confined to religious cliques, but found poetical expression in Byron's *Earth and Heaven* and Moore's *Love of the Angels*, and artistic expression in the pictures of Danby and Martin. In religious circles, however, the tendency to dwell on the future was intensified. For there, Christianity was conceived of as "a scheme of salvation authenticated by miracles, and, so to speak, *interpolated* into human history. And so Philosophy, Literature, Art and Science were conceived of apart from religion". Prejudice could, therefore, do its work. Radicalism and infidelity were closely associated; the Whigs, associated with the *Edinburgh Review*, were deemed sceptical and latitudinarian, ready to play into the hands of Roman Catholics craving for Emancipation; Toryism was the bulwark not only of the Constitution but of religion, for as Lord Cockburn said: "Devotion has changed its place and gone to the higher ranks." And, not least, the success of the Continental Catholic Revival after the fall of Napoleon provoked a widespread fear of "Popery".

There was a general demand for books dealing with "unfulfilled prophecy". But works like Faber's *Dissertations* were general rather than particular in application. The ingenious Hatley Frere had for some years been looking for a man who had the ear of the public, through whom he might broadcast his special interpretation. The receptive ear he found in Irving, who (as we have seen) was only too ready to hear, adopt and preach the new doctrine.

"He had crossed the Rubicon. Henceforth the gorgeous and cloudy vistas of the Apocalypse became a legible chart of the future to his fervent eyes" (Ol. II, 222).

The new influence was only too evident in a sermon preached before "The Continental Missionary Association", and published under the title of *Babylon and Infidelity Foredoomed*. The keynote was struck in the Dedication to Frere—"I had no rest in spirit until I offered myself as your pupil." There was little originality in the book. Millenarian tenets had never disappeared in the Christian Church; with modifications in each age, they stood for:—

"(1) A final impending battle with God's enemies; (2) The speedy return of Christ; (3) Who will judge all men; (4) and establish His kingdom on earth, which would last 1,000 years. (Rev. 20 being only N.T. reference.)

"In spite of Augustine's teaching that the millennial kingdom was already an accomplished fact, having commenced at the appearing of Christ,—the old millenarianism was transmitted in an undercurrent, suddenly bursting out from time to time in the Middle Ages (e.g., Joachim of Floris), its adherents generally assailing the Papacy and a secularised Church. It appeared in uncompromising strength in sixteenth century Anabaptism, and though disowned as "opiniones Judaicae" by the orthodox Reformers, found its way in a milder form into Pietistic circles of Protestant Churches, where it was closely associated with belief in Verbal Inspiration and "Revivalism." (*Ency. Britan. art. Millennium.*)

The common stock of Irving worked into a Philosophy of History by elaborate symbolisation, Daniel and Revelation being regarded as puzzles verifying each other's predictions. For 1,260 years the Saints were to be delivered over to the "little horn" (the Pope) i.e. A.D. 533—1793. The French Revolution, with its proscription of Christianity, the new Missionary Movement, mechanical progress, all were regarded as "signs of the end". The Second Coming was fixed seventy-five years following 1793 (1868). With a little re-adjustment the scheme might have been taken from a modern "British Israelite" pamphlet. Notice the "Superior Spiritual Blessings of God on the British Nations!

One is struck by Irving's sectarian bitterness and reckless dogmatism:—

"The Reformed Church hath set aside faith in the Scriptures, and builds upon the common sense of mankind and were better to acknowledge Paine's 'Age of Reason' than the Gospel. The whole philosophy of Europe serveth infidelity. . . . There is nothing but rationalism in religion and liberalism in politics." "Even among such as are spiritual there is a constant appeal to *the useful*. The intellect hath become all sufficient." "The Church is in the Laodicean state."

"The cloudy German and the phlegmatic Hollander and the hardy Switzer" are accused in particular of choking the seed with "the wild weeds of the human understanding". (British Evangelicals were active at this time trying to "revive" Continental Protestantism—efforts not always appreciated by Continental Protestants.) The British

Government through "wicked patronage is endeavouring to keep" down every spiritual minister as if he had the plague-spot on his forehead, while the dissenter is too full of political grievances, a sad declension from "the Puritan or Seceder of the ancient spirit". As an opponent of political Reform and Catholic Emancipation, he loathes the "specious name of *toleration* and liberality". "When our rulers permit to the worshippers of the beast, the same honours, immunities and trusts which they permit to the worshippers of the true God—that day our national charter is forfeited and we are sealed no more."

It is unnecessary to quote more to illustrate Irving's growing alienation from the best thought of his age, intensified by his translation of the work of (strange to say) a Spanish Jesuit, to which he contributed a lengthy Introduction (Lacunza, Pseudonymn "Ben Ezra," *Coming of the Messiah in Glory and Majesty*, 1827).

"O Edward Irving! O Edward Irving!" cried Coleridge. "By what fascination could your spirit be drawn away from passages like Thess. 2 (1–10), to guess and dream over the rhapsodies of the Apostle . . . to befit a dreaming Talmudist not a Scriptural Christian."

"I preclude all prognostication of time, event, mode, persons and place of the accomplishment. It may be long before Edward Irving sees how much grander a front his system would have presented had he trusted to the proof of Scripture, of undisputed catholicity, to the *spirit* of the *whole* Bible, its fitness to satisfy the needs and capacities of mankind, and its harmony with the general plan of the divine dealings with the world—and left the Apocalypse in the background. But alas! He has made the main strength of his hope to rest on a vision. . . ." (Notes on Irving's "Ben Ezra," *English Divines*, II, p. 337).

It is one of the tragedies of Church History that one who had the ear of the public like Irving should have adopted the obscurantist views then so popular, instead of popularising the rich seminal thought of Coleridge, Erskine, and the Oriel School; they had the treasure but could not unlock it. Had he done so, he might have modified and enlarged English and Scottish Evangelicalism without impairing their ardour, thus preparing the Churches for the sudden outburst of Criticism later in the century. But Irving was carried along by the swirling torrent of impulse, undirected by logic or consistency. "He had many thoughts pregnantly expressed, but they *did not tend all one way.*" His thought flowed along, "not as a swift rolling river, but as a broad, deep and bending or meandering one. Sometimes it left on you the impression almost of a fine noteworthy *lake.*"

His conceptions were too often merely the raw material of impressions made on him by circumstances, and by those with whom he was intimate, unsifted and coloured by a restless, imaginative and rather morbid temperament.

Carlyle describes his visit in the Spring of 1827 at Edinburgh:—

"He was very friendly, but had the look of trouble, of haste, and confused anxiety; sadly unlike his old good self. He talked with an undeniable self-consciousness, and something which you could not admit but to be religious mannerism. 'Farewell! I must go then and suffer persecution as my fathers have done'. It made one drearily sad" (*C.R.*, 285f.).

While in 1831

"He was surrounded by weak people, mostly echoes of himself. . . . He found Democracy a thing forbidden, leading to outer darkness; I, a thing inevitable" (p. 293).

It is only right, however, that the age should bear part of Irving's blame. We find so sane a man even as Dr. Arnold writing in 1831:—

"Whether this be a real sign or not" (i.e., the first "Tongue" manifestations at Port Glasgow), "I believe that 'the day of the Lord' is coming, i.e., the termination of one of the great $αἰῶνες$ of the human race. The termination of the Jewish $αἰών$ in the first century, and of the Roman $αἰών$ in the fifth and sixth, were each marked by the same concurrence of calamities, wars, tumults, etc. And society in Europe seems going on fast for a similar revolution." (Stanley's *Life*, p. 174, Ed. Ward Lock & Co.)

Napoleon's lurid words, "I have always followed fortune and the god of war," seemed but portents of what was to follow. As 1830 approached, strikes and unrest became chronic in Britain, and on the Continent Revolution shook the thrones that had been re-established in 1815. Irving was merely obsessed with a question with which everyone was concerned. It is significant that his *Last Days* was edited as late as 1850 under the orthodox auspices of Dr. Horatius Bonar.

Irving's dogmatism was now intensified through the adverse decisions of the Presbytery of London and the Scottish General Assembly that his *Orthodox and Catholic Doctrine of Our Lord's Human Nature* contained errors subversive of the great doctrines of Christianity. This undoubtedly strengthened the fatalistic strain in his character and drew him closer to the "Albury Circle", which first met in 1826 to discuss "Unfulfilled Prophecy".

The presiding genius of this circle was the remarkable Henry Drummond. Drummond conceived the project of inviting a group of those interested in "Prophecy" to a week's conference at his country house—Albury Court, Surrey. There were present nineteen clergy of the Church of England, two Dissenting and four Church of Scotland ministers including Irving and his friend, Robert Story of Rosneath. Of the members, Hugh McNeil, the Irish Rector of Albury, became alienated from the Irvingite Movement some time after the appearance of glossolalia, and was for many years the leader, politically of the Conservative Party and ecclesiastically of the Evangelicals, in Liverpool. Daniel Wilson became famous later as Bishop of Calcutta. Joseph Wolff (1795-1862), was a German Jew, converted to Roman Catholicism which he left in favour of Anglicanism; he was a born enthusiast, setting out in 1828 in search of the "Ten Tribes" and spending most of his life travelling in India, Armenia and Abyssinia. (See H. P. Palmer, *Joseph Wolff, His Romantic Life and Travels*. Heath Cranton, 1935). Then there were Hatley Frere, Spencer Perceval (son of the murdered Cabinet Minister), and Tudor (a Welshman), editor of the *Morning Watch*, the official organ of the movement.

These Conferences ("retreats" they would be called to-day) were held annually. The host was the historian and published the proceedings (three octavo volumes entitled *Dialogues on Prophecy*). The movement also produced an ambitious quarterly entitled *The Morning Watch*. For six days there were daily meetings at Albury. Everyone took careful notes.

"No appeal was allowed but to the Scriptures, of which the originals lay before us; in the interpretation of which, if any question arose, we had the most learned Eastern scholar perhaps in the world to appeal to, and a native Hebrew. I mean Joseph Wolff" (Ol. I, 393).

In the evening this "School of the Prophets" wound up the business of the day in arm-chairs round the library fire. Within the grounds of the mansion a "Catholic Apostolic Church" was one day to rise, to intertwine the names of Drummond and Irving.

There was

"perfect unanimity on the following points:—(I) That the Christian Dispensation was to be terminated, ending in the destruction of the *visible* Church, like the Jewish; during which 'judgements' the Jews were to be restored to Palestine. (II) 'The judgements' were to fall principally, if not exclusively, upon Christendom. (III) That 'the 1,260 years' commenced with Justinian and terminated in 1793, and that the vials of the Apocalypse *then* began to be poured out; that our blessed Lord will then appear, and that therefore it is the duty of all to press these considerations on the attention of all men" (*v.* E. Miller, *History of Irvingism*, 1878).

Academic views of the Second Coming soon gave way to a thorough-going Millenarianism. The Rev. N. Armstrong (an Irishman) preached in St. Anne's, Blackfriars that the New Jerusalem was to be on the site of Rome. "Our inheritance shall be dominion over the creation: we shall rule angels: we shall rule the earth."[1]

Irving's views were expressed in *Last Days*:—

"O ye niggardly spiritualisers, ye pharisaical contemners of the *material* creation! For my part I expect to see the Lord eye to eye, in bodily form, not in *spiritual drapery*. I do expect to look upon, and to *rule* over this world purified and redeemed, and possessed by living creatures in flesh and blood."

(It will be observed that Judaistic conceptions, current in the Early Church, and persisting in Montanism, were revived.)

This emphasis on the *material* is in striking contrast to a parallel stress on the *spiritual*, e.g., "Confessions are but a veil cast over the face of God" (Irving on *Larger Catechism*). Here, needless to say, he is unfaithful to the Orthodoxy

---

[1] This was the Protestant lecturer whom Dean Church heard, as a schoolboy at Bristol (1832). He relished Mr. Armstrong's "highly spiced tropes and elaborate similes." "I remember buying a 'Council of Trent' that I might emulate him in finding passages to confound possible Popish controversialists, who at that time were in the softening and minimising mood."

on which he elsewhere so sternly insists (e.g., "Notes on 1560 Confession", etc.). But it is hopeless to look for consistency in Irving.[1]

As 1830 approached, the Albury School tended to stress the *preparations* ("signs") of the Second Coming, rather than the event itself. Hence the *material* aspect of the Millennium was thrust into the background, and the spiritual came to the front.

"If the period be not actually arrived, it is fast approaching when it will be necessary for the *Holy Ghost to make himself manifest* to God's children by visible signs, as it was in the first ages of Christianity" (*Morning Watch*, No. 7, p. 621).

"The anti-intellectual prejudice already noted, is found in expectation that 'an order of men will be raised up to use Christ's eyes with Christ's heart', the opposition consisting of 'clear headed men, men of sleek speech, of clear understanding but little faith', in whom 'the Spirit speaks not'" (*Morning Watch*, No. 7, p. 633).

"We seem," said Irving, "to be relapsing into the condition of those disciples in *Acts* who did not know there was a Holy Ghost. The Spirit must be present *personally* to produce any change upon the heart and life of men. Where are the rich outpourings of doctrine—where the large manifestations of varied truth—where the huge volume of fat and savoury food, which rejoiced the former ages of the Church?" (*Idolatry*).

There was a craving for the Gifts of the Spirit and an atmosphere conducive to charismata. It was therefore not surprising that on the last day of the last Albury Conference, July, 1830, on knowledge reaching the gathering of manifestations having occurred in the West of Scotland, it was proposed and agreed:—

"That it is our duty to pray for the revival of the gifts manifested in the primitive Church,—healing, miracles, prophecy, kinds of tongues and interpretations of tongues, and that a responsibility lies on us to enquire into the state of those gifts said to be now present in the west of Scotland."

This was the crucial moment. We stand on the threshold of the revival of "The Gift of Tongues".

---

[1] One of his orthodox friends was Rev. E. T. Vaughan, St. Martin's, Leicester, "who yielded nothing which could even pluck a hair from Calvin's head." Note his pamphlet—"*The Calvinist Clergy defended . . . in a Letter to Rev. Jas. Beresford*" (London 1818, 2nd ed. 1820. Personal friendships between Anglican Evangelicals and Scottish Ministers were not uncommon then.

CHAPTER IX

LIGHT FROM FERNICARRY

" The light that never was, on sea or land."—WORDSWORTH.

IT will be remembered that Irving took with him to the Albury Conference Robert Story, minister of Rosneath. Little did he realise the importance of Rosneath in the development of his career, when in 1828 he visited his friend's parish by the "sweet half-Highland waters of the Clyde". When he stirred the whole neighbourhood by his preaching, he little dreamt of the peasant girl, in all probability in the congregation, whose utterances were to start the "speaking with Tongues", for which he had so sincerely prayed.

On the same occasion Irving crossed the water to Row to see McLeod Campbell, a friend of Story, who as a stranger had several months earlier called on him in Edinburgh, when Irving had declared: "God may have sent me instructions by your hands".

At Rhu he met, though not for the first time, Alexander J. Scott, who was destined to exert considerable influence over Irving in the earlier stage of glossolalia. This "Sandy Scott, a most precious youth" with "the finest and strongest faculty for pure theology" Irving had "yet met with", a Probationer of the Church of Scotland and son of Dr. Scott of Greenock, he at once engaged as his assistant.

The soft shores of the Clyde provided an atmosphere conducive to intense religious experience of a kind untypical of Scottish piety. For the Calvinistic theology of Scotland had now ceased to have much living influence on the popular conscience.

It had deeply engraved itself on the popular understanding certainly, with the result that preaching tended either towards mere moralism divested of spiritual basis, or the working out of an abstract and rigid doctrinal system, which took little account of the changing wants and questionings of humanity. Original thinkers who suggested a better way, somewhat on the lines of Coleridge, were regarded with suspicion by the dominant and growing Evangelical Party.

There was the devout layman, Erskine of Linlathen, meditative and introspective, a seeker after light, who replied to one who sought infallible authority:—

"O no! Such a thing, if it could be, would destroy all God's purpose with man, which is to educate him, to awaken a growing perception in the man himself of what is true and right, which is of the very essence of spiritual discipline."

Erskine could never conceive of Christianity as a formal revelation or external institution. His religion has been described as "all heart", as internal light flooding the soul. Salvation was the "healing of the diseases of the soul," Eternal Life "the communion of God with the soul". Men are "already pardoned" if they only thought of it, and "have only to realise what is theirs".

"I have heard to-day the true Gospel," said Erskine of McLeod Campbell, after hearing him preach in 1828.

McLeod Campbell's Gospel was new to his age. So long as the individual was uncertain of being the object of God's love, and was without any sure hold of his personal safety, it was vain to induce him to serve God under the power of any purer motive than the desire to win God's love for himself, and so secure his own happiness.

As Principal Tulloch has said, in *Movements of Religious Thought in the Nineteenth Century*, the keynote of the period is "Expansiveness". The theological mind is seen opening in all directions. There is a breaking up of the close traditional systems inherited from earlier ages. There is a new sense of the Fatherhood of God and recognition of the Religious Consciousness; a desire after a more concrete and living faith; a hankering after both the mystical and the majestic. No wonder, then, that an abnormal movement like the Irvingite was enabled to arise and claim a large measure of popular support, which was only gradually withdrawn as eccentricities became marked.

Nor was this thirst for a more *spiritual* religion confined to thinkers. There was much popular demand for simple preaching such as that of Robert Story of Rosneath— no genius, but an earnest parish minister, a large-hearted brotherly soul. McLeod Campbell's warm and single-minded proclamation of an uncomplicated Gospel had roused the antagonism of the local Presbytery, but had aroused the enthusiasm of the countryside.

This smouldering fire might have become extinct but for A. J. Scott, who, "being called down to Scotland and residing at his father's house, which is in the heart of that district of Scotland upon which the light of Mr. Campbell's ministry had arisen, was led to open his mind to some of the godly people in these parts".

Irving was gradually coming to believe that the Apostolic charismata belonged to all ages, and had been in abeyance through want of faith alone.

Yet he was inclined to hold that they would only be restored at the time of the Second Advent. Mr. Scott's convictions as to the present possibility of their revival were much stronger.

"He used often to signify to me his conviction that the spiritual gifts ought still to be exercised in the Church; that we are at liberty, and indeed bound, to pray for them as being baptised into the assurance of the 'gift of the Holy Ghost', as well as of 'repentance and remission of sins' . . . Though I could make no answer to this, I continued still very little moved to seek myself, or to stir up my people to seek these spiritual treasures. Yet I went forward to contend and instruct whenever the subject came before me in my public ministrations of reading and preaching the Word, that the Holy Ghost ought to be manifested among us all, the same as ever he was in any of the primitive Churches" (Irving in *Fraser's Magazine*, January, 1832).

Scott undoubtedly laid the "splendid train of mischief"—the *ignis fatuus* which was later to lure and obsess Irving. His preaching in Greenock and the neighbourhood produced a feeling that the revival of the "Gift of Tongues" might be possible.

He had to deal with people whose religion was fluid, if not molten. The atmosphere was favourable to revival, and the people suggestible. This is evident from the veneration with which a certain farm girl, Isabella Campbell, was regarded. Her admirers resorted to the farmhouse of Fernicarry, near Rosneath, and she would certainly have been canonised had she been living in a Roman Catholic country. The religion of this young invalid was a simple pietism. To her sister she one day cried:—

"O that the Lord would pour down His Spirit upon the land, for it is a land of darkness and deceit! Men think themselves alive. All think themselves Christians, but, alas! few there are who worship God in the Spirit, rejoice in Christ and have no confidence in the flesh."

These words are quoted from *Peace in Believing*, a memoir of Isabella Campbell by Robert Story, her minister, a book which secured an immense local circulation, though without any literary value or narrative interest, being simply the record of rapt and ecstatic communion with God.

On her death, her sister, Mary Campbell, stepped into her place. Mary's character was somewhat dissimilar. She was the "young woman" to whom A. J. Scott was led "to open his mind" during his holiday in the west (1830). She was

"at that time lying ill of a consumption, from which afterwards, when brought to the very door of death, she was raised up instantaneously by the hand of God. Being a woman of very fixed and constant spirit, he was not able with all his power of statement and argument, which is unequalled by that of any man I have ever met with, to convince her of the distinction between regeneration and baptism with the Holy Ghost; and when he could not prevail he left her with a solemn charge to read over the Acts of the Apostles with that distinction in her mind, and to beware how she rashly rejected what he believed to be the truth of God.

"By this young woman it was that God, not many months after, did restore the gift of speaking with tongues and prophesying to the Church" (*Fraser's Magazine*, January, 1832).

Expectation was in the air. Just as at Pentecost, fermentation would soon lead to explosion. "I remember," said an eye-witness, "hearing the cry in the Spirit, 'Send us Apostles! Send us Apostles!' The room used to ring with it."

The manifestations first occurred in the household of the Macdonalds. Robert Norton, M.D., in his *Memoirs of James and George Macdonald* (pp. 58, 59, 78) gives the following account of the brothers. They were plain men, shipbuilders. Their religion was of a quiet and unobtrusive type; it was said they read no book but the Bible. The ministry under which they sat was unimpressive, yet even when the clergy preached at them for holding peculiar views, they did not cease from churchgoing. As Erskine of Linlathen testified:—

"Although they soon became classed among the disciples of Mr. Irving, who at that time was beginning to be stigmatised as heretical, the fact was that, so far as I can ascertain, they never read a single volume of his, or not at least for years after their own views were established. And although after a time they began to attend the preaching of Mr. McLeod Campbell, it was because they had *previously* been taught of God the same truths, and were attracted to Rhu by their love of them.

"Until the eve of the miraculous manifestations in them, the subject of spiritual gifts did not at all occupy their attention, much less their expectations and desires; nor did it even when their prayers, in common with those of other Christians, for an outpouring of the Spirit, began to be answered by the pouring out of a very extraordinary if not marvellous spirit of prayer upon themselves" (Erskine's *Letters*, I, p. 176).

Margaret Macdonald was dangerously ill. She had scarcely been able to have her bed made for a week. Dr. Norton says:

"Mrs. —— and myself had been sitting quietly at her bedside when the power of the Spirit came upon her. She said: 'There will be a mighty baptism of the Spirit this day!' and then broke forth in a most marvellous setting forth of the wonderful work of God; and as if her own weakness had been altogether lost in the strength of the Holy Ghost, continued with little or no intermission for two or three hours in mingled praise, prayer, and exhortation."

"At dinner time James and George came home as usual, when she addressed them at great length, concluding with a solemn prayer for James, that he might *at that time* be endowed with the Holy Ghost. *Almost instantly* James *calmly* said, 'I have got it'. He walked to the window, and stood silent for a moment or two. I looked at him and almost trembled, there was such a change upon his whole countenance. He then, with a step and manner of the most indescribable majesty, walked up to Margaret's bedside, and addressed her in these words of the Twentieth Psalm—'Arise and stand upright'. He repeated the words, took her by the hand, and she arose, when we all *sat down quietly* and *had our dinner* (Cp. Exodus 24:11: 'They saw God, and did eat and drink'). After it, my brother went off to the building yard as usual, where James wrote over to Miss Campbell, commanding her in the name of the Lord to arise.

"The next morning, after breakfast, James said, 'I am going down to the quay to see if Miss Campbell is coming across the water' (the Clyde), at which we expressed our surprise, as he had said nothing to us about having written her. The result showed how much he knew of what God had done, and would do for her; for she came as he expected, declaring herself perfectly whole."

The following is Mary Campbell's account of her experiences:—

"Two individuals who saw me before my recovery said that I never would be strong, that I was not to expect a miracle being wrought upon me, and that it was quite foolish in one who was in such a poor state of health, ever to think of going to the heathen.

"I told them that they would hear of miracles very soon, and no sooner had the last-mentioned individuals left me than I was *constrained* of the Spirit to go and ask the Father, in the name of Jesus, to stretch forth His hand to heal . . . *to ask in faith*, nothing doubting, that by the next morning I might have some miracles to inform them of.

"It was not long after that I received James Macdonald's letter. . . . I had scarcely read the first page when I became quite overpowered, and laid it aside for a few minutes; but I had no rest in my spirit until I took it up again and began to read. As I read, every word came with power, but when I came to the command to rise, it came home *with a power no words can describe*; it was felt to be indeed the voice of Christ . . . such a voice of power as could not be resisted.

"I felt as if I had been lifted up from off the face of the earth, and all my disease taken off me. At the voice of Jesus I was surely made to stand upon my feet, leap and walk, sing and rejoice. O that men would praise the Lord . . .!" (Reported by Rev. A. Robertson of Greenock in *A Vindication of the Religion of the Land.*)

After her recovery Mary Campbell spent the summer of 1830 at Helensburgh. Meetings innumerable were held, and manifestations extraordinary were made. To ecstatic speech was added automatic writing. On the moment of inspiration she would seize a pen, and with rapidity "like lightning" would cover sheets of paper with characters believed to be letters and words. Story, in reply to Chalmers' queries, stated that not only did she utter "sounds altogether new to my ears for nearly an hour" on taking her by the hand to bid her adieu, but referred to the "inconceivable rapidity" of her automatic writing, which she described as in every respect independent of her own volition . . . and as if she herself was unconscious of the exertion. "I am persuaded you will be prepared to conclude that these things are of God and not of men". Story was later to revise his opinion.

Mary Campbell was a young woman of intense psychical

power, which found expression in charismatic Christianity. Had she lived at the end of the nineteenth century instead of at the beginning, her energies would probably have found expression as a "medium". She was one of the few members of the Irvingite circle who combined automatic writing with glossolalia.

The Rev. A. Robertson described how people of all classes gathered round her at Helensburgh.

"Writers to the signet, advocates who rank high in Society come from Edinburgh, join in all the exercises, declare their implicit faith in Mary Campbell's pretensions, ask her concerning the times and seasons . . . and bow to her decisions with the utmost deference as one inspired by heaven."

There was the same excitement at Port Glasgow. "Ever since Margaret was raised and the gift of tongues given," wrote one of the Macdonald sisters (18th May, 1830), "the house has been filled every day with people from all parts of England, Scotland and Ireland."

Special interest was awakened where special hopes in this direction had been for some time cherished. Several people connected with the Albury Circle came from London and stayed three weeks at Port Glasgow, among whom were Thompson (a doctor) and Cardale (a lawyer).

Mr. Cardale, besides co-operating in the report drawn up of the manifestations, was quoted as an entirely competent witness by a writer in the *Edinburgh Review* (*Pretended Miracles*, Irving, Scott, and Erskine, June, 1831).

"These persons, while uttering the unknown sounds, have every appearance of being under supernatural direction. The manner and voice are (generally speaking) different from what they are at other times. This difference does not consist merely in the peculiar solemnity and fervour of manner (which they possess), but their whole deportment gives an impression, not to be conveyed in words, that their organs are made use of by supernatural power.

"Their own declarations, as the declarations of honest, pious, and sober individuals, may with propriety be taken in evidence. They declare that their organs of speech are made use of by the Spirit of God, and that they utter that which is given them, and *not* the expressions of their own conceptions.

"In addition, I have only to add my own most decided testimony, that so far as three weeks' constant communication and the information of those in the neighbourhood can enable me to judge—the individuals thus gifted are living in close communion with God and love towards all men; abounding in faith, joy and peace, with an abasement of self, such as I have never witnessed elsewhere, and find nowhere recorded but in the history of the early church. . . . And just as they are fervent in spirit, so they are diligent in all the religious duties of life. They are devoid of fanaticism, but are persons of great *simplicity of character* and of *sound common sense.*"

Erskine of Linlathen followed in the track of these delegates from London—staying no less than six weeks in the Macdonalds' house. His immediate impressions are embodied in the tract *On the Gifts of the Spirit* (Greenock, 1830):

"Whilst I see nothing in Scripture against the re-appearance or rather continuance of miraculous gifts in the Church, but a great deal for it, I must further say that I see a great deal of internal evidence in the West country to prove their genuine miraculous character, especially in the speaking with tongues. . . . After witnessing what I have witnessed, I cannot think of any person decidedly condemning them as impostors, without a feeling of great alarm. It is certainly not a thing to be lightly or rashly believed, but neither is it a thing to be lightly or rashly rejected. I believe that it is of God."

Three facts emerge:—

(a) "The voices struck me very much, perhaps more than the tongues. It was not their loudness, although they were very loud, but they did not sound to me as if they were the voices of the persons speaking; *they seemed to be uttered through them by another power.*"
(b) "The languages are distinct, well-inflected, well-compacted languages; they are not random collections of sounds; they are composed of words of various length, with the natural variety, and yet possessing that commonness of character which marks them to be one distinct language. I have heard many people speak gibberish, but this is not gibberish." (Specimens preserved as taken down by hearers:—O Pinitos, Elelastino Halimangotos Dantita, Hampooteni, Farini, Aristos, Ekrampos.)
(c) "The tongues were unintelligible to the hearers unless the additional gift of interpretation was vouchsafed.

"After James Macdonald had prayed for a considerable time, first in English and then in a tongue, the command to pray for interpretation was brought to his mind, and he repeated—'It is written: let him that speaketh in a tongue pray that he may interpret.' He then prayed for interpretation with great urgency, until he felt he had secured the answer, and when repeating over the concluding words of what he had spoken in the tongue, which were 'disco capito', he said, 'And this is the interpretation: the shout of a king is among them'."

The impression Erskine received was—

"That the passage spoken in the tongue had concluded with the prophecy of Balaam, in which these words occur. I conceived that the words 'disco capito' had been given to us as words of reference, directing us to the beautiful passage of which they form part, Numbers xxiii: 19–21" (Erskine's *Letters*, Vol. I, pp. 182–86 and Appendix, viii).

Erskine was to revise his estimate of the movement. He never ceased to regard the Macdonalds as sincere, and he never forfeited their confidence. But he seems to have felt later that their prophesying was in some measure due, in modern terminology, to the uprush of ideas matured in the subconscious. He ascribes two instances of James Macdonald's prophecies "to seed . . . in the newspapers". E.g.:

"He had read there some foolish rumour about the time of George IV's death, that the Ministers would probably find it convenient to conceal that event, until they had made some arrangements. This remained in his mind, and it came forth at last as an utterance *in power*, but wrapped in such obscurity of language as not to expose it to direct confutation; but on reading the paragraph I recognised such a resemblance that I could not doubt it, but put it to him; and although he had spoken in perfect integrity, yet he was satisfied that my conjecture as to its origin was correct."

Another utterance, clothed in the language of Daniel, chapter 11, was also traced to a newspaper paragraph.

"James Macdonald did not say he was conscious of anything in these two utterances distinguishing them from the others.

"I thus see," concludes Erskine, "how things may come into the mind and remain there, and then come forth as supernatural utterances, although their origin may be quite natural. . . . Is there not a great perplexity in this? Does the control of a church solve it?" (*Letters*, I, p. 209f.).

Erskine of Linlathen in 1837 retracted his former opinion that

"The remarkable manifestations which I witnessed eight years ago were the miraculous gifts of the Spirit, of the same character as those of which we read in the New Testament. Since then I have come to think differently. But I still continue to think that the disappearance of these gifts from the Church must be a greater difficulty than their reappearance could possibly be."

Nor were the characters of the individuals concerned in any way the cause of the change of view; James and George Macdonald received the highest praise. (Appendix to *Election*.)

Had Erskine known Mary Campbell as intimately as he knew the Macdonalds, it is improbable that he would have exonerated the *personal* element in the manifestations. He would have found room not merely for the divine and the "natural" in the subconscious sphere, but also for the malignant and the false.

He would have seen that (in William James' phrase) "snake and seraph abide there side by side". For Mary Campbell's character contained elements of vanity, restlessness and selfishness evident from even a cursory perusal of her minister's account of her career.

Mr. Story remonstrated with Mary for filling her tired mother's farmhouse of Fernicarry with her admirers, while her dying brother Samuel had no peace in the midst of the babel of talking and psalm-singing. He rebuked two young men present with him, who asserted it was their object to serve the Lord as missionaries, and who objected to the learning of Eastern languages as "carnal". Shortly afterwards Mr. Story received a singular letter from Mary, asserting that *now* God suffered her to write only what *He* pleased.

"There is now to me a delightful depth of meaning in the words being *Bidden* and *Forbidden* by the Holy Ghost.

"Should she send away her friend (Mr. Caird)? 'The answer I received was: See thou do it not; I, not thou, broughtest him to this place, and it is I, not thou, who have a right to send him away.'

"I besought him," she continued, "to spend most of his time in prayer and fasting; but I could not urge him to commence the study of languages, *seeing I look every day for the gift of tongues being poured out upon the Church*. I look upon the system of education for the ministry to be of the devil. If God has promised to furnish his servants with every necessary qualification, what have they to do but step into the field, depending on Him for all? The eloquence of the unlearned fishermen drew from the multitudes glory to God, and were such eloquence again heard . . . etc.

"There is another consideration. *The time is short.* I expect to see the Redeemer on earth long before *he* (Caird) could be fit, according to the judgement of men, for entering the field of Christian labour.

"All the signs of the latter day are now manifest. O that a sinful world would be warned! O my dear, dear Mr. Story, cry these things in the ears of your people, for they believe them not" (R. H. Story, *Robert Story*, p. 198).

Soon after this letter was written, Mary spoke with tongues. She desired to ascertain what the tongue was that she might go to the country where it was intelligible. By and by she announced that she believed it to be the language of a group of islands in the South Pacific Ocean (a safe suggestion). Her handwriting was submitted to Sir George Staunton, whose judgment agreed with Dr. Lee's of Cambridge, i.e., "It contains neither word nor language known in any region under the sun." In reply to Chalmer's query (24th April, 1830) Story replied:

"Many here say it is of the devil. . . . She knows when the languages change—and the articulations are obviously different—some of them exceedingly musical—others not so. Sometimes she has the impression that what she is uttering is the language of a particular people. . . e.g., Turkish and the language of the Pelew Islanders.

"She seemed greatly oppressed in spirit that the power of interpretation was not given. On Saturday last Lady C——— G——— was constrained to interpret various sentences. Macdonald, who commanded Mary to *rise*, was at first very sceptical concerning the gift which he heard. She had received, but now the same power rests on him and his brother and they mutually interpret. The fact of a numerous band of young persons going forth with the Gospel so sanctioned, is well fitted to reprove our dead Church . . . but if a delusion, the more speedy it is given to the winds the better."

Several points emerge from his foregoing account of Mary Campbell. Her letter to her minister is interesting. It contains in crystallised form ideas which were strongly characteristic of the Tongues Movement under Irving. The perspective is dominated by the imminent Second Coming. There must be an immediate evangelisation of the world in preparation of that event: the "Gift of

Tongues" is the means towards that end, as well as being one of the "signs" of the Last Days. There is a strong anti-intellect bias, a belief in the positive rightfulness of ignorance, which is conceived of as Apostolic, and through which the Holy Ghost may speak without being dimmed by mere human learning.

Robert Norton, M.D., a man of considerable education, though sympathetic to the "manifestations" (author of *Memoirs of James and George Macdonald*) declares in fact:—

"It is a melancholy instance of perversion and prejudice that the assertion should be so continually persisted in that the Gift of Tongues is to enable men to preach the Gospel to foreigners, —when the Apostle commences his description of the gift by asserting the very contrary. . . . The Gift of Tongues is *not evangelistic, but devotional*" (*Neglected . . . Scriptural Truths . . . the late revival in the west of Scotland*, 1839).

Norton was perfectly right: the critics too hastily assumed that *all* Gifted Persons aimed at miraculous preaching in foreign languages—an imitation of Pentecost, as popularly interpreted.

The belief in "permanent endowment" has died hard. An article in the *Baptist Argus* (Louisville, Kentucky, 23rd January, 1908) cites eighteen different instances of men and women gifted with "tongues", who had gone to India, China and Japan in the past few years trusting to these gifts instead of the knowledge of the languages necessary, and how several of these deluded people were saved from starvation by the missionaries.

Mary's idea of religion was somewhat akin to that of the American Southern negro: noise and excitement were religion—any ethical and intellectual backbone spelt degeneration—"It's all booklarnin', dey ain't no Holy Ghos' in it at all."

The Holy Ghost has nearly always been interpreted in "Pentecostal Communities" in its primitive Hebrew and pagan sense, as a possessing "energy" suddenly descending on men, and immediately superseding "fleshy ordinances". It is interesting to note that she was conscious of changing over from one tongue to another. *The Morning Watch* also ascribes to James Macdonald the power of speaking "two tongues, both easily discernible from the other". Davenport, in discussing Mormon frenzy, described many of the people at Palmyra, N.Y., as having "fits of speaking all the *different* Indian dialects, which none could understand" (*Primitive Traits in Religious Revivals*, p. 188).

It will be seen, as our narrative develops, how similar in general outline are outbreaks of glossolalia, in different countries and in different periods.

Mary Campbell, on her recovery, married W. R. Caird, the law clerk whom Mr. Story had rebuked.

"The persons who quitted Scotland" to go into "some region of heathendom where the difference of language had hitherto proved a barrier to all missionary labour . . . have for nearly two years been resident in my little parish, and edify a congregation of from fifty to two hundred persons. The Missionary project having been abandoned, they found out another use for the tongue".

These are the words of Hugh McNeile, the Evangelical rector of Albury, Surrey, who had been a member of the "Prophetic Circle" and had welcomed the "Gifts" on their first manifestation; he afterwards became their vigorous antagonist though the Lord of the Manor (Henry Drummond) stood out as enthusiastic champion of the Tongues.

The Cairds had also been for a time lay chaplains to Lady Olivia Sparrow, of Brampton Park (an influential supporter of the Irvingite cause), between whom and Irving they had passed to and fro. Some time after their marriage Mary and her husband visited Scotland, passing and repassing Rosneath, but (significantly) never calling at the manse. Story tells how one day he saw a group of elegantly dressed women and among them Mary, where not long before one of her sisters had been seen loading a dung-cart. He had no opportunity of private conversation. He had an interview with her later, in the presence of Lady Harriet Drummond, at Greenock, with whom she was staying, which resulted in the following letter:—

"Several years before you heard a voice, that unless you arose and proceeded without delay to declare the Gospel to the heathen, you and your father's house should perish. The command was God's or it was not. As you have carefully avoided a personal interview, I must judge of appearances . . . as your former pastor.

"Of all persons I ever knew, *you* are liable to be excited by the presence of others, and originally having a strong love of approbation. I therefore trembled, especially . . . when you became (after your marriage), the guests of dear Mr. Irving. I knew you would, without any intentional deceit, be led to do whatsoever was pleasing to him.

"For you know, you were by *his own writings first led to expect* what you thought you had received when the gift of tongues came upon you. At London, amidst the adulations of an excited people, at Albury amid the splendid hospitality of your godly host—you have come to the conclusion that this is *not* the time to obey the voice of God. When these gifts and powers came upon you, you were poor and destitute. *You owe everything to your reputation for Christianity.* Had the Spirit indeed left you? Had you indeed become a tinkling cymbal?" (Story, pp. 214-17.)

Mrs. Caird vouchsafed no reply, but an answer came from Henry Drummond:—

"19th June, 1834.

"Sir, Mrs. Caird, in absence of her husband, has put into my hands, as her pastor, a letter in which you charge her with professing religion from mercenary motives. Partly through Mr. Irving and from my own knowledge, I can prove the charge as false as it is base; and it comes with peculiarly bad grace from a man notoriously holding opinions which have drawn Mr. John Campbell out of the Church of Scotland, contrived . . . so as to retain his stipend."

To an angry tirade on the part of Mr. Caird, Story replied:—

"Is the first exhibition of speaking in tongues to confirm in their sinful and dishonest idleness some foolish boys . . . is it to command their stay in her poor oppressed mother's house? Is the agony of suffering which a patient sufferer endured through the noise night after night,—spiritual joy? Or the perfect things transacted in the chamber of the dead?" (A horrible and vain attempt to 'raise' Samuel Campbell's corpse.)

So stung was Caird by Story's disbelief in the "fruits of the Spirit" manifested by his wife, that he converted the correspondence into one about money, demanding more than the £600 which the minister had paid to the Campbell family as proceeds of the *Memoir of Isabella Campbell*. Story's firmness, however, led to the collapse of the lawsuit.

The devoted parish minister had tried to rescue Mary from "perilous fellowship" during "those tumultuous meetings in Helensburgh", and "with much ado succeeded in prevailing on her to live in the quiet of the cottage at Mamore", where his family was staying.

"Then—away from scenes where such gross familiarity was dared with the name of the Eternal, she came to herself, and confessed that she had spoken and prophesied in the name of the Lord God Almighty, when only giving vent to her own fancies."

But such a confession was remorse rather than repentance.

At an earlier period she and her husband had refused to go to Prince Edward Island when Story laid before them a letter urgently calling for preachers. And she afterwards fully identified herself with every excess of the Irvingite movement in London. She died in 1840, still a young woman. She was not even fully trusted by the Irvingites themselves. *The Edinburgh Review* (June, 1831) commenting on the later part of No. 8 of *The Morning Watch*, states:

"It seems allowed that it may be necessary to give up the case of Mary Campbell, and that of other persons of weak judgement, who shall have proved, by their extravagant and unwarranted presumptions, that they have mistaken false confidence for faith."

In 1832 Edward Irving wrote to Story:

"Oh, Story, thou hast grievously sinned in standing afar off from the work of the Lord, scanning it like a sceptic, instead of proving it like a spiritual man. Draw not back, brother, but go forward. *Keep your conscience unfettered by your understanding.*

The biographical details given in the foregoing pages may appear to be in the nature of a digression. But they reveal the character of Mary Campbell as seen through the eminently fair eyes of Story, and throw light on Edward Irving's lack of insight into human nature. From her he received in absolute faith what was virtually the result of his own speculations developing in her sub-conscious mind, and surging up in the form of revelations. Thus was he built up in his belief, mistaking the echo of his own voice for the voice of God, as the traveller on the Brocken mistakes his own shadow in the clouds for a phantom giant.

The later career of the Macdonalds is very different from that of Mary Campbell. A reaction against the manifestations led to their narrow escape from being mobbed, as Dr. Norton relates. But when the cholera came to Port Glasgow, they were almost the only individuals who would enter the houses of the sick—which secured them "at least a silent respect".

Another characteristic feature was their refusal to accept "the pressing invitation made by some of the affluent and influential members of Mr. Irving's congregation, to go up to London". Neither of the brothers could see the Lord's hand in this call—even when backed by generous financial support. They believed that the "gifts" were liable to be abused there. "At its commencement, the work bore every scriptural mark, as far as we knew." But regarding "Mr. Irving's apostles appealing almost solely to an assumed prophetic gift calling them to such an office, we find no parallel to this in Scripture."

James Macdonald became seriously ill during the autumn of 1834. A friend who came from a distance to visit him asked if he *still* had no doubt that the extraordinary manifestations in him had been from the power of the Holy Ghost resting on him. He simply replied: "I can no more doubt it than I doubt that God is my God." He died on 2nd February, 1835. His brother followed him (14th September, 1835). The twins were born in 1800. It is a striking fact that (like Isabella Campbell) they *both died of consumption and that it was of this disease that Mary Campbell was cured.*

Their abnormality was probably a combination of the physical and psychological, but a genuine religious passion was the controlling factor in the lives of the brothers, though this was mixed with baser elements in the case of Mary Campbell.

The Irvingite Movement has been examined in its birth-place. It now emerges into the wider setting of thought and experience in London.

CHAPTER X

CHARISMATIC CHRISTIANITY

"Dim as the borrowed beams of moon and stars
To lonely, weary, wandering travellers, is *Reason* to the
soul."—DRYDEN, *Religio Laici*.

On the return of the Albury delegates from the west of Scotland, a meeting was held in October, 1830, to consider results.

The "Gifted Persons" had declared "that their organs of speech are made use of by the Spirit of God, and that they utter what is given them, and not the expression of their own conceptions or their own intention". "But I had numerous opportunities," said Mr. Cardale,[1] the leader of the delegation, "of observing a variety of effects confirmatory of this. I repeatedly observed that it had no exhausting effect upon them—neither loudness of manner nor vehemence of action."

The Committee's report was approved, and throughout the autumn of 1830 prayer meetings were held in private houses in London, "for the outpouring of the Holy Ghost". Several of these meetings were held weekly in Mr. Cardale's house. They were not confined to any one congregation, nor does Edward Irving appear to have taken any part in them. The "miraculous" cure of Miss Fancourt in England (a clergyman's daughter) on 20th October, 1830, a case remarkably parallel to that of the Macdonalds and Mary Campbell, though entirely independent, was a "sign" which stimulated the craving for the revival of Apostolic "gifts". "Miracles," commented the *Morning Watch*,

---

[1] J. B. Cardale (1802–77), succeeded his father as head of Cardale, Iliffe & Russell, solicitors to Rugby and Gray's Inn. The *Dict. of National Biography* notes his proficiency in Greek, Latin, French and German; "his strength of will, calmness and clearness of judgment, kindness of heart and manner added to the prestige of his long rule," when he became an Apostle of the Catholic Apostolic Church. All this was to mitigate Irving's future suffering.

CHARISMATIC CHRISTIANITY

"have occurred in all ages of the Church, depending only *upon the faith at any particular time.*" Mr. Martin, at Kirkcaldy Manse, was not impressed. He wrote to his daughter, Anne, of several local parallels, e.g., Miss Nairn of Pittenweem lost her power of speech. Expensive treatment did no good. One day she woke up, talked and sang. "I never heard a miracle mentioned as a solution of this difficult case," observed Mr. Martin.

At length on 30th April, 1831, the first case of speaking in tongues occurred in London, when Mrs. Cardale uttered "with great solemnity" three distinct sentences in a *tongue* and three in English interpretation ("The Lord will speak to His people—the Lord hasteneth His Coming—the Lord cometh"). She repeated the last words several times, with gradual increasing and then diminishing strength and loudness. At a later meeting a Miss Hall (governess in the family of Spencer Perceval) "sang in the Spirit".

These events were notified to Rev. the Hon. Baptist Noel, clergyman of the parish (subsequently a Baptist Minister), who not only refused his sanction, but preached against the gifts. The Cardales for some time continued to attend his church, then "went elsewhere," and finally found in Irving a man of note who was ready to lend his patronage and sympathy to the manifestations.

We can trace Irving's connection with the manifestations to the prayer meetings which were held in Regent Square Church at 6-30 a.m. for a fortnight preceding the General Assembly of 1831, when Scottish Churchmen and puzzled English adherents joined in supplication on behalf of the ecclesiastical authorities who were about to brand him and his friends as heretics. At that General Assembly McLeod Campbell was deposed, Irving's doctrine of our Lord's human nature was condemned, and his protégés were disciplined (c.f., p. 117–20).

The effect of this reverse, the condemnation of a Churchman for what he deemed orthodoxy, the rejection of a prophet who had declaimed against the errors of the age, was to strengthen Irving's fatalistic belief that he must suffer as his fathers had done, and to make him all the more ready to welcome new light. The "prophetic" and the "priestly" had always been strangely mingled in Irving; the "prophetic" element was now to prevail, though several years after his death the "Catholic Apostolic Church", which rose out of the nucleus of his congregation, swung back to the "priestly" extreme in their compilation of an eclectic High Church Liturgy (1842).

After the General Assembly of 1831, those who met early every morning at Regent Square during the crisis resolved to continue the meetings, and direct their prayers to interests more immediately their own. This is the origin of the early services so characteristic later of "the Catholic Apostolic Church". As May brightened into June, they prayed for the bestowal of the miraculous gifts of the Spirit, about which they had heard so much. Continual and persistent prayer, in which the worshippers ceased to be units, setting their minds on one object, produced the desired fruit. The very atmosphere of the early morning—and the fasting which was usual, were powerful stimulants. The first intimation that the manifestations had occurred in answer to prayer is contained in an incidental reference in a letter of Irving to Story (July, 1831): "Two of my flock have received the gift of tongues and prophecy." Not till four months later, however, did the new wonder manifest itself publicly.

During the interval Irving assumed the part of an investigator. The whole process of examination he explained in a speech before the London Presbytery a year later. Speaking of the prayer meetings he said:—

"We cried unto the Lord for apostles, prophets, evangelists, pastors, and teachers . . . because we saw it written in God's Word that these are the appointed ordinances for the edifying of the body of Jesus.

"The Lord was not long in answering our prayers. He sealed first one, and then another; and gave them enlargement of spirit in their own devotions when their souls were lifted up to God. He then lifted them up to pray in a tongue which the apostle Paul says he did more than they all. . . .

"I say as it was with Paul at the proper time . . . namely, in their private devotions, when they were wrapt up nearest to God, the Spirit took them and made them speak in a tongue, sometimes singing in a tongue, sometimes speaking words in a tongue;

"and by degrees, according as they sought more and more unto God, this *gift was perfected until they were moved to speak in a tongue, even in the presence of others.*

"but while it was in this stage I suffered it not in the church, acting according to the canon of the apostle; and even in private,

REGENT SQUARE CHURCH
Interior in Irving's day

[*To face page* 154

in my own presence, I permitted it not; but I heard that it had been done. I would not have rebuked it, I would have sympathised tenderly with the person who was carried in the Spirit and lifted up; but in the church I would not have permitted it.

"Then in time, perhaps at the end of a fortnight, the gift perfected itself, so that they were made to speak in a tongue and to prophesy; that is, to set forth in English words for exhortation, for edification, and comfort, for that is the proper definition of prophesying as was testified by one of the witnesses.

"Now when we had received this into the church in answer to our prayers, it became me, as the minister of the church, to try that which we had received. I say it became me, and not another, as minister of the church; and my authority for that you will find in the 2nd chapter of Revelation."

[Here we can see that, so far, the priest in Irving has not yet vanished in the prophet.]

"I then addressed myself to the task of putting them to the proof . . . I durst not shrink from it.

"The first thing towards the trial was to hear them prophesy before myself; and so I did. The Lord in His providence (*I cannot remember the particulars, nor do I charge my memory with them*), gave me ample opportunities in private prayer meetings (of which there were many in the congregation for this purpose established) of hearing the speaking with tongues and prophesying;

"and it was so ordered that every person whom I heard was known to myself, so that I had the double test . . . *first*, the blameless walk of persons in full communion with the Church of Christ; and *next*, privately hearing the utterances, in which I could detect nothing contrary to sound doctrine . . .; and *beyond these* there are *no outward* or visible signs to which it can be brought.

"Having these before me, I was still very much afraid of introducing it to the church. . . . For look you at the condition in which I was placed. I had sat at the head of the church praying that these gifts might be poured out. Was I to disbelieve that which in faith I had been praying for?" . . . "I, as Christ's dutiful minister, standing in His room and responsible to Him (as are you all) have not dared to believe that, when we asked bread, He gave us a stone, and when we asked fish, He gave us a serpent."

It is clear, knowing Irving's mind, that in him the critical faculty was weak. He examined the candidates to satisfy his conscience, but he had strong prepossession in favour of the gifts. It was true that he might be able to detect cases of obvious imposture. But he could scarcely differentiate between the genuinely inspired and those weak-willed, suggestible people who are so often the passive victims of revival mania. To differentiate between true and false candidates would be beyond the power even of one who combined intense psychic power, psychological insight, and spiritual intuition. It would require the power of reading men's souls which only One Man has ever possessed.

Irving's faith was simple and absolute: he had neither historic sense nor knowledge of the maze of motives and cross-currents which are found in men's minds and hearts. He was unable to control the current of prophecy he had set in motion. Warning and reproving voices interrupted his prayers and exhortations in private meetings, telling him that he was restraining the Spirit of God. One morning in March, 1831, he yielded.

"I went to the church, and after praying, I rose up and said in the midst of them all, 'I cannot be a part in hindering that which I believe to be the voice of the Holy Ghost from being heard in the church'. (After reading 1 Cor. xiv: 23.) 'I permit . . . that everyone who has received the gift of the Holy Ghost, and is moved by the Holy Ghost, shall have liberty to speak,'—and I pointed to those whom I had heard in private.

"Now, observe, I took to myself, according to the commandment of Jesus, the responsibility of trying the prophets in private, before permitting them to speak in the Church. I then gave the Church an opportunity of fulfilling its duty; *it belongeth not to the pastor alone, for beyond question, it belongeth to every man to try the spirits.*"

Before this decision the utterances were restricted to private meetings. The Rev. David Brown has revealed what took place at these meetings in his *Personal Reminiscences of Edward Irving*. He presided whenever Irving was absent, serving as assistant after Mr. Scott's resignation, from the close of 1830 till the beginning of 1833. His future career developed along normal lines; he afterwards became Principal of the Free Church College, Aberdeen. It is a pity that he did not publish a fuller account of the Irvingite Movement in London.

"After the morning meetings a select number of us would go to breakfast with Mr. and Mrs. Irving. At one of these breakfasts, a sweet, modest young lady, Miss Emily Cardale, began to breathe heavily and increasingly so, until at length she burst out into loud but abrupt short sentences in English, which after a few minutes ceased. The voice was certainly beyond her natural strength, and the subject-matter of it was the expected power of the Spirit not to be resisted by any who would hear. Other such utterances followed . . . first by Miss Hall, *and then by a man who rather repelled me* (a teacher of the name of Taplin) who professed to speak in an unknown tongue.

"All that was uttered in English seemed to be so poor, and the same thing over again, that I was kept in uneasy suspense; and the only thing that might seem to indicate a 'power not their own' as its source, was the unnatural—I could not say preternatural—strength of it" (*The Expositor*, vol. VI, p. 216 ff).

The matter was, however, soon taken out of Irving's hands. The "tongues" soon burst their banks, dragging Irving and his restrictions with them. Publicity soon became a feature of the movement, which suddenly attracted universal attention.

The following article, extracted from *The World*, appeared in *The Times* of 19th November, 1831[1]:—

"On Sunday, the Rev. Edward Irving delivered two sermons on the extraordinary gifts of the Spirit, on each of which occasions the congregation was disturbed by individuals pretending to the gift of tongues. During the sermon in the morning, a lady (a Miss Hall) thus singularly endowed was compelled to retire into the vestry, where she was unable, as she herself says, to restrain herself, and spoke for some time in the unknown tongue to the great surprise of the congregation, who did not seem prepared for the exhibition."

Miss Hall, as Mr. Pilkington (then one of the Irvingite circle) relates in his *Narrative*, so acted—"respecting the regulation of the Church", "whilst another, from the same impulse, ran down the side aisle, and out of the church".

"The sudden, doleful, and unintelligible sounds, being heard by all the congregation, produced the utmost confusion; the act of standing up, the exertion to hear, see, and understand, by each of perhaps 1,500 or 2,000 persons, created a noise which may easily be conceived.

"Mr. Irving begged for attention, and when order was restored, he explained the occurrence, which he said was not new, except

[1] There is some confusion as to dates. The manifestations that attracted most attention were on 16th October and 6th November, 1831.

in the congregation! He expounded 1 Cor. xiv. 'in order to elucidate what had just happened'. The sister was now returning from the vestry to her seat, and Mr. Irving, observing her from the pulpit, said, in an affectionate tone, 'Console yourself, sister! Console yourself!' He then proceeded with his discourse."

It was a Communion Sabbath. Irving's sister-in-law, Mrs. Hamilton, an elder's wife, said that in the evening:—

"There was a tremendous crowd and from the commencement of the service there was an evident uproariousness, men's voices continually mingling with the singing and praying in the most indecent confusion. Mr. Irving had nearly finished his discourse, when another of the ladies spoke. The people heard for a few minutes with quietness comparatively. But on a sudden, a number of the fellows in the gallery began to hiss, and then some cried 'silence!' and some one thing and some another, until the congregation, except such as had firm faith in God, were in a state of extreme commotion. Some of these fellows (who afterwards appeared were a gang of pickpockets come to make a 'row') shut the gallery doors, which I think was providential . . . for many lives might have been lost.

"Mr. Irving immediately arose and said, 'Let us pray'—'O Lord, still the tumult of the people', over and over again in an unfaltering voice. . . . Certainly the Lord did still the people.

"Before the blessing, Mr. Irving intimated that henceforth there would be *morning* service on the Sunday, when those persons would exercise their gifts, for he would not subject the congregation to the scenes they had witnessed.

"Some called, 'Hear! hear!' others 'down! down!' The whole scene reminded one of Paul at Ephesus."

"Most of the Session dislike all this," wrote Irving to Mr. Macdonald on 7th November, 1831, "and had I not been firm, the voice of the Holy Ghost would, ere this, have been put down by one means or another. Our morning worship is attended by nearly 1,000 persons. I seek the blessing of God, then we sing. Mr. Brown or I read a chapter, and the Spirit confirms our interpretations, or adds and exhorts in a few words, without interruption, but with great strengthening; then one of us, or the elders, or the brethren prays, and then I fulfil the part of the pastor or angel of the church with short instructions, waiting at the intervals for the Spirit to speak, which He does sometimes by one, sometimes by two, and sometimes by three— which I apply, and break down, and make the best use of for edifying of the flock and convincing the gainsayers; with short prayers as occasion serveth; and I conclude with prayer, and with the doxology, and the blessing.

"Every Wednesday night I am preaching to thousands 'the Baptism with the Holy Ghost', and the Lord is mightily with us. But many adversaries. Oh, pray diligently that Satan may not be able to put this light out! . . . Farewell! P.S. The Cairds are with us again."

What was Irving's own idea of the manifestations? They were God's answer to his prayer for direct intervention in the world, challenging the advance of "the mechanical philosophy" that reduced everything to "cause and effect". Unwilling to cast pearls before swine, he recognised the need of sowing seed beside *all* waters and therefore gave the public a careful account of the movement in a series of articles written for *Fraser's Magazine* (1832). He had prepared the way by "the full preaching of Christ's coming in the flesh and His coming again in glory", the two great doctrines that had gone "out of sight and out of mind".

"Thus we stood when the news of the restoration of the gift of tongues in the west of Scotland burst in upon us like the morning star, and turned our speculations upon the true doctrine into the examination of a fact."

Irving claimed to have left no stone unturned as an investigator. What impressed him chiefly was Mary Campbell's realisation that Christ did mighty works as a man anointed by the Holy Ghost, "and not by God mixing himself up with the man". "She straightway argued that, if Jesus as a man in my nature thus spake and performed by the Holy Ghost, which he even promised to me, then ought I, *in the same manner*, to do likewise." A peasant girl's interpretation of Acts x: 38 and Mark xvi: 17 was thus accepted by the theologian because it confirmed what he had been preaching for "six or seven years"!

Irving's use of picturesque, popular phraseology was notorious. At heart he probably adhered to the "Catholic and Orthodox" view of the Person of Christ. But the Irvingite circle received his teaching at its face value, teaching that (*a*) practically reduced Christ to a human being, endowed by the Holy Spirit with power and (*b*) conceived of the Holy Spirit an energy, similar in kind though different in degree, inspiring human beings who might thus attain unheard-of heights of holiness. Irving's doctrine, as received by those who actually practiced tongues and prophesying, was dangerously simplified. He argued that:

"As there was but one giving of the Law, and one Incarnation, so there is but one Day of Pentecost . . . and to expect another is folly and delusion. The gifts *then* came into the Church and are in the baptised Church *now as ever*."

He denied that the gift of tongues in his own time was viewed as a short cut to the speaking of foreign languages; on the contrary, it was "a sign" to the outsider (as in 1 Cor. xiv). Most of his followers followed this interpretation, though the ignorant Mary Campbell believed that the gift of speaking foreign languages (e.g., Turkish and Pelew Island tongue) had been miraculously bestowed on her! One feature of this January article in *Fraser's Magazine* was significant:

"If Apostles were raised up again, as I believe they will be—they shall stand humbly under Christ, as prepared channels through which His virtues may pass."

That suggestion led later to Irvingism becoming a polity as well as a system of doctrine and practice.

In the March Number of *Fraser*, we have Irving's own impression of the manifestations. It is impressive.

"The whole utterance, from the beginning to the ending of it, is with a power, and fullness, and sometimes rapidity of voice, altogether different from that of the person's ordinary utterance in any mood; and I would say, both in its form and in its effects upon a simple mind, quite supernatural.

"There is a power in the voice to thrill the heart and overawe the spirit after a manner which I have never felt. There is a march, and a majesty, and a sustained grandeur in the voice, especially of those who prophesy, which I have never heard even a resemblance to, except now and then in the sublimest and most impassioned moods of Mrs. Siddons and Miss O'Neil.

"It is a mere abandonment of all truth to call it screaming or crying; it is the most majestic and divine utterance which I have ever heard, some parts of which I never heard equalled, and no part of it surpassed, by the finest execution of genius and art exhibited at the oratorios. And when the speech utters itself in the way of a spiritual song, it is the likest to some of the most simple and ancient chants in the cathedral service, insomuch that I have been often led to think that those chants, of which some can be traced up as high as the days of Ambrose, are recollections and transmissions of the inspired utterances in the primitive church.[1]

---

[1] Prof. R. Will thinks that Church Music has taken the place of Glossolalia. "Is not J. S. Bach's fugue the gushing up of a religious sentiment that cannot be inspiringly expressed in words?" (*Le Culte*, II., p. 360.)

"Most frequently the silence is broken by utterance in a tongue, and this continues for a longer or a shorter period, sometimes occupying only a few words, as it were filling the first gust of sound; sometimes extending to five minutes, or even more, of earnest and deeply-felt discourse, with which the heart and soul of the speaker is manifestly much moved to tears, and sighs and unutterable groanings, to joy, and mirth and exultation, and even laughter of the heart.

"So far from being unmeaning gibberish, as the thoughtless and heedless sons of Belial have said, it is regularly-formed, well-proportioned, deeply-felt discourse, which evidently wanteth *only the ear of him, whose native tongue it is*, to make it a very masterpiece of powerful speech."

For the present, we may continue considering Irving's own account, bearing in mind the fact that the descriptions of his opponents were sometimes as one-sided in scepticism, as his in credulity.

"Useful, brother?" he asks his opponents: "It is most useful for thee, in order to get the better of thine unbelief and irreverence, to abate thy trust in thine own understanding, by showing thee a thing which it cannot enter into—to make thee feel and acknowledge God speaking by His Spirit.

"It is the standing symbol of the communion of the saints, and their fellowship with the Father and the Son, not by means of intelligence, but by means of the Holy Ghost.

"But because intellect cannot grasp it, intellect would dash it to the ground, and deny that there is a spirit in man deeper than the intellect—that there is a Holy Ghost binding God to Jesus, and Jesus to the Church, and the Church with one another.

"*The unknown part of the discourse is the symbol of the fountain secret*, unseen and unknown. Doth a man refuse to drink of the clear, flowing stream, because he knows not the hidden and secret cavern from which it hath flowed out!"

Irving tells of a "Gifted Person" who described his inmost experience of the Tongues:

"When I am praying in my native tongue, however fixed my soul be upon God, and Him alone, I am conscious of other thoughts and desires, *which the very words I use force in before me*. I am like a man holding straightforward to his home full in view, who, though he diverge neither to the right hand nor to the left, is ever solicited by many well-known objects on every hand of him.

"But the moment I am visited with the Spirit, and carried out to God in a tongue which I know not, it is as if a deep covering of snow had fallen on all the country round,—and I saw nothing but the object of my desire and the road which leadeth to it. I am more conscious than ever of the presence of God. He and He only is in my soul. *I am filled with some form of the mind of God*, be it joy or grief, desire, love, pity, compassion or indignation; and I am *made* to utter it in words which are full of *power* over my spirit, but not being accessible to my understanding, my devotion is not interrupted by *associations or suggestions from the visible or intellectual world*: I feel myself, as it were, shut in with God into His own pavilion, and hidden close from the invasions of the world, the devil, and the flesh."

This is very similar to the account of glossolalia as observed at Greenock by Archibald McKerrell (*Apology for the Gift of Tongues*, 1831). He was in touch with Alan Ker, relative of David Ker (deacon at Regent Square, and staunch supporter of his minister).

Irving continues:—

"In the same breath, in perfect continuance, sometimes in constant sequence, sometimes with such a pause as a speaker makes to take his breath, *the English part* flows forth in the same fullness, majesty and grandeur. As God speaketh in the Church for edification—this is always the largest part, four or ten times as much being known as is unknown. The *un*known is the sign that the known is a message from God, prophesying under the power of the Spirit—and not any offering of the enlightened and pious mind for the benefit of the brethren—it is *Jesus occupying the speech*, and using the tongue of his servant, to speak the things which he desireth at that time to be spoken and heard."

At this point Irving proceeds to qualify this statement by one which virtually annuls it: "*The person is not used as a trumpet merely for speaking through*, but as an *intelligent conscious* creature, to be possessed in these his inward parts and *used* by the Lord of all". A little further on, however, he speaks of "Jesus *using his will*, and through the spirit and tongue of the man, uttering forth what words He pleaseth". And yet again: "In uttering the unknown and the known, he is alike under the power of Jesus, equally conscious in his speech to the thing which is uttered". This is contradicted unmistakably in a sentence which follows: "There is no difference in the state of the speaker—he is equally *un*conscious, equally *un*intelligible" . . .

"This seems to me," he concluded, "to realise the views of man's being that I was wont to hear from the mouth of that most profound thinker, our dear Coleridge, as he hath blessed me more instruction than any other uninspired man."(!)

Two alternatives could end glossolalia:—

(*a*) A man might either *refuse* his will, and thus quench the Spirit.

(*b*) Or being commanded by those who rule over him, he can cease to *give* his Will, and so arrest the utterance of the Spirit.

These conflicting statements, within a few sentences of each other, show that Irving was of all men the least logical.

On the whole, considering his writings and the actual course of the movement, we may say that he believed the inspired person to be a passive instrument of the divine voice; a man's own piety was temporarily deflected, in order that the absolute and perfect holiness of the Deity might communicate uncontaminated messages.

Irving believed that there was no difference between the actual state of the speaker in uttering the known and the unknown words, the one being as pure an utterance of the Holy Ghost as the other. As to the virtue of the unknown tongue, not only did human associations prevent a full "absorption in God;" there was the temptation of learning beforehand what to say. Further

"A man's faithfulness is put to a sterner proof, for as word draweth on word, and sentence followeth sentence, he may shrink from the consequences of going forward, e.g., his feelings of love, friendship and favour to those whom he is called upon to rebuke may arrest the current of his willingness. Every prejudice, every passion, every fibre of the flesh which remaineth uncrucified, will now arise to prevent the spirit from uttering what it is his mind to say, for the flesh lusteth against the spirit.

"I can conceive a thousand temptations in the way of hindrance. *The utterance in English is far more trying than the utterance in the unknown tongue.* It is only by the strong hand of the Lord that the utterance is not marred or mangled."

In the words of one of Irving's greatest contemporaries:—

> " Life, like a dome of many-coloured glass,
> Stains the white radiance of eternity."

The final article in *Fraser's Magazine* appeared in April, 1832. He opens by claiming that tongue-speech was the *same* form of utterance given at Pentecost; whereas in his March article he distinctly denied that glossolalia in his time was designed as a miraculous way of evangelising by languages unlearnt—Pentecost being unique and modern manifestations resembling rather those at Corinth. Quite seriously, he describes God as "raising up weak women and uneducated men", resulting in the "driving away, in utter disgust, all but simple-minded, single-hearted disciples. These it is building up, rooting and grounding them in love, and it will, like good food, bring the Church into a perfect man". The "gifted persons" had asked for bread—would God give them a stone?

To "this suspicious generation, which examineth religious questions as an Old Bailey lawyer doth a thief" he addressed two parting challenges.

(1) "If, as Scripture teaches and all orthodox divines have given their verdict, there is a real union between Christ and His Church, the wonder is, not that there should in our time be like manifestations, but that they should ever have ceased. For the gifts of the Spirit are as much the property of the Church as are the graces; nay, these two are not separated, but are the *outward* and *inward* forms of the same indwelling of Christ."

(2) "Again, no one doubteth that Christian baptism doth convey to the believer the gift of repentance towards God, and the remission of our sins by the regeneration of the Holy Spirit; and why should they doubt that it doth convey also the baptism with the Holy Ghost for speaking with tongues and prophesying? Nay, far more specifically do the supernatural manifestations of the Holy Ghost belong to Christian baptism than repentance and remission. For speaking with tongues and other gifts accompanied the establishment of the Church at Jerusalem (Acts ii), at Samaria (Acts viii), and among the Gentiles (Acts x)."

Irving's argument has been treated fully in order that a "composite photograph" of his mind may be produced, as his thoughts on the Gift of Tongues revealed themselves in his writings. This biography could scarcely claim to be "a psychological study", if it failed to do justice to the complexity of his thoughts, motives and feelings—the cross-currents which mingled in his fertile mind and generous heart.

CHAPTER XI

THE TONGUES—VARIOUS VIEWS

> "His speech was like a tangled chain;
> nothing impaired but all disordered."

"BODILY effects", "speaking in the power", and cognate phenomena, have usually been associated with movements among the uneducated. (Kentucky backwoodsmen, Mormons, etc). The Irvingite Movement was largely supported by people of culture. The leader was Henry Drummond,

"a singular mixture of all things—of the saint, the wit, the philosopher—swimming, if I mistake not, in an element of dandyism".

Carlyle adds that in spite of Drummond's "fine qualities and capabilities", he was

"well-nigh cracked by an enormous conceit of himself, as pride and vanity seemed to pervade every fibre of him and render his life a restless inconsistency. That was the feeling he left in me, nor did it alter afterwards. . . . He, without unkindness of intention, did my poor Irving a great deal of ill".

"Henry Drummond is in all chairs—I fear for him", said Irving once. "His words are more witty than spiritual; his manner is *spirituel*, not grave. . . ."

Then there were Robert Baxter and J. B. Cardale, both eminent lawyers, Robert Norton, a doctor, and A. J. Scott, a minister of high intellectual calibre. Pilkington was obviously an educated man, Taplin a schoolmaster. People like Lady Olivia Sparrow were drawn to the movement by its very novelty, as such women of leisure are to-day drawn to Spiritualism or Christian Science. It is a striking fact that women took an important part in the actual manifestations, as in the Montanist Movement. Those who *practised* the gifts were generally of a lower class than the "noble women" who patronised the movement.

§ 1

How did the speakers react to the "power"?

"Anti-Cabala" describes how "a man of placid demeanour", after expounding Chapters xxxiii. and xxxiv. of Exodus on a certain occasion—paused. And presently, in startling dissonance, burst forth in an unknown tongue.

"I could not see the speaker, or to be more correct, the roarer. I should judge, by its harshness, that it was the voice of a man. It lasted but a minute or two, and *ran off into English words*, "Abide in Him! Ye shall behold His glory! Ye shall behold His glory!" etc.

"The whole was uttered in a tone of varied cadence, but so loud, revolting and unnatural (not *unearthly*) that it operated on me like a shock from which I could not immediately recover.

"The second speaker was a female. Her utterance was accompanied with considerable heaving of the chest and head —the loudness towards the end *in both cases*, and the heaving also, like a gentle subsidence of breath and motion in a pair of bellows when allowed to expire of itself, as though the exciting influence within were mechanically operative and insensibly withdrawn.

"The speakers at Mr. Irving's appear to lose all self-control, and to be operated on by a foreign influence."

Anti-Cabala notes the "tones of terror calculated to shock and derange the nervous system of many persons", and cites one case mentioned in *The Times* of the fatal effect on a young lady's mind ("past recovery").

Mr. Pilkington in his pamphlet speaks of a terrific "Crash! (cras-cras-cra-CRASH!!!)", the vociferation being sudden and rapid. Sentences were short, and it was difficult to distinguish the "Tongue" from the English part, as both were chanted.

"Power and authority" were characteristic of male utterances, "plaintive and affectionate emotion" of female speech.

The speaking was "mechanical", thus agreeing with Anti-Cabala's account. Pilkington was informed by Irving that the gifted persons had informed him that the power "operated on the *end* of their tongues". He describes the physical process as follows:—

"Her whole frame was in violent agitation, but principally the body from the hips to the shoulders, which worked with a lateral motion. The chest heaved and swelled—the head was occasionally raised from the right hand, which was placed on the forehead, while the left hand and arm seemed to press and rub the stomach.

"She was but a few seconds in this state when the body swayed, the neck became stiff, the head erect; the hands fell on the lap, the mouth assumed a circular form, the lips projected, and the 'Tongue' and 'English' came from her in an awful tone.

"During the utterance I noticed a violent exertion of the muscles at the back of the jawbone; and that the stiffened lips never touched, to aid the articulation of the 'Tongue', but they closed sufficiently to express the labials of the English part of the delivery, and *instantly resumed the circular form.*"

George Grenville adequately represents the "incredulous layman" (ἄπιστος ἢ ἰδιώτης), of whose unfavourable judgment Paul warned the Corinthians:—

"The speaker after ejaculating three 'ohs', one rising above the other in *tones very musical*, burst into a flow of unintelligible jargon, which whether it was in English or gibberish, I could not discover. This lasted five or six minutes, and, as the voice was silenced, another woman, in more passionate and louder tones, took it up. This last spoke in English, and words, though not sentences, were distinguishable. She spoke sitting, under great apparent excitement, and screamed on till, from exhaustion, as it seemed, her voice gradually died away, and all was still" (*Memoirs*, III, Ch. 22).

A private letter from a visitor from Aberdeen is quoted in the anonymous pamphlet *The Unknown Tongues or Rev. Edward Irving and Rev. Nicholas Armstrong arraigned.* The letter is dated November 3rd, 1831:—

"I went at 6 a.m. to Mr. Irving's . . . it was full, containing at least 700. The dim, gray light, scarcely sufficient to permit the distinction of one individual from another, gave a sepulchral solemnity to the scene, which was heightened by the awful, breathless silence. A paraphrase was sung, and Mr. Irving stood up with his hands raised as far as possible above his head. Then Mr. X—— read from Isaiah, during which he broke out every few verses into the most unintelligible gibberish. He ended, and the rev. gentleman explained the meaning of the unknown tongues, after which he said: 'Now let the Lord do as seemeth Him fit among the people.'

"An awful stillness prevailed for about five minutes. Suddenly an appalling shriek seemed to rend the roof, which was repeated with heart-chilling effect. I grasped involuntarily the bookdesk before me; and then, suddenly, a torrent of unintelligible words, for about five minutes, followed by—'When will ye repent? Why will ye not repent?'"

The account of the difference in process is interesting.

"The young lady who uttered 'the above words was' quite scarlet. She was close to me; she sank down exhausted.
"In an instant another mild-looking girl, two seats behind me, began the 'Unknown Tongue', but like a schoolboy saying his lesson. She soon sat down.
"A man beside me seemed working himself up, but said nothing!
"The minister then rose and said: 'It was visible that the Spirit of the Lord was actively at work.' He asked a blessing and we departed. *I was ill all day afterwards.*"

The same pamphlet also gives a long utterance delivered in the tongue, but in English. It is like the burning admonition of a Hebrew prophet.

Carlyle's opinion of the Tongues was, as we might expect, decidedly adverse, but was based on observation.

The first reference we find to Glossolalia is in a letter to his wife (22nd August, 1831):—

"Friday I spent with Irving in the region of the supernatural. Understand that the 'gift of tongues' is here also (chiefly among the *women*) and a belief that God is still working miracles in the Church—by hysterics. I learned that poor Dow (minister) of Irongray is a wonderworker and a speaker with tongues. His autograph letter was read to me detailing all that the 'Laart' had done for him. Poor fellow! it was four days after his wife's death.

"Irving hauled me off to Lincoln's Inn Fields to hear my double (Mr. Scott). For a stricken hour did he sit expounding in the most superannuated dialect (of Chroist and so forth). The good Irving looking at one wistfully, so piteously as though he implored me to believe."

"Poor Edward Irving," Carlyle wrote to his mother (20th October, 1831); "His friends here are all much grieved. For many months he has been puddling in the midst of certain insane jargonings of hysterical women, and cracked-brained enthusiasts, who start up from time to time in public and utter confused stuff, mostly 'oh's' and 'ah's', and absurd interjections about 'the body of Jesus'; they also pretend to work miracles, and have raised more than one weak bedrid woman, and cured people of 'nerves', or as they themselves say, 'cast devils out of them'.

"All which poor Irving is pleased to consider as the 'work of the Spirit', and to janner on at great length, as making *his* church the peculiar blessed of heaven, and equal to or greater than the primitive one at Corinth. This, greatly to my sorrow, has gone on privately a good while with increasing vigour; but last Sabbath it burst out publicly in church; for one of the 'prophetesses', a woman on the verge of derangement, started up and began to speak with tongues and *as the thing was encouraged by Irving,* three or four fresh hands started up in the evening. Whereupon the whole congregation got into foul uproar, some groaning, some laughing, some shrieking, not a few falling into swoons—more like a bedlam than a Christian church.

"Happily, neither Jane nor I were there. We had not even heard of it, when going next evening to call on Irving, we found the house all decked out for this same 'speaking with tongues'; and as we talked a moment with Irving, who had come down to us, there rose a shriek in the upper story of the house, and presently he exclaimed, 'There is one prophesying, come up and hear her!'

"We hesitated to go, but he forced us up into a back room, and we could hear the wretched creature raving like one possessed: *hoo*in and *haa*ing, and talking as sensibly as one would do with a pint of brandy in his stomach, till after some ten minutes she seemed to grow tired and became silent. Nothing so shocking and altogether unspeakably deplorable was it ever my lot to hear. Poor Jane was on the very verge of fainting and did not recover the whole night.

"Irving, with singular calmness, said only, 'There, hear you; there are the "Tongues"!' and we two, except by our looks . . . answered him nothing. . . . Why wasn't there a bucket of cold water to fling on that lall-lalling hysterical mad-woman? thought we" (*C.R.*, p. 298).

As to the actual words purporting to be in "Tongue", we have the statement of the *Morning Watch* itself that they contained "many Greek and Latin radicals, and with inflections also much resembling those of the Greek language". "I heard Mr. Taplin, and what I heard was this," declared the Rev. Hugh McNeile in his "Letter to a friend."

"I write in all seriousness before God, without scoff, or sneer. Neither more or less than jargon, uttered 'ore rotundo', and mingled with Latin words, among which I distinctly heard more than once, 'amamini, amaminor'."

This is certainly confirmed by written specimens which have been preserved. The first is one collected on various occasions at the beginning of 1831 by Archibald McKerrell, in which he heard "the same individual speak in a Tongue, written down" by him on the spot "while the individual was speaking". Only words marked in inverted commas are in the order in which they were spoken:

> Hippo gerosto—Hippo—Booros—Senoote—
> "Foorime—Gorin Hoopo Tanto Noostin."
> Noostarin—Niparos—Hipanos—Bantos—Boorin—"O Pinitos" "O Fastos Sungor O Fastos Sungor". Deripangito—Boorinos—Hypen—Eletanteti—Eretini—Menati (*Apology for the Gift of Tongues*, 1831).

So readily did the tongue-speakers swing into rhythm, even in their English utterances, that it is not surprising to find writers of pamphlets resolving utterances in the power into verse. It should be understood, in reading the following "hymns", that the actual recitation must have been much more irregular:—

> " Hippo gerosto niparos
> Boorastin farini
> O fastor sungor boorinos
> Epoongos menati."

The following is quoted by A. Robertson in *A Vindication of the Religion of the Land:*—

> " Hey amei hassan alla do
> hoc alors loore
> Has heo massan amor ho
> ti prov his aso me."

§ 2

"Tongue-speech" almost suggests to us Esperanto, with its mixture of Greek, Latin, Italian, etc. But Esperanto was not evolved till 1887. Mr. Pilkington, who published a pamphlet on becoming disillusioned, gave it the following title:—

"THE UNKNOWN TONGUES
  Discovered to be English, Spanish and Latin
    And the Rev. Edward Irving
proved to be erroneous in attributing these utterances to the
    influence of the HOLY SPIRIT

Various interesting colloquies between the writer and Mr. Irving and his followers, and observations which manifestly show that they are all under a delusion.
By George Pilkington,
Who interpreted before the congregation,
London, 1831."

Mr. Pilkington was apparently a very "suggestible" person. He attended Mr. Irving's prayer meetings at 6.30 every morning for nearly three months before Sunday, 16th October, 1831, when there were manifestations in church. He then began

"to think more seriously of the gift, not because it was:
(a) relied on by such a devout man as Mr. Irving (whose method of praying and argumentative way of expounding the Scriptures had a very powerful effect on my mind and feelings),
(b) but because those persons were themselves remarkably pious, and I concluded that they would scarcely have ventured to utter such direct and remarkable prophecies, if they were not so gifted."

On the day after these manifestations he declared that he was "strongly excited by a very powerful feeling", which he was "unable to describe", "to exhort and forewarn them of impending difficulty; but resisted it, until Mr. Irving in his discourse said it was sinful to suppress such movements."

"I could no longer restrain, and with a sudden burst of utterance, used the following detached sentences: 'The second sword is now drawn in this church.' 'Deny me no more', etc.

"Mr. Irving praised God for opening 'another mouth', and said, 'We have heard the voice of the Shepherd'. I now concluded that the excitement I felt was the same as that which influenced the 'gifted persons', but that *they experienced it in a higher degree*, which produced the utterance of Tongue."

Irving afterwards took Pilkington back to his house for a talk; the latter explained that he had previously been a Deist, before attending services at Regent Square. (No doubt the attraction of the manifestations was due to the neglect of the Holy Spirit in his former arid faith.) Irving observed "that he was deficient in theology, but had a deep sense of his duty to God".

Then turning to his secretary (Mr. A.), he said:—"Our brother fancied he understood the tongues."

The stranger replied:—"Such an occurrence happened in Scotland, and the gentleman who interpreted spoke by the power of the Spirit, *without the agency of his own understanding.*"

"That was not as it occurred to me," replied Pilkington boldly.

"I explained that as I knew several languages, I might have heard some familiar sounds."

Irving replied that he had not the least idea of the meaning of Tongues, and "aspired to be no more than the humble pastor of the flock". ("This humility filled my heart with a mixture of love and admiration for him.")

Pilkington left Irving's at 1 p.m. and spent the time till 3 in earnest prayer, tortured by the fear of being considered an outsider. At the 3 o'clock prayer meeting in the vestry there were nine or ten people present, the "missionary" presiding. On catching four words in the utterance which followed from a woman, he wrote down as an interpretation of "gthis dil emma sumo"—"I will undertake this dilemma" ("but afterwards recollected that the word was 'assume', and that the first syllable was lost by the preceding word ending in a vowel").

The paper he gave to Mr. A (whom he had already met); it was passed on to the missionary, who asked with surprise "What did he intend by it?"

"This is what I understand the Tongues to mean," answered Pilkington.

"How *can* you, sir! undertake to interpret the words of God? Do you wish to upset the Church?"

Pilkington replied that he came simply for the purpose of interpreting, as Brother A would testify.

The missionary gave an inquiring look at Mr. A who appeared to be ignorant of the circumstance!

At which Pilkington, exceedingly hurt, turned to the missionary: "I offer the words in all humility—if they be of no value I trust you will believe that I have merely done what was required of me."

He replied: "You cannot interpret by human understanding; interpretation must be given by the Spirit."

A few days later, Pilkington accosted Mr. A on his way home from a meeting. The latter appeared as if he wished to avoid him.

Then a "gifted brother" came up: "Pray, Sir, are you the gentleman who spoke in the church on Monday?"

Pilkington admitted the fact.

"How do you feel, sir? Could you avoid it, sir?"

"I think I could have avoided it."

"Well, since you have confessed *that*, allow me to advise you not to speak again, unless you cannot help it."

It is clear that here we have an organised group, united on a given basis, and hostile to the intrusion of individuals and ideas out of harmony with its principles. Yet Pilkington was extraordinarily persistent, in spite of his one-sided interpretation of the movement. We find him again taking part in a meeting of the inner circle in the Regent Square vestry. Sister No. 1 utters the words "Hozequin alta stare". He first translates this as "Hosanna in the highest". But on comparing it with a following utterance ("Hozehamenanostra"), he decides it should be "Jesus in the highest". He does not clearly remember the remaining words, but quickly jots down their supposed meaning—"Will take care of this house". She afterwards repeated it three times—"Hozehamenanostra". The interpretation he gives as: "Jesus in the highest will take care of this house".

On being challenged by Irving, he declared that "Hoze" was Jesus; "ha" a contraction of habeo; "mena"= hands; "nostra"=ours.

"Say no more about it," replied the minister, anxious to know the truth, yet fearing the opinions of the circle.

Sister No. 2's utterance, "Holimoth holif awthaw", Pilkington dismissed as bad enunciation of "Holy, most holy father". ("I didn't speak in English, did I?"—he heard No. 2 ask her neighbour.)

On a member suggesting that if the Gifted were to speak in Church, they should be "well-placed" and should endeavour to say as little as possible, Sister No. 2 cried out in English: "Do you not know that it burneth in the bone—burneth in the bone?"

A final utterance came from Sister No 3: "Casa sera hastha caro." He whispers to Irving that it is Spanish; "the house will be in my care"—Irving anxiously listens and both try to keep the unsympathetic group from hearing. The meeting ends, and Pilkington remembers that he has eaten nothing all day—a significant stimulant to ecstatic religion!

Pilkington now began to have definite doubts as to the soundness of the movement. "I was neither a mocker nor a scoffer—God forbid! But He has given me understanding." Had not "the missionary" rebuked him for "presuming to interpret"? And had not Mr. A refused to admit that he had been invited by Mr. Irving to take part in the meetings, although it was but two hours since he had united with the minister in prayer for the perfection of the Gift?

"As the sap passes through the trunk and branches and each contributes relief in proportion to its luxuriance. . . . I reasonably expected that the 'Gifted Persons' would sympathise in the feelings of a spirit so wantonly afflicted, but all were silent.

"Nor did my suspicions want authority when I remember how instantaneously they burst forth, as if the trigger of a loaded gun had been pulled, when Mr. Irving declared that the law permitted them to speak by the Spirit (if the power was so very overpowering!);—and how suitably they could *restrain* the Spirit till the 'second service' of the prayer meeting, apparently with as much ease as the owner makes of a stop-watch."

(Irving divided the prayer meetings into three parts, one of which was specially reserved for utterances in the power.)

The secrecy, the sectarian spirit, and disinclination of the gifted persons to make use of his interpretations—confirmed Pilkington's suspicions of the movement.

Decisions in the spiritual world, however, are seldom reached without a struggle. Pilkington's faith in the Tongues was temporarily confirmed shortly afterwards, when he "stood up and holding his hand above his head, was influenced to utter words other than his own", giving as interpretation of a "gifted sister's" utterance "yeo cogo nomo"—"I know the law." He added:—"Let that which is *of the Spirit* be proclaimed on the housetops, and *that of the flesh* confessed; for there is one fold and one door, and those who would climb over the fence are thieves and robbers."

"Now Mr. Pilkington," Irving called, "I believe you really *are* in the Spirit." This seems to indicate that anything was welcomed which confirmed the supernatural character of the gifts in the eyes of the distinctly subjective "triers". Pilkington himself realised this after that meeting:—

"I thought less of 'discernment' than of other gifts—but now I perceive that, as it involves a knowledge of the human heart, it cannot be possessed by any but the omniscient. I would have Mr. Irving recollect that he endeavoured to persuade his congregation that these persons were gifted *because* he *prayed* for the gift, and argued ('egg: scorpion') that the Almighty would not give an impure spirit.

"He prayed that I should be gifted with interpretations, but rejected it, because I acknowledged that I translated by the understanding. Was not this a proof that the supposed Tongue was a *known* language? Might not this be considered the opportunity afforded by God, in answer to prayer, for Mr. Irving to discern by another test, the impure spirit of these supposed Gifted Persons?"

"A full confidence in Mr. Irving's zeal and discernment induced me to believe in the reality of the gifts."

On 19th October, 1831, he wrote to Irving stating that he wished to state his position before witnesses. Next morning a meeting was held in the presence of the "inner circle", witnesses on whom the minister declared "he could depend". Pilkington had not proceeded far, when he was interrupted rather hastily by Irving:—

"You will occupy all our time, sir!" ["I must confess that I was very much surprised; for I thought that Mr. Irving's time could not be better spent than in paying very minute attention to any information that would help him to discern the purity of the Spirit."]

Irving:—

"I wish to refer to what you said in the church:—*was it by your own understanding or by the Spirit?* Were you in the Spirit, you would know; because the Gifted Persons say it is impossible to mistake the feeling."

Mr. P:—

"I felt that I was under the powerful feeling of piety and devotion."

Mr. B (Baxter):—

"If I understand you rightly, it was a mere *excitement of the flesh*, under the influence of devotion, which compelled you to utter expressions dictated by your own *understanding*."

Mr. P:—

"Certainly, it was so, *except when I interpreted*."

Mr. B:—

"But were your interpretations merely translations?"

Mr. P:—

"They were, from expressions which I heard in English, Spanish and Latin" (1 Cor. xiv, 2 urged).

Mr. B:—

"I am very glad that you are *now* satisfied that you are not in the Spirit."

Mr. Irving:—

"But you say that you heard the Tongue in English; pray, how did you know where the English commenced?"

Mr. P:—

"By the same means you would know the first from the second part of a tune. Also, 'broken English'."

Later, Pilkington was reprimanded by Mr. B.:

"Should you ever feel so disposed again (i.e., to speak), I would recommend you to keep silence, and tell Mr. Irving what you intended to say."

Pilkington:

"You may depend upon it that I will never speak again in the church." (All seemed pleased).

Irving added (who ever appeared to be conscientious on this point):—

"Unless you cannot possibly avoid it."

Mr. A.:

"Not even then! for the Gifted Sisters tell me they *can restrain* themselves by *prayer*."

(How then, asks Pilkington, is it a *power*?)

After the minister's prayer, Mr. B. (one of the witnesses on whom Irving "could depend") told Pilkington "Not to repeat publicly what had happened because there was a *difference of opinion* on the subject". This, Pilkington indignantly notes, was the man whom he heard talking in a corner of the church to Mr. A.,—"Truth is such a comprehensive word, and so beautiful. Purity is also a word I am fond of using in prayer—it flows from the mouth so sweetly"; and he repeated it once or twice as if honey on his lips.

Pilkington tells us he was "encouraged by two very pious persons to attend the prayer meetings for the remainder of that week". "On Sunday I determined to go to some other church. But something whispered to me to see the end of it." The church was crowded to excess, but the "gifted persons" were silent because "God did not wish to speak". The Monday morning prayer meeting was fairly full. The "gifted persons" having spoken, Irving declared:—

"Brethren, you have heard the words of God." ("I felt an involuntary tremor and my mind was filled with horror") "I afterwards read 12 and 14 I. Cor. under guidance of my own reason, divested of the bias it had acquired in the deep theological attainments of Mr. Irving, whose persuasive eloquence and transcendent ability are so attractive and irresistible."

Pilkington met Irving in private immediately after this prayer meeting. He pointed out that when the individual takes upon himself to declare that his words are words from God, any sect might produce a Spirit to establish its particular doctrine, till at length there would be nothing but a confusion of tongues; whereas the Holy Spirit would declare but one doctrine in any church or country.

What about 1 Cor. xiv. 13 and 28? Interpretation alone could justify speaking in a tongue in public, particularly with verse 36 in view: "What! came the word of God *out from you?* or came it *unto you* only?"

Irving was evasive: "You do not understand; let me teach you. You are a stranger to me, but I conclude you are enthusiastic; and believe me, that is sinful." Irving wrote to *The Times* (27th December, 1831), giving his explanation of Mr. Pilkington's disclosure. This letter, rejected as "trash" by England's greatest newspaper (indicating his fall in the eyes of the public) was substantially reproduced in *Fraser* (March, 1832).

I thought it was no use to prolong the interview, so I determined to ascertain, by a plain and direct question, the difference between our ideas and that which acted on the "gifted persons", and said:

"Pray, sir, allow me to ask if they speak by the same power and influence as that which acted on Balaam's ass?"

"No, sir," replied Irving. "The ass had no *understanding* and no sympathy with God; do you observe the plaintive and affectionate manner in which the words are uttered by these persons?"

He conceived of the "gifted persons" as mere mechanical mediums, but in not withholding understanding from them, stopped short of an absolute denial of their normality.

As Pilkington was about to retire, Irving said "stop!" and prayed for the eternal and temporal prosperity of his family.

"I have discontinued all intercourse with Mr. Irving and his followers; because I have discovered error and discrepancy in their proceedings, which cannot exist in any work that emanates from God." So closes a remarkable account, which fails, however, to do justice to the manifestations, in narrowing down the inquiry to the tracing of known languages in the tongue speech, though it cannot be denied that this element contributed to the movement.

§ 3

There is a vast literature of pamphlets and sermons bearing on the Gift of Tongues in the time of Irving, both in support of the movement and in opposition to it. Of these a large number, on both sides, are written from preconceived opinion, without serious first hand examination of the phenomena, and are therefore of little value beyond indicating the general feeling of the public.

Considering first, the "literature" adverse to Irvingism. We find that the Rev. Hugh McNeile in his "Letter to a friend . . ." (1834), written when the movement had reached maturity, has indeed first-hand information about the earlier stage of the movement, but soon rules out any possibility of good, by his hard-and-fast adherence to rigid "Verbal Inspiration"; e.g., he exhibits what to us would appear lack of imagination unfitting an educated man, in stressing the fact that when Mr. Taplin read 1 Peter "in the Spirit", his ear was "struck by deviation from our authorised version"! The ground generally taken by the critics was rather different from the typically eighteenth century position of Lord Shaftesbury's *Letter concerning Enthusiasm* (1707). The opposition was more often orthodox than rationalistic.

We are constantly met with three arguments directed against the Tongues:—

(1) The Canon is closed, and the revival of "the Gifts" after they have served their appointed end, means a New Dispensation.

(2) "The Gifts" are associated with heretical Doctrines.

(3) The "Gifted Persons" do not show forth the "fruits of the Spirit".

Not much is to be gleaned from sermons of the period, except sidelights on Irving's unpopularity with his clerical contemporaries—Presbyterian, Anglican, and Methodist. A few suggestive sentences occur in a discourse of Irving's nearest neighbour, the Rev. Wm. Harness of St. Pancras'

Parochial Chapel, Regent Square (6th November, 1831). He diagnoses the movement as—

"Not the result of premeditated imposture, but the effects of a strong and much to be lamented delusion. For the sake of charity and as a part of Christian duty, I would entreat you not to be led to these services from motives of *curiosity*.

"Nothing can put an end to these excesses but their meeting with neglect. Fanaticism, like every other malady of a fevered imagination, is heightened by the presence and supposed sympathy of numbers."

But the manifestations seem to have been taken advantage of by many of the clergy for the purpose of displaying their own flowers of rhetoric, as in the following:—

"Thus the turbid visions of phrenzied enthusiasts, and the idle rhapsodies of delirious fanaticism, assume the privilege of celestial inspiration, and array themselves in the hallowed garb of prophecy . . . etc." (Rev. A. C. L. D'Arblay, M.A., 8th January, 1832, at Camden Chapel, St. Pancras).

Of greater value is a sermon by the Rev. David Thom of the Scots Kirk, Liverpool—"Miracles of the Irving School shown to be unworthy of serious examination".

If the Irvingites possessed the power of working miracles, there was but one alternative—"to bind up the lucubrations of Mr. Irving with our Bibles" or "by the word of God to beat down every pretention to miraculous power". Secondly, the "gifted persons" ignore the fact that 1 Cor. xiii alone is a warrant for holding that charismata were of a transient nature: they revert from the maturity of Paul to the childishness of the Corinthians. Thirdly, Irving in his *Last Days* was quite wrong in identifying the foretold time of miracles with his own age; the "latter days" referred to the old age of the Jewish Dispensation, which in Apostolic times was "ready to vanish away".

As far as the last point is concerned, Mr. Thom was undoubtedly in advance of his generation. "The religious world" of Irving's day might reject the revived miracles as conducive to disorder, but it shared with him generally a belief that the end of world would be preceded by signs and portents. It has already been noted, that as late as 1850 Dr. Bonar edited Irving's *Last Days*. And Dr. Cumming, who criticised his vagaries, afterwards gained no little notoriety in London himself by confident predictions of the "End of the World". (See p. 236f.).

Had Irving been born fifty years later, when eschatology was studied more carefully in its Jewish setting, and literalism more discredited among educated men, he would not have been so easily led to believe in the restoration of Apostolic charismata, lacking a common *point de départ* in a theologically conservative background.

One of the forces most bitterly opposed to "our modern pretenders to spiritual gifts" was the Edinburgh *Christian Instructor*, the organ of the Evangelical Party in the Church of Scotland. This journal made little attempt to find out what exactly the "gifted persons" believed. The September Number for 1832, e.g., accuses them of

"Endeavouring to show that Corinth was a parallel case . . . finding they cannot bring forward as much evidence as in Acts ii. *That* gift (at Corinth) was not for the end of teaching, but to serve as a sensible sign that those to whom it was given, were under a divine influence and acted under a divine commission."

This was precisely what the "Gifted Persons" professed the Tongues were for, in London at least: they were for a "sign"—not for preaching the Gospel. Sometimes the opponents of the movement were hardly fair, as McLeod Campbell rightly complained, in his criticism of *The Modern Claims to the Possession of the Extraordinary Gifts of the Spirit stated and examined*, by W. Goode, M.A., (subsequently Dean of Ripon).

Yet the *Christian Instructor* was not without a sturdy common sense:

"If a man tells us that spiritual gifts should be revived and should never have been discontinued . . . we shall tell him that he has not a particle of scriptural ground for his persuasion, that a cry for miracles argues an unbelieving and unspiritual state of mind, and that he is acting like a man who should urge that the scaffolding should not be removed from the beauty of a new house, because the house being built by means of it, cannot stand without it.

"If, however, men come forward bristling with anathemas, advancing an exclusive claim to the possession of the Spirit, and meeting our slightest expressions of doubt or hesitation with the direct assurance that we are blaspheming the Holy Ghost, we begin to doubt whether there be in such men aught of the Spirit of God."

Many of the pamphlets are full of complaints such as:

"The bitter spirit of censoriousness, and of arrogant assumptions concerning other churches, and especially of other ministers than Mr. Irving. . . .

"Holiness moreover, is prayed for as a means to an end, viz., that the miraculous operations of the Holy Ghost might be manifested in the recipients" (*A Morning Visit to Rev. E. Irving's*, 1832).

The New Apostles pamphlet points to "the noble army of martyrs" and the millions of witnesses who have had no guide but the will of God, as revealed in Scripture. The expectation of Spiritual Gifts on the part of "the weary and disheartened children of God" is condemned as restless discontent with God's natural order. "Blessed are those who have *not* seen, but have believed."

"In search for spiritual food, these fanatics were not very careful of its quality or source."

The New Apostles was published about 1860 and is virtually a criticism of a late Irvingite book, *Events affecting . . . the Church* (1847). Like many anti-Irvingite pamphlets, the *New Apostles* was not marked by any liberality of thought.

Dean Stanley, indeed (who had just published his epoch-making *Commentary on Corinthians*), is attacked for

"having tried to throw the light of Paganism (! !) on the subject, and illustrate the gift of tongues by the ecstasies and ravings of the Montanists, the prophets of the Cevennes, and most important—the Irvingites, declaring at the same time his disbelief in their divine authenticity: in fact he illustrates by parallelism truth by falsehood."

Another characteristic of many of these pamphlets is their way (common to the controversialists of all ages), of wrenching sentences from their context and putting them in such a setting as would render them doubly grotesque or blasphemous.

Another class of pamphlet (on both sides) is distinguished for its portentous learning. The Rev. Henry Blunt, rector of Streatham, quotes Chrysostom, Augustine, Isidore of Seville, etc., to prove that the Gifts died out in the Early Church when they had served their object. "Nor did the Prophets lose their understanding in ecstasy" (Origen). He cites Richard Baxter to some purpose:—

"I must confess that we have been much to blame in not making known to common Christians somewhat more of the nature of the heresies of the first ages and the effects of them, by which they might have been better fortified against them; for now, for want of such information, the poor wretches take old, rotten, damned heresies, and many are ready to run after them to their own perdition, little knowing that ever these heresies were in the world before."

He also quotes Luther's reply to Melancthon's query about the "Celestial Prophets," who claimed "to be on the same footing as the Prophets and Apostles"; "Try the spirits . . . their bare *assertion* of a Divine afflatus is not a sufficient ground for receiving them."

Of the "Literature" which appeared in defence of the revival of spiritual gifts, Robert Norton in his *Neglected and Controverted Scriptural Truths* follows much the same method as that of the writer just cited.

Dr. Norton was able to find the Fathers as sound exponents of Glossolalia and kindred gifts, as Mr. Blunt had found them opponents. The Apology of Athenagoras, for example, is confidently cited:—

"I call them prophets, who, being *out of themselves* and their own thoughts, uttered forth whatsoever by the impelling power of the Spirit, He wrought in them; while the Divine operator served himself of them and their organs, even as men of a trumpet."

Dr. Norton was evidently a man of considerable education. For he traced (as modern students of Abnormal Religious Psychology have done) the history of Glossolalia through the centuries to Irving's time, referring to the Camisards and the "Great Revival". He quotes an interesting segment from Wesley's Journal (15th August, 1750):—

"By reflecting on an old book . . . I was fully convinced of what I had long suspected; that the Montanists were real scriptural Christians; and that the grand reason why the miraculous gifts were so soon withdrawn was that . . . dry, formal, orthodox men began even then to ridicule whatsoever gifts they had not themselves . . . as either madness or imposture."

When Dr. Norton wrote this pamphlet in 1839, the Tongues had already run their course, and yet the events were recent enough to be clearly imprinted in his memory:—

"As regards the present constitution of that church, I am altogether unfavourable, but nevertheless entertain the most undoubting conviction that there was originally within it, a real miraculous work of the Holy Ghost. Amidst the many snares of a great and mixed congregation, the gifted individuals in it appear to have been led into much abuse of their gifts, gradually terminating in the withdrawal from them of the Spirit's presence."

One is more inclined to believe, however, that Glossolalia died out naturally, than was quenched, as Dr. Norton asserts, by "the rising up among other members of the church of men assuming the apostleship".

William Harding, a member of Regent Square Church, in his *Word for Inquiry previous to decision in the matter of the present manifestations* (1832), agrees with Dr. Norton in admitting excesses among the "gifted persons", but urges:—

"That if there was a Judas amongst the Twelve (no doubt as fully endowed with miraculous powers as the rest), it would necessarily happen that the gifts of the spirit would extend beyond the number of the true members of Jesus Christ."

(Here follows a warning against "those who seek gifts for mere pride, power, and notoriety".)

Mr. Harding does not seem to realise the confusion which this qualification introduces. It was almost universally asserted by members of the Irvingite circle that the advantage of "speaking in the Spirit" was that degrading human associations were cut off, and the subject (one in very truth "baptised with the Holy Ghost") would deliver a message direct from God. Though a zealous supporter of the Movement, he contradicts a common article of Irvingite faith in declaring

"That without *both the understanding* and the application of the Holy Ghost, as a model to all the baptised therewith . . . I perceive that the gifts now bestowed upon the Church will not be without peril and evil as at Corinth."

Harding protests against popular misconception of the Tongues as a short cut to missionary success, and quotes Conyers Middleton, the liberal eighteenth century divine, in confirmation; but follows this up by a typical Irvingite tirade against "liberalism, reform, and intellectual millennium—or rather the forces under the banner of the man of sin".

Pulpit and pamphlet strife merely strengthened Irving's convictions; would the healing touch of an old friend effect what controversy could never solve? In a letter to Mrs. Carlyle (10th November, 1831) Carlyle notes that

"Irving comes but little our way. He was here once taking tea, since the work of the 'Tongues' began. I told him with great earnestness that it was no special work of the Holy Spirit, or of any spirit save of that black, frightful, unclean one that dwells in Bedlam. He persists, mildly obstinate, in his course, *greatly strengthened by his wife, who is reckoned the beginning of it all.*

"I do not think it will spread ever among the vulgar here at this time of day; only a small knot of ravers now rave in that old worn-out direction." (13th November. To John Carlyle):—"On the whole, the Cockneys are too old for such lullabies—they simply think he is gone distracted, or means to 'do' them; and so, having seen it once come back no more."

In his *Reminiscences* Carlyle describes how he told Irving

"With all the delicacy, but also with all the fidelity possible to me—

"'That the 13th of Corinthians to which he always appealed, was surely too narrow a basis for so high a tower, or quasimast, piece added to piece, till it soared far above all human science and experience, and flatly contradicted all that, founded solely on a little text of writing in an ancient book!' I did not expect that he would at once, or soon, renounce his fixed views, connections and methods for any of mine; but perhaps at some future time of crisis and questioning dubiety he might remember the words of a well-affected soul, and they then might be a help to him. All this lasted about twenty minutes. He then began with the mildest low tone, and face full of kindness and composed distress—'dear friend'—in a style of modesty and friendly magnanimity and endeavoured to make his apology and defence. Which done he went silently on his way" (p. 299f.).

CHAPTER XII

THE STRANGE CASE OF ROBERT BAXTER

NARRATIVE OF FACTS characterising the SUPERNATURAL MANIFESTATIONS
in
MEMBERS OF MR. IRVING'S CONGREGATION
and other individuals in England and Scotland
and
FORMERLY IN THE WRITER HIMSELF
BY ROBERT BAXTER

LONDON:
JAMES NISBET, BERNERS STREET.
MDCCCXXXIII.

§1

IT is surprising that this astounding document has not received greater attention, if not from the compilers of "devotional classics", at least from students of abnormal religious psychology. Robert Baxter seems to have had a modified "dual personality". He belonged to a legal firm of high standing at Doncaster. He was also a writer on public questions, e.g. *The Panic of 1866, with its Lessons on the Currency Act* (Longmans, Green). And his son, R. D. Baxter (1827–75), was an economist of sufficient weight to be mentioned in the *Encyclopaedia Britannica*.

Robert Baxter was a deeply religious man, teaching in Sunday School and visiting the poor of the parish at Doncaster where his brother was clergyman. He belonged to the old High Church Party (soon to give way to the Tractarians), and was a Tory and State Churchman of a rather obscurantist type, penning a "Layman's Appeal" on behalf of the Church of England, which appeared to many to be about to succumb to the forces of infidelity and radicalism at the time of the Great Reform Bill.

Theologically, however, Baxter seems to have been a fervid evangelical, using the jargon of that school, and rigidly differentiating between the sacred and the secular.

His *Narrative* smacks of the Middle Ages or of the Puritans and Covenanters, rather than of the prosaic nineteenth century, so vivid are spiritual things to him, and so naïvely are they related. Had he been a mere religious adventurer, venturing his all on the successful establishment of a new sect, we would not be so surprised at his extravagant visions and revelations. But he was not merely a man of good position, but a successful lawyer. It will be gradually seen, as his story is unfolded, how the two departments of his life were kept apart.

Mr. Baxter had heard of the manifestations at Port Glasgow in 1830 from a near relative who had a friend, a Church of England clergyman, who lived in the neighbourhood. He believed that "nothing but an abundant outpouring of the Spirit of God could quicken the Church, could stem the torrent of infidelity; I longed greatly, and prayed much for such an outpouring".

In the summer of 1831 Mr. Baxter was called up to London on business and having obtained an introduction, attended the prayer meetings privately held by those who spoke in the power and those who sought for the gifts.

"Mr. T. (Taplin?) was made at one of these meetings to speak two or three words very distinctly, and with an energy and depth of tone which seemed to me extraordinary, and it fell upon me as a supernatural utterance which I ascribed to the power of God.

"Miss E. C. broke out in English in an unnatural and unaccustomed tone, an intense and riveting power of expression— with a very cutting rebuke to all present, and *applicable to my state of mind in particular.*

"In the midst of this awe and reverence, I was myself seized upon by the power; and *in much struggling against it*, was made to cry out, and myself to give forth confession of my own sin for which we were rebuked; and afterwards to utter a prophecy that the messenger of the Lord should go forth, publishing to the ends of the earth in the mighty power of God, the testimony to the near coming of the Lord Jesus."

Baxter was overwhelmed by this occurrence, and "continued many weeks weighed down in spirit", lest he should "mistake the will of God in this matter". He was conscious of a power "acting upon him beyond the mere power of excitement", a power "unlike anything he had ever known before", to fall down and "acknowledge that God

THE STRANGE CASE OF ROBERT BAXTER

was amongst them of a truth". The next day he spent in fasting and prayer.

"Malachi iv. 5 and St. Luke i. 17 were brought before me, and it was written upon my mind by a power wholly new to me; 'The Lord is now pouring out upon the Church the spirit and power of Elias, to prepare for the second coming of Jesus.' I could not see the propriety of this so fully as to clear up my doubts . . . but it worked in me a persuasion that this was the Lord's answer to prayer."

Before Baxter left town he "argued upon the impropriety of shutting up the manifestations",—which had not yet been allowed in public.

"One thing I was much struck with. I knew the views of these with whom I was associated were 'High Church'. I was told that the Spirit had spoken very strongly of the Churches of England and Scotland as 'Babylon'."

(Another mark of the sectarian spirit already noted.)

For five months he made no utterances in public, though in private prayer "the power would come down upon me and cause me to pray with strong crying and tears for the state of the Church"; especially on one occasion in his study, when his "thoughts were wandering to worldly concerns". On lifting a short prayer for deliverance, "suddenly the power came upon me, my wandering thoughts at once riveted, and calmness of mind at once given me".

"By a constraint I cannot describe, I was made to speak—at the same time shrinking from utterance, and yet rejoicing in it. The utterance was a prayer that God would give me 'the gifts of wisdom, faith, miracles, prophecy, tongues, etc., and that He would open my mouth and give me strength to declare His glory'."

He had to put his handkerchief in his mouth so as not to alarm the house, but when he reached the last word "the power died" in him. With the power came an overwhelming conviction that he had received what he had been praying for . . . "which was never shaken until the whole work fell to pieces".

Reflecting on these experiences, he tells us he reached convictions "irrespective of the slow processes by which the mind ordinarily reaches them, though an apparently logical chain of proof was . . . always given". Secondly, the utterances were often accompanied "with the flashing in of conviction on the mind, like lightning rooting itself in the earth".

These five months of absence he spent at Doncaster, where the power on one occasion constrained him at Sunday School to return to his study, and conveyed to him "very distinctly the impression that he might be called to utterance during public worship that day. In spite of natural misgivings, he sought direction in 1 Cor. xiv, and found that it was his duty to yield to the power.

"The ordinary service passed without any visitation of power. But after the Sacrament had been administered, when kneeling, to return thanks, the power came upon me largely, *though the impulse was not to utterance*—my tongue was riveted, and my soul filled with joy and thanksgiving."

In January, 1832, Baxter was in London again. By this time Glossolalia had been permitted in church, and he took a leading part in the manifestations.

"The power which then rested upon me was far more mighty than before . . . carrying me on without confusion or excitement. The things which I was made to utter, flashed in upon my mind, without expectation, and without any plan or arrangement: all was the work of the moment, *and I was the passive instrument of the power which used me.*"

He also was

"Made to bid those present ask instruction on any subject . . . and to several questions asked, answers were given by me in the power. One in particular was so answered, with such reference to circumstances of which I was wholly ignorant, as to convince the person who asked it that it was the Spirit speaking. This however troubled the pastor, who came up to me and said, 'Faith is very hard'. I was immediately made to reason with him in the power until he was fully convinced that the Spirit was of God."

It is unnecessary to give an exhaustive account of the numerous utterances and revelations of Baxter, as they bear a strong family resemblance. A few that are representative are selected by way of illustration.

He used "to preach in the Spirit", usually at evening meetings in Irving's house, when "young men were present who taught in schools and houses in different parts of

London". In one of these utterances, he described the Apostolic Church as Samson in the days of his strength. The world was Delilah who seduced the Church to surrender its secret source of strength (the teaching of the Spirit), receiving instead the applause, opinion, and learning of the world. But the locks had been growing in the dungeon, the teaching of the Spirit was again bestowed, and the Church was now rousing itself to lay hold of the pillars and bring down the strongholds of wickedness on the heads of the wicked.

More immediate injunctions were given.

"Very distinctly we were commanded to 'count the days one thousand three score and two hundred'—1,260—the days appointed for testimony, at the end of which the saints of the Lord's should go up to meet the Lord in the air."

We have already noticed a sectarian spirit at work in the Irvingite Movement. In the career of Baxter we see this at its worst. Not merely did he utter "judgements" after the style of O.T. prophets on the Pope, the Protestant Churches, Bible Societies,—but also his associates, sometimes for the most trivial reasons, he "sharply rebuked in the power". E.g., When about to give utterance, on one occasion, "Herod" was in his mind, "Pharaoh" in his mouth. Capt. G. told him in private that "Herod" was in accordance with the context. Baxter turned on him:—
"So you would rather be unfaithful to your heavenly Father than shame your poor brother? Is this the love you bear to your Father?"

On another occasion, when Irving expressed his doubts as to Glossolalia in church, and Brown advised "Don't do it whilst you have a doubt", Baxter cried out "in the most fearful voice" "that if the utterances were of God, who could hesitate to argue on them?" ("This was so strongly put, that, as Mr. Irving on a future occasion observed to me, he was tempted to doubt whether the Spirit bearing testimony in such a manner, was God's way of teaching us submission.")

Such being Mr. Baxter's inner experience and lurid apocalyptic background, it is not surprising to find a series of revelations, followed by ecstasy, misery, delusion, and renewed confidence. He was tortured, however, not so much by a Bunyan-like consciousness of sin, as by repeated misgivings as to whether his wonderful experiences were really God-given. It is strange indeed to read of a man of education experiencing what would be natural enough in an earlier day, when village was isolated from village, when witches and warlocks, the devil and his angels, were vividly conceived of as personally present in the world.

§2

At one of his breakfast parties, Mr. Irving remarked that Mr. T. when in the Court of Chancery, had found the power mightily upon him, but never a distinct impulse to utterance. Suddenly Baxter was made to declare:—

"There go I, and thence to the prison house."

This was followed by a prophetic setting forth of the darkness of the visible Church. That testimony would be borne which would make the nation tremble. That the abomination of desolation should be set up, and Satan sit in the high places of the Church. "I went out under the constraint of the power . . . which was overwhelming."

"As I shaped my way towards the Court, the sufferings and trials I underwent were almost beyond endurance. Might it not be a delusion? Ought I not to consider my own character in the sight of the world . . . and the ruin of all worldly prospects? But confident that the power speaking in me was of God, I entered the Court.

"Now power came upon me. I stood in the Court three or four hours . . . and as the time lengthened, more and more perplexed at its absence. I was tempted to speak in my own strength *without the power*, but I judged this would not be faithful to the word spoken. I came out of the Court.

"The mental conflict was most painful. I went at once to Mr. Irving, who welcomed me as delivered from prison. 'We are snared—we are deceived!' He enquired particulars but could give no solution" [Nor could he meet Baxter's objection that if *he* was deluded, they all must be.]

At the early morning prayer meeting, he took the message of Miss E.C. as applying to his own case:—"It is discernment—it is discernment ye lack—seek ye for it—seek ye for it."

His "heaviness was not removed till breakfast", when the text from Jeremiah was quoted: "Thou hast deceived me, and I was deceived. Then said I, I will not speak the

THE STRANGE CASE OF ROBERT BAXTER

word of the Lord any more; but the word of the Lord was unto me as fire in my bones."

"When I had read this and *was thinking of it*, I was made to say:—'The word of God is as fire, and if ye, O vessel! refuse to speak the word, ye shall utterly perish. Ye went to the place of testimony. The Spirit was quenched before the conscience of the king. Ye lack discernment—ye must read the word of God spiritually . . . etc. Then followed a command to flee to the mountains, to come out of Babylon and be separate. . . . This acted like electricity. My satisfaction was complete.

"As I journeyed home in the coach the following morning, the power came upon me in the form of a revelation, that God had *set me apart for a special purpose*. I should be taken away from my wife and family, and become a wanderer without habitation. And that this separation should be, in God's hand, a visitation upon my wife for her opposition to the work of the Spirit. That I should find my brother at home as I entered the paddock gate, and he would receive the Spirit and speak in same power in which I spoke, and that I should be made to deliver to him two messages—one to be carried to my wife, to declare to her God's purpose . . . the other to some relations, enjoining the winding up of all my worldly concerns and the future provision for my wife and family; that a child of my brother should be called as a prophetess, and that I should minister on the ensuing Sunday in my brother's church. The conclusion I gathered was that I should never see my wife and children again."

On his arrival at Doncaster, there was his brother at the gate—"this confirmation so unmanned me that I could not for some time speak to him."

"Without mentioning anything of the revelation, we spent the night discoursing. *He* had that evening, for the first time, assembled some of the people to pray for the gifts of the Spirit. 'I attended the meeting, but no power came upon me to utterance.' It had been for some time his habit to observe Friday as a fast day (a survival of the old High Church Practice soon to be galvanised into life by the Oxford Movement). Telling his brother he wanted to be left undisturbed, he added: 'If the Lord should make you His messenger, you will not be disobedient'."

On Saturday, his brother's wife asked him if the Lord had revealed to him what he had done. Baxter replied, no. She added,

"He has given X (my brother) the Spirit; he spoke much in the night in power. My brother shortly afterwards called me into his room, and in the supernatural utterance said: 'Every spirit that confesses Jesus Christ is come in the flesh is of God. Jesus Christ is come in the flesh.'

"After a pause, I asked him if the Lord had shown him what he had for him to do, and on his answering 'no', I added: 'Let us go to breakfast, the Lord will declare it in due time'.

"At breakfast I opened a letter: 'It is a worldly matter'. 'Aye, such were we at one time', said my brother misunderstanding me. About to correct his mistake,—I was made to declare that the Lord had set me apart, etc.; accompanied with my putting my hands upon the head of his child, and declaring her set apart for the office of a prophetess, and with a command to him to baptise my infant with the Holy Ghost.

"After family prayers, he called me into another room to speak to his wife, who had mistaken part of the message as rebuking her. Then the power came upon me to give the second half of the message. That I should minister in his church on Sunday, and *then should begin the spiritual ministrations which should never cease till the Lord should come.*"

Even more fantastic messages he received that day, "communicating in a distinct manner" that he should be called on to bear witness at Cambridge and in the House of Commons; that this might be accomplished immediately, he would be "caught up in the Spirit", as Philip was. No sign was vouchsafed, and nothing happened. Whereupon he came to the conclusion that the communication was from Satan. "The next day, being Sunday, we were all of us somewhat tried in faith."

The congregation that Sunday morning must have been astonished, as Anglicans, to see a layman officiating, especially when he laid aside "the stated service", having told the clerk he would have no part to take. In gown and bands he entered the reading desk, "a minister of the Spirit, not of the flesh". "By myself I have sworn, saith the Lord, I will not fail thee." After praying for an hour, the "power ceased."

"While they sang, I went into the vestry to fetch a Bible. Here I was wholly impotent. When I returned I had no power. My sister was seized with a hysterical fit. All my confidence in God seemed for the moment to desert me, and I felt as though my mouth was shut for ever.

"It was, however, but for a moment. I read in great power the 61st chapter of Isaiah, and preached in the power for upwards of an hour."

In the afternoon he preached from "Behold the bridegroom cometh", asserting that within three and a half years simple believers would be caught up, and the world delivered over to judgment.

On Monday the power was at its height. Baxter tells us that he would feel it coming upon him, welling up, before the actual utterance came, his whole frame throbbing as though a fire was burning in it. He was to bear testimony before William IV and Queen Adelaide, that he would lay his crown before the King of kings to whom his heart would be turned, that he would refuse to remain king of Babylon (this nation), but would retain power for the present as protector of God's people. "There was a mysterious allusion to the three children in the fiery furnace of Nebuchadnezzar", and an intimation that before he reached the king's presence, he, too, would have to pass through a fiery trial.

When Baxter returned to London he underwent trial indeed, though not in the manner he had expected. He returned in the greatest confidence. But the members of the Irvingite circle had not been "carried away" in ecstasy to anything like the same extent.

For Miss E. C. warned him in the power; "Did ye not feel the touch of the enemy? ... It is not yet—it is not yet. It shall be a plain way; the way shall be plain."

While the common sense of Irving urged: "Well, dear brother, be not puffed up with the abundance of revelations."

Said Baxter: "I know not what it is; I am overwhelmed; I have yet to break my connection with my professional engagements here, and it seems as though Satan would not suffer me."

Miss E. C. (In power): "To the word—to the WRITTEN word!" (to Baxter's confusion).

Irving then said (*not in the power*) that a passage was brought to his mind: "If any man provide not for his own, he hath denied the faith." He added: "It seems strange that you should leave your wife."

"Ye *must* not leave her", echoed Miss E. C. in the power.

The bubble was pricked.

Baxter had been building spiritual "castles in Spain", with

which he had become so obsessed that they alone seemed to him to possess reality. He had built up a wall between everyday life and religion, which only a shock could destroy.

"If a thunderbolt had burst at my feet, it could not have created half the pain and agonising confusion. The impression rushed upon me like a flood:—I have betrayed my brother into a Satanic embassy and ensured his expulsion from the Church. I have sent my wife a lying torture, and shall seem to her as a monster and I shall have forfeited all my professional pursuits, contrary to God's will. I paused a little under the revulsion of feeling which always succeeds any violent excitement . . . racked with the most fierce mental conflict, I endeavoured to lift up my soul in patient waiting upon God, and, in a little time, I seemed to have light upon the subject, which spoke peace, in a measure, to me."

But this revulsion proved to be merely a temporary reaction from visionary extremes out of touch with actuality.

"The messages *were* from God, but I had mistaken them, in supposing they called for my immediate cessation from all worldly labour.
"Relieved in a measure, I went to my coffee-house, and found there a letter which greatly confirmed my previous persuasion. This was from my wife, to say her brother had delivered to her (in power) the message that the work was of God; that she recognised it even at the cost of great sacrifice. This spoke to me as God's seal of His work: as I had, for months past, seen the utter inability of human efforts for her conviction."

In the evening his brother returned, somewhat startled at the non-fulfilment of the prophecy that his infant would speak in the Spirit after Baptism. When he arrived at the home of certain relatives to deliver his message, he was ready to burst into tears with the confession that he had been deluded. Suddenly the power came upon him, and he gave utterance, "*all the time trembling at what he was saying*". As one would expect, the relatives tried to lay hands on him. But when the power ceased, "he fell just into the former state" and told them of the failure of his revelation. Their disbelief in the work confirmed his suspicions of being deluded, and after a few hours' consideration, "he wrote to his wife, begging her to forget all that had passed."

Baxter decided that he had better return home; his wife, he discovered, had relapsed into unbelief of the work as divine, but could not wholly shake off the feeling that God's hand was in the movement to some extent. He himself felt the power much with him, though not to the same extent as in London. On 3rd February, on noticing in a newspaper that the Government had appointed a "general fast" on the motion of Spencer Perceval, he was made to declare in the power that it was merely "to avoid clamour"; it was the prayer of the prophets of Baal on Carmel, whereas the cry of "spiritual" believers would receive an answer *by fire*. "I was not then at all aware what was intended by this allusion to fire; but it was to prepare the way for the doctrinal masterpiece of delusion."

§ 3

Utterances became more and more frequent with reference to fire. He received a letter from a friend at a distance ("who was unconscious of what was going on here") who mentioned his having met two ladies in a northern county, who alleged themselves to have been baptised, not only with the Holy Ghost but with FIRE.

Knowing Baxter's mind as we now do, we are not surprised that he first brooded over this novelty, and then prayed steadily and repeatedly for the new gift. This culminated in his declaring "in the power" to his wife that they would both be baptised with fire; sin would be completely burnt out of them. The forty days during which he should be "tried" and found faithful had well-nigh elapsed, when he should be endowed with power as an apostle. On the fortieth day he was to go back to the church in London; the sick would be healed, the deaf hear, the dead be restored, and apostles sent forth to the ends of the earth to give warning of the rapture of the saints and to prepare a people for the Lord.

We must remember that at this time cholera was sweeping over Britain. And just as religious ecstatics used to parade the streets of the City during the Plague of 1666, on Biblical analogy, crying, "yet forty days and London shall be destroyed!" so the cholera fanned the flame of Irvingite fanaticism in 1832. Chalmers took practical measures for the ending of the plague in Edinburgh. In London, Irving followed the older method of appointing fasts and prayer meetings for the avoidance of what was regarded as a judgment on the sins of the people. At these meetings Baxter's confident utterances produced a tremendous effect.

"Mr. Irving embraced me . . . and his elders broke into a thanksgiving for having sent such light into the church. Mrs. C. took my hand, when the power came upon her, and she declared that Jesus . . . had touched my lips with a living coal . . . and I should speak with authority as a prophet".

That does not mean that a holy and perfect unity pervaded the circle of "Gifted Persons". On the contrary, suspicion and jealousy were constantly breaking out, under the cloak of utterances in the power. There constantly recurred a group-feeling that there was someone present who was quenching the Spirit. One example may be taken as an illustration:—

On the Saturday evening before Baxter was expected to receive baptism of the Holy Ghost, in Irving's house—
"Mrs. C. was made to cry out in a most piercing utterance that there was someone in the midst of us who was provoking the Lord by jealousy, envy and hard thoughts. A feeling of dismay seemed to run through the company. The accusation was reiterated that the person should step forward and confess. The agony expressed on many countenances was intense; one man was so overcome that his head fell on the chair, as though he were paralysed, uttering an unnatural moaning cry. . . .
"I turned . . . to pray, when Mr. Irving silently pointed to a person who was struggling to give utterance. But instead of articulate words nothing but muttering followed, and *this with an expression most revolting*. An utterance broke from Mrs. C. and myself: 'It is an unclean spirit'!"

But the man continued "muttering and speaking nonsense", in spite of Baxter's attempted exorcism.

"Lady X, who had once or twice spoken in the power, rose up and with outstretched hand, cried out: 'Greater is he that is in you than he that is in the world!' and repeating this several times, sank down on the floor. We all paused. Mr. Irving suggested: 'This kind goeth not forth but with prayer and fasting.' Baxter could only say 'that in due time the man would be delivered'; and so we parted."

Instances similar to the above might be quoted in illustration of the suspicious attitude of the "Gifted Persons".

Miss H., who had for some time been received as a prophetess among them (one of their earliest tongue-speakers), had been charged by Miss E. C. and Mrs. C. with forging utterances, which they asserted in the power, were "of the flesh".

To Baxter, "her utterances seemed at times as full and as clearly supernatural as Miss E. C.'s". Miss E. C. would frequently take up and complete utterances in power, begun by Miss H., so as to cause Mr. Irving to remark how manifestly one spirit spoke in both.

The collision occurred over a message sent to an M.P. regarding the national fast, Miss H. being convicted of meditating utterances purporting to be spoken in the power . . . "Explained in any way, however," comments Baxter, "it involved all of us in lack of discernment."

It is impossible to draw hard-and-fast conclusions either of telepathy on the one hand, or of fraud on the other, owing to the fact that the movement was not impartially investigated under strict conditions. It seems clear that there was a certain amount of "thought transference" and intuitive reading of the minds of those professing spiritual gifts. We must also bear in mind the fact that the inner circle of the movement consisted of Miss E. C. (Emily Cardale), Mr. T. (Taplin), Mrs. C. (Mary Caird, the initiator of Glossolalia), and Baxter (who, in spite of his revelations, was only in London when called up on business, etc.), with the mysterious Irishman. Mr. A., who aroused Pilkington's suspicions, in the background (probably the Rev. N. Armstrong).

We cannot go so far as to doubt the sincerity of these people. But they held together as a "Group", keeping the leadership of the movement in their own hands, preferring private to public meetings as we shall see later (though taking full advantage of public meetings for manifestations), and claiming the right to admit would-be "gifted persons" to the exercise of their craft!

We can see that Miss E. C. enunciated the views of the group when in the power she forbade Irving to allow Baxter to conduct the Sunday service falling several days before the expected baptism with the Holy Ghost. For was not Baxter an outsider in two senses; neither a founder of the movement, nor one who was continually "on the spot"? Was he not getting puffed up with these extravagant visions, and being looked up to as the "leading light" by the soft-hearted, muddleheaded Irving? Ambiguous utterances in the power purporting to come direct from God untainted by human motives, were only too often the cloaked aspirations either of individuals or of "the group mind". Sudden and unpremediated utterances were often fruit unconsciously matured in the sub-conscious.

Baxter wrote, with deeper insight than he was aware of, on becoming finally disillusioned, "that facts which have lately occurred have been broad enough to show the active workings of a spirit; also, that though a supernatural power is with us, we are not therefore, of necessity, receiving it of God".

He was a better psychologist than one would suppose the subject of such delusions would ever be.

"Oh! the deep subtilty—the hollowness of our hearts—the awful justice of our God, who, because of the craving after something more than the gentle dew of the Spirit, gave us indeed meat to our lust, by leaving us under a spiritual power, which was supernatural and sweet to the taste, but afterwards wormwood and ashes."

We might add: "He gave them their request, but sent leanness into their soul!" (Psalm cvi: 15).

Resuming the thread of the narrative, we find ourselves on the threshold of the expected new dispensation. It was the Sunday preceding the expected baptism with fire. Irving's sermon acted as fuel to Baxter's craving, for his text was from Rev. xi: 5: "Fire proceedeth out of their mouth, and devoureth their enemies." He himself was but a "fleshly minister", but Baxter was a "spiritual minister".

Baxter notes that

"the same distinction was carried through the Church also—the Church receiving the ministry of the prophets speaking by the utterance of the Spirit, was called the *spiritual* Church, in contra-distinction to the *visible* Church; and cutting short the fleshly ministry, by cancelling the ordination by laying on of hands, was shown God's rejection of the visible; and in the gift of utterance and the sending prophets . . . was shown the bringing out of the spiritual church".

This applied also to the Sacraments. When the fullness of power was come in, the baptism of water (John's baptism) would be discarded in favour of baptism with the Holy

THE STRANGE CASE OF ROBERT BAXTER 199

Ghost and fire. Irving was not yet prepared to admit that the new dispensation had already been ushered in. When an infant was brought forward to be christened and an utterance broke from Baxter—"Jesus receiveth thee into his church, thou little one, and baptiseth thee with his spirit!"—the minister proceeded to baptise in the usual way, merely returning thanks for the utterance. Baxter concealed his chagrin by "rationalising"; Irving would have to continue using *the form* till he received full endowment as a "spiritual minister".

The next step was an utterance in reference to the text, "Behold I stand at the door and knock, if any man hear my voice and open the door, I will come in unto him, and sup with him, and he with me".

Christ was *now* knocking specially by his Spirit; He was soon to come as the reality, which the Communion elements merely typified. For had not the apostle declared, "As oft as ye eat of this bread and drink of this wine, ye do show forth the Lord's death, UNTIL HE COME".

This spiritual coming, Baxter admits, was not to preclude a personal coming at the end of the three years and a half. But now Christ, in the full power of the Spirit, with the baptism of fire, was to pass through the world in His "*spiritual* ministry" as he did in the land of Judaea for the same space of time in his "fleshly ministry". The parallel is carried further—As Christ was slain and rose from the dead, so also would his witnesses suffer; "they who remain alive unto the coming of the Lord shall be caught up to meet him in the air".

Baxter was still in some doubt as to the time when the Spiritual Church would be fully constituted, and all visible elements discarded. Subsequent utterances, however, convinced him that this would not be until the full powers of an apostle were given, and he was daily—nay hourly—expecting this event.

He was now obsessed by eschatology. The book of Revelation was his forecast of world history on the eve of fulfilment. Everyday events he related to the cosmic plan, which assumed vivid reality. One evening, for example, he met a missionary from America who declared that the American Indians were the lost ten tribes of Israel, and asked him if he (Baxter) had any teaching on that question. Having never thought of the problem, Baxter replied in the negative. But the matter matured in the sub-conscious, and as one might expect, an utterance broke from him several days later when he was at breakfast at Irving's: Not only were the American Indians the ten lost tribes, but within the appointed three and a half years they should be settled in Palestine before the days of vengeance set in. One evening he was made to address an Indian chief (present at an evening meeting at Irving's) "in a most triumphant chaunt" as the vessel chosen by God for Restoration.

"The chief did not believe in the message, or in the gifts, though he was apparently astounded; and as I conversed with him, his *tout ensemble* was so strangely of the Tartar caste that my confidence was shaken . . . however, my conscience was clear of all wilful mistakes" [as if godliness and enthusiasm were the only tests of truth!].

It is strange to think of this theory of the "Ten Tribes" being rejected by the simple Indian and a parallel delusion adopted by a considerable number of educated people to-day, under the name of "British Israel". There have been (and probably always will be) pietistic circles among whom the intellect has been at a discount; they have claimed to accept nothing but the Bible, but in reading it in the light of contemporary events, have allegorised it grotesquely. Thus Baxter makes Revelation viii. yield the following:—"The third part"=Protestantism. The other "two thirds" =Papists and Infidels. Hail represented the Tories; fire—the Liberals, who throughout Europe burn up the green grass (the good order of Society). The sea was the military, the earth the civil state. The casting of the mountain into the sea was the collision between liberalism and the military. The third trumpet applied to the ecclesiastical state—the wormwood bitterness of the star—false doctrine, etc. There is no doubt that Baxter's ingenuity, in flashing "limelight" on obscure parts of Scripture made a strong appeal to certain minds, who, taught to accept the whole Bible as the direct Word of God, were only too ready to welcome solutions which seemed to bring Holy Writ into closer touch with contemporary life.

Baxter returned to Doncaster "deeply depressed" at not receiving full endowment as an apostle in London, to find that his wife had relapsed into disbelief of the work.

A revelation, however, suddenly came upon her, calming all her irritation and distress, and in a moment filling her mind with peace, giving a reason why the prophecy had not been fulfilled on the fortieth day. Had the church in London manifested greater love, this baptism and power would have been given *there;* but now it should be given *here* (at Doncaster). A most emphatic declaration was revealed in the power that on the day after the morrow, both Mr. and Mrs. Baxter would be baptised with fire. The day arrived and in the evening an utterance came from the power—"kneel down".

"We knelt down, lifting up prayer to God continually. Nothing, however, ensued. Again and again we knelt, and again and again we prayed, but still no fulfilment. Surprising as it may seem, my faith was not shaken . . . but for *six weeks* I continued to seek after it. My wife ceased to follow it."

Baxter found relief, again, in "rationalisation". Non-fulfilment had previously been explained by backsliding in London: *now* baptism with fire was "spiritualised", and declared in power to denote the burning out of the carnal mind, resulting in the perfect holiness of true believers. An interesting trait which increases the similarity of Montanism and Irvingism already noted, is that during this period Baxter receives messages in power, that "the marriage state would no longer be blessed with increase", but the energy of both sexes would be concentrated on warning the world, till the expiry of the days of testimony should summon them to the glory of the Lord.

After a short interval he received a letter from Irving, stating that Miss E. C. had commanded him to write that "you must not expect this in the flesh" (referring to baptism with fire). Irving added:—

"Here I leave it without any comment whatever—I am not equal to the work of commenting upon these words of the Lord—I am content to walk in the darkness. . . . The Lord lead us aright . . . the day is not known and it is a mystery."

Baxter was amazed. He afterwards asked Miss E. C. why they recognized his prophecy, but in practice set it aside; "she would not speak upon the subject". The "Group Mind" was once more calling a rebellious member of the herd to heel: the shepherd was impotent.

§ 4

Baxter still continued to treat every doubt as a temptation, for the supernatural nature of his experience seemed so clear, in spite of the failure of his prophecies; he had undoubtedly experienced communion with God such as few men attain to. His faith in verbal confession as an unfailing means of "trying the spirits" was strengthened on hearing the case of two twins, a girl and a boy, "children of a pious and exemplary clergyman" in Gloucestershire. They were seven years of age, and "nothing of a religious turn had been remarked" in them. (Baxter does not seem to realise the influence imitation exerts over the child mind, in stating the significant fact that the parents had gone in for the manifestations—many children love "playing at church".)

Their utterance was most astounding according to Baxter, "preaching with such recital of Scripture and power of argument, as might be supposed to surpass many able ministers, and certainly quite out of the compass of children of their age". Encouraged by their parents, they proceeded to prophecy and utter commands, until they uttered things which seemed contrary to Scripture, finally astonishing everyone by an utterance *forbidding to marry*.

They called the boy "who seemed much wrought upon by the power" and cried in power: "Ye may try the spirits in men, but ye may not try the spirits in children. Ye shall surely be punished."

The curate was called in, and demanded a confession that Christ was come in the flesh. "Paleness and agitation increased over the child, till an utterance broke from him, 'I will never confess it'." The curate persisted in his efforts: "I command thee, thou false spirit, in the name of Jesus, to come out of the child."

The child afterwards described his feelings: he felt as though a coldness was removed from his heart, and passed away from him. On being told to resist it, he did so several times. Once, some time afterwards, he mistook something his parents had said to him, to be a direction to yield to the power, and did yield, speaking supernaturally as before; but on being corrected, and henceforth resisting the power whenever it came upon him, he was entirely freed from it.

Caroline Fox, whose *Journals* were published in 1882, gives a full account of the twins, some interesting details being given in addition to the facts mentioned by Baxter.

"The parents placed themselves entirely under the direction of these chits, who trotted about the house, and everything they touched was immediately to be destroyed or given away as Babylonish! This poor deluded man's house was dismantled, his valuable library dissipated and himself and family thoroughly befooled. At last the younglings pointed out Jerusalem as the proper place for immediate family emigration, and everything was packed up, and off they set. The grandfather of the sprites was infinitely distressed at these goings-on and goings-off, and intercepted his son at the commencement of the pilgrimage, and confined him to the house, inducing him to write to Irving to inquire how they were to find out whether they were influenced by a true or false spirit.

"Just before this letter reached him, a Miss B., under whose care these children first became possessed, had an interview with Irving, and instead of being received by him with open arms, heard the terrible sentence, 'Thou hast a lying spirit'. She flew into a vehement rage, and such a 'spirituelle' scene took place between them as is indescribable."

Caroline Fox thinks that Irving had been told of the failure of many of Miss B's. prophecies. He then wrote to the parents advocating such tests as "Try the Spirits". The letter was read by the parent (Mr. P.) in the presence of Lord R., Mr. W., and others. As soon as it was read the children burst in upon the assembled relatives as they were rehearsing the tests. Suddenly the father's eyes were opened, and he ordered the children upstairs.

"By a judicious discipline these children were rescued from what is considered, with some show of reason, to have been a demoniacal possession. The father, however, became insane ultimately from what he had passed through, and died in that state" (Fox, p. 40 f).

This is an interesting corroboration of Baxter's account from a lady who was obviously an onlooker, but one who had her information at first hand. Another case of children prophesying will be considered later (p. 263 ff).

The above incident temporarily resuscitated Baxter's faith in the manifestations. He became finally disillusioned not so much through the failure of prophesies, as by being "providentially led to an examination of doctrines, for neglecting which, at an earlier period, I justly suffered what came upon me".

"The word was made flesh" was one day being discussed at a devotional meeting; Baxter gave an exposition of his view that Jesus took fallen flesh, but took it free from the law of sin, which we are all born under. A friend (not named) assented to this definition, but charged Mr. Irving with holding a contrary view—i.e., That the *law of the flesh was in Jesus, and only kept down by the Spirit.*

A few days later a clergyman from Staffordshire had a long discussion with Baxter, in which he argued that if Irving's theology was unsound, the Spirit of God could not be speaking in him (a natural conclusion, granted the theory of "rigid mechanical accuracy").

On that occasion Baxter cried in the power,[1] "He has erred! He has erred!" He examined Irving's whole position more carefully and came to the conclusion that he was unsound on the imputed righteousness of Christ, besides holding the possibility of the believer's perfect holiness in the flesh.

He wrote to this effect to Irving—who appeared to be more and more under the influence of his female conclave; Irving replied as follows:—

"It being wonderfully ordered that Mrs. C. should be in town for a day or two and Miss E. C.—these two prophetesses of the Lord, who have been his mouth of wisdom and warning to me and my church in all perplexities; I called along with my wife . . . and proceeded to read your letters."

On coming to the words "he has erred," Miss E. C. declared in power that Mr. Irving had maintained the truth, *and must not draw back;* he had erred in some ways, but the Lord had forgiven him. Mrs. Irving mentioned a doubt—whether it should not be left simply to the Lord, when Mrs. C. "with great authority and strength" declared both in Tongue and English that Mr. Baxter had erred in "bringing carnal understanding to spiritual things" and in "*making a distinction between Christ's holiness and that of his Church*".

Irving is, however, perfectly right in pointing out that Baxter himself had been only too full of the passage he particularly criticised in his *Day of Pentecost:*—

"Baptism of the Holy Ghost doth bring to every believer the presence of the Father and the power of the Holy Ghost, according to that measure, *at the least*, which Christ, during the days of his flesh, possessed."

He concludes by suggesting that if he had a meeting with Baxter, their differences would not bulk so large.

"This letter," said Baxter, "was a great blow to me." It was difficult to throw aside what had lain at the very heart of his religion. But he decided that the only course was to go up to London for a final interview with Irving, who relied mainly on the argument that the utterances that had failed were of the devil, and those which were successful were of God, in reply to the objection that it was impossible to distinguish true utterances from false (the external demonstration being the same). Every message would have to be decided on grounds of origin, and who knew whether or not a man had the gift of discerning spirits? Had not Irving preached that messages delivered in the power were "pure unadulterated water without admixture", in which entire and implicit confidence might be placed?

Yet he was driven from this position by the fact that before the whole congregation a man had denounced him, the pastor, "this denunciation coming with every demonstration of power and tongues".

It was then attempted to decide the origin of the utterance by prescribing a certain poise in the subject—a calm sense of the love of God in Christ and of our abiding therein, as a proof of divine inspiration; and an opposite state of mind as a proof of the utterances being deceitful. But in Baxter's case, several utterances had been confirmed, spoken when he was in a disturbed state; and others, which had proved false, were given under the prescribed frame of mind. "I was fully persuaded that no such line of distinction could honestly be drawn."

Baxter interviewed not only Irving (then before the Presbytery of London—26th April, 1832), but also Miss E. C. and Mrs. C., who argued that non-fulfilment of prophecies made under the power was simply due to mistaking their meaning. "A most miserable subterfuge," is Baxter's comment. Irving pointed to Jeremiah xv: 18, 19, where the prophet, on expostulating with God for non-fulfilment of his word, is told to separate the precious from the vile. Also Jer. xx: 7 and Ezekiel xiv: 9—"If the prophet be deceived when he hath spoken a thing, I the Lord have deceived that prophet". He forgot, however, to complete the text, which is to the effect that such a prophet will be destroyed!

Some months after Baxter's recantation, he received a letter from Irving (6th July, 1832), pleading with him to cease "blaspheming the prophets and church of God", and reasserting his views as to Christ's "habitation" of human nature, believers receiving "the power of regeneration, which is the continuance unto us of the power of generation in Jesus."

This letter completed Baxter's alienation from the Irvingite Movement, and led to the summing up of his objections to it, which may be presented as follows:—

(1) Irvingite prophecies were generally "crude undigested thoughts", prompted by "the strong cravings of curiosity, and the restlessness of an excited imagination". The substitution of a branch of truth for the tree was the result, —the Second Coming assuming a disproportionate place in their working theology.
(2) Baxter objected strongly to the secrecy of the meetings. He had several times rebuked Irving for this "in the power", but select meetings were eventually restored, on the ground that in a miscellaneous assembly the spirit was quenched.

In a favourable atmosphere "Satan can develop the subjects of his delusions; and going on, step by step, can unwarily lead his victims into extravagances, first of doctrine, and next of conduct, *which they themselves would, without such gradual preparation,* shudder to contemplate."
(3) The personal morality of the individuals concerned seems to have been beyond question, but there was a distinct antinomian tinge in the movement, a marked tendency towards "perfectionism". The notion that absolute holiness was attainable in this life might produce a spiritual glow and sense of successful endeavour, but the result was a lowering of the standard, undue confidence, and hardening until the conscience might, in extreme cases, be "seared as with a hot iron".
(4) Baxter began to examine the Scriptures apart from preconceived ideas, and discovered the extent to which the N.T. stresses the understanding, being greatly impressed with such passages as: "The Lord give thee understanding in all things."

"Now I am assured, both from the remembrance of my own utterances, and from those of others, that the spirit

THE STRANGE CASE OF ROBERT BAXTER

manifested in us all has always striven to put aside the understanding, and bring its followers into an absolute submission to the utterances."

(5) A result of this following of mere impulse was the grotesquely subjective character of so many utterances; e.g., Baxter's stern and remorseless denunciation typified by his "burden against Scotland for casting off episcopacy." "Ye know not what spirit ye are." Further, there was the casting off, under the name of Babylon, of the Church Universal and the setting up of the new sect as alone "apostolic", the treatment of all who rejected the Tongues as blasphemers. His eyes were opened to this blind Sectarianism.

(6) "Mr. Irving is a man of God . . . but his mind is so imaginative as almost to scorn precision of ideas, and his views will thus continually vary, without himself being aware of it. His energy and activity, swelling into impetuosity, leave him peculiarly open to error, in all subjects which require deep thought and patient and continued investigation. No man was ever perhaps less qualified to investigate and unfold the deeper mysteries of religion. With him one line of truth swells over its parallel line, and converging lines cut where they should only meet.

"Yet with all this, there is much real candour—real devotedness—real love to God, and charity towards all men. In the matter of the manifestations I believe him to be much tried. He cannot shut his eyes to facts which are daily rising up before him, and yet he is afraid to entertain doubts, and deals with them all as temptations.

"It is one thing to lead men on into the power of the enemy, and quite another thing to deliver them. For the sake of those whom I may have hardened or betrayed into a false faith, I feel called upon to publish my own shame. . . . The 'gifted persons' are deceived, and not deceivers, save instrumentally."

"She is one of the lambs of my flock—she is carried in my bosom. And shall I bring one of the lambs of my flock, who may have been led astray, before a public court? Never—never, while I have a pastor's heart!" This was received with involuntary applause. Irving's single-minded sincerity never failed to impress his harshest critics.

"Is there anything in the constitution of the Church which forbids the exercise of the prophetic gift, supposing it to be real?" asked Mr. William Hamilton. The Presbytery confined themselves generally, however, to the assertion that unauthorised persons "neither ministers nor licentiates of the Church of Scotland", and in some cases "neither members nor seatholders" of the congregation, had been permitted to "interrupt the public services of the church".

Prophesyings, pleaded Irving, had been provided for by the *First Book of Discipline;* but "ye are ministers of the Word of God and not ministers of the standard of any Church." [Compare this with his previous eulogies of Creeds and Confessions.] Further,

"I say that it is *not persons but the Holy Ghost* that speaketh in the church. . . . This is what I rest my case on. This is the root of the matter. Come and hear for yourselves. The church is open many times in the week; and the Lord is gracious to us, and speaks *through his servants very often.* Therefore the decision must entirely depend on this; whether it be of the Holy Ghost—or not. For if it be, who dare gainsay it?"

Irving regarded the "gifted persons" as the passive instruments on which the Spirit played. In a "Letter to his opponents" he admitted the possibility of deception, which he ascribed to the devil. He scarcely seems to have appreciated the difficulty any human being would at once encounter, who should essay "trying the Spirits".

The verdict was inevitable. On 2nd May, 1832, Irving was declared "unfit to remain the minister of the Scottish National Church", though he continued to be still a minister of the Church of Scotland. In pronouncing sentence, the Moderator of the Presbytery of London paid tribute to "the earnestness of the man and (I will say) the man of God". Irving was now "cast out"—as he himself recorded in the Kirk Session Book of the National Scotch Church, which he took with him. But with characteristic devotion

EDWARD IRVING
Painted by Faithful Pack, 1832

To face page 211]

he spent the day after the trial in preparing for his Communion Season. The sacramental Tokens, which he had had struck on 11th May, 1827, were distributed as usual—"to be kept (if not delivered up at the Table) as a bond of union till such time as the Lord shall guide the flock to some other place of refuge". On Sabbath, 6th May, 1832, Irving and his followers found the gates of the National Scotch Church barred against them when they sought to hold their early morning service. Mr. William Hamilton tried in vain to persuade the Trustees to allow the last solemn sacrament to be held in Regent Square; they felt it would strengthen the position of their former pastor and bring him a strong accession of friends (two hundred persons having applied for admission as members).

That fatal Communion Sabbath, Irving preached in Britannia Fields to a spellbound congregation, within sight of the twin towers of his old church which could be seen gleaming white in the summer sunshine among the trees. Britannia Fields soon became known to the public as "The Field of the Tongues". The police were kept busy with some of the demonstrators.

Among Irving's hearers was an artist, F. C. Pack, R.R.P. To him we owe the portrait of Irving preaching in the open air, which came into the possession of the Presbyterian Historical Society in 1925 and now hangs in the hall immediately behind Regent Square Church. A trained portraitist, he included on his canvas in miniature the face and character of the leading men and women who accompanied Irving in his Exodus into the Wilderness. They were no passive hearers, but responded actively in Tongues to the preacher's eloquence. Several can be identified from the picture and the painter's notes on the back, e.g., Miss Cardale, Henry Drummond and Taplin. Faithful Christopher Pack (1759–1840) was of Quaker stock, but as a young man plunged into the fast life of the artist quarter in London. He entered the studio of Sir Joshua Reynolds, and after practising in the provinces and at Dublin, returned to London in 1821 where he led an interesting and varied life as painter, lecturer and chiropodist. For many years his contact with religion had been slight, but in his old age he came under the spell of Irving; he became a member at Regent Square and a "sub-deacon" in the new church. In declining health and with insufficient means, he found new life and inspiration in the preaching of Irving (*v*. art. by Miss L. W. Kelley, M.A., Presbyterian Historical Society *Journal*, May, 1932). The picture of the preaching in Britannia Fields belonged to the Carré family and was probably commissioned, purchased or given to the "dear Carré" (d. 1854), whom Irving met at Aberystwyth on his last journey northwards, and heard holding forth "at the head of the Marine Parade".

. . . . .

Mrs. Oliphant hardly does justice to the Trustees of Regent Square Church. They would have been compelled to act sooner or later. Mr. John Hair, in a clear and sympathetic chapter, has pointed out how the conflict was "waged with mutual courtesy and affection".

"On the one side the minister of God resting on the Word of God, and on his own strong faith that the manifestations were divine; and on the other his own dearest friends, trustees of the church and members of session, disbelieving in the so-called 'gifts', and resting on the requirements of the trust-deed and the arm of the civil law to make an end of them" (*Regent Square*, p. 113).

They must have read with sad hearts his last appeal (17th March, 1832) :—

"MEN AND BRETHREN,—As a man, and the head of a family, bound to provide for himself and those of his own house, I am enabled of God to be perfectly indifferent to the issue of your deliberations this night, though it should go to deprive me of all my income, and cast me, after ten years of hard service, upon the wide world with my wife and my children, forth from a house which was built almost entirely upon the credit of my name and primarily for my life enjoyment, where also the ashes of my children repose. . . . I am still assured that my God, whom I serve, and for whom I suffer reproach, will support and richly reward me, even though ye also should turn against me, whom the Lord set to be a defence and a protection around me."

The trustees were deeply touched, but what could they do? They had already offered their minister every loophole; had he been willing to disallow the manifestations at the ordinary Sunday services, they would not have interfered with the weekday early prayer meetings (recognising that there must be *something* in a movement that drew many hundreds daily out of their beds into the yellow London fog at 6.30 a.m.). They had further appealed to his good sense by procuring from Sir Edward Sugden, the eminent counsel, an opinion entirely adverse to the practices that he considered lawful on the grounds of being essentially Christian. The more influential elders were also trustees, and of the kirk session only Mr. Horn had resigned owing to the "tongues". His elders were old friends, yet only Mr. Mackenzie entirely agreed with his point of view.

What Irving really needed was at least six months leave of absence in a country where he could neither understand the language of the people nor be understood by them. On 19th July, 1828, he had written to his wife—"Next Sabbath is the first of my Sabbatical year". Would that he had taken that "Sabbatical Year" as some American professors do—a year of complete change abroad! A fallow year might easily have led to renewed fruitfulness that was not "forced". Mental hygiene was not understood a century ago, so he was allowed to get utterly worn out, and then—when his nerves were on edge—he was "cast out". As early as 24th February, 1824, we find him writing to Collins, the publisher:

"I am at present worked beyond my strength, and you know that is not inconsiderable. My head! my head! I may say with the Shunamite's child. If I care not for it, the world will soon cease to care for me, and I for the world."

Henry Drummond, seeing that he looked run-down in the summer of 1828, proposed a visit to Harrogate; but his doctor told him the water would do him little good, as "his complaints proceeded rather from an excess of health and disarrangement of the functions through much thought".

Irving had been brought up in the country and the city was quite unsuitable for a man of his physique, who used every ounce of energy to tackle activities that never ceased to expand. He would retire from London to a mansion like Brampton Court, where he would find no rest from city toil. It took Mrs. Irving some time to realise that her husband was literally working himself to death. We find her writing in October 1830, of his visit to Lady Olivia Sparrow's:

"Dear Edward hurried down from London again, to be with me as soon as possible. There are a goodly number of hearers, and hearers *all day long here*; so that yesterday Edward spoke constantly from nine in the morning till nine at night, what with expositions, dictating, and answering questions."

During the manifestations he went on as usual with his writing and his pastoral visitation; he would concern himself with the needs of the population around his church, though his assistant was specially charged with "mission" work. Even after the crisis, when he had no certain provision for his own necessities, his house would be crowded with thoughtless callers.

"I verily believe he offered to God the sacrifice of a broken heart." He must have been sorely wounded by the contemptuous attitude of the Press after his ejection by the Presbytery. In a leading article, *The Times* rejoiced that "the blasphemous absurdities" had been brought to an effectual conclusion.

"It would, indeed, have been a subject of wonder had they come to a different conclusion, though they had had the benefit of a concert upon the 'tongues' from the whole male and female band of Mr. Irving's select performers. So long as the rev. gentleman occupied the stage himself he was heard with patience —perhaps, sometimes with pity . . . but when he entered into partnership with knaves and impostors to display their concerted 'manifestations'—when he profaned the sanctuary of God by introducing hideous interludes of 'the unknown tongues', it was impossible any longer to tolerate the nuisance" (3rd May, 1832).

That was the judgment of the world at large and the judgment of the "religious world" was scarcely milder.

But Irving did not act in isolation. He was followed by over six hundred communicants. They found temporary refuge in a large room in Gray's Inn Road, which at other times was occupied by the social reformer, Robert Owen (to the pious horror of the *Morning Watch*, the Irvingite organ). After the break with Regent Square, and the last burst of publicity, Irving became comparatively unknown outside the new sect in which he insulated himself. He was a shadow of his old self, yet he held forth in the open air on the green at Islington, outside Clerkenwell prison and even at Charing Cross. Some heard him gladly, but he complained of a multitude of "strangers and gazers who do insult me daily".

DARK DAYS

Neither Cockney crowds nor police regulations damped the ardour of disciples like Spencer Perceval. Irving even called on Lord Melbourne and eloquently urged that

"They only asked the same licence that was given to puppet-shows and other sights not to be prevented; that the command was express, Go into the highways, and that they must obey God rather than man" (Greville's *Journals*, 5th September, 1824).

Mrs. Oliphant pictures him pausing with wrapt looks when the burst of utterance comes upon some obscure person in the crowd; for that utterance is to him the voice of God, and for it he has borne "deprivation of everything save life itself"; therefore he gives magnificent thanks in unconscious humility, for what he believes to be confirmation from heaven;

"a sight, if that voice were true, to thrill the universe; a sight, if that voice were false, to make angels weep with utter love and pity; any way, whether true or false . . . an attitude noble and affecting" (Ol. II, p. 303).

In the June Number of the *Morning Watch*, with reference to the cholera scourge that was sweeping over England, there appeared a long letter from Irving advancing the opinion that disease itself was due to sin or was a test like "Job's affliction, and that no man with faith should be overpowered by it". The keynote was 1 Cor. xii: 9: "To another the gifts of healing by the same Spirit". A personal experience of his own is given in confirmation (Ol. II, pp. 309-313). I allude briefly to this as a late attempt of Irving's to reproduce another charisma of the Apostolic Church in addition to Glossolalia.

The *Morning Watch*, a quarterly review, abounding in discussions and expositions of the "gifts", served to hold the new community together. It was also the visible sign of the control which Henry Drummond and other wealthy and influential men began to exert over the movement, which had so far been "Irvingite" owing to the prestige of the great preacher who had thrown the cloak of his patronage over the infant "denomination". When West's picture gallery in Newman Street (Owen's "Infidel Covert") was taken over by the evicted congregation, the very arrangements intimated a far-reaching change.

"Instead of a pulpit," says Baxter in a second pamphlet *Irvingism*, "there was a raised platform, on the front of which are seven seats; the middle seat is that of the angel; the three on each side are elders. Below them are seven other seats belonging to the prophets, the middle seat being allotted to Mr. Taplin as their chief. Still lower, in a parallel line, are seven other seats appropriated to the deacons.

"The angel ordered the service, and the preaching and expounding was generally by the elders in order, the prophets speaking as utterance came upon them."

Baxter might eventually proclaim his experiences a delusion, but many of his principles took hold; particularly the authoritative way in which he interpreted prophecy, and uttered predictions. Up to this time, the speakers (of whom the majority were women) seem only to have given stray gleams of edification. He declared "in the power" that the Church no longer retained the privilege of ordaining, but that all spiritual offices were henceforth to be filled by the "gifted", or by those called by the "gifted". As Mrs. Oliphant remarks:—

"This new development introduced, instead of the steady certainty of an established law, the unsettled and variable condition naturally resulting from dependence upon a mysterious spiritual authority, which might at any time command an entire change in their proceedings, and was besides liable to be intruded upon by equally mysterious diabolic agencies, which could with difficulty be distinguished from the real influence of the Spirit" (II, p. 320).

The last act in which Irving presided over the new congregation was the opening service at Newman Street (24th October, 1832). On his describing the Church as barren—"conceiving, but not having brought forth" (during his exposition of 1 Samuel 1) an ecstatic voice interposed "in the power"—"Oh, but she shall be fruitful, oh! oh! oh! she shall replenish the earth! Oh! Oh! she shall replenish the earth and subdue it—and subdue it." Other utterances followed—few of them adding in any way to the sense of what was said, and some of them having little apparent point.

Thus, while Irving is exhorting his hearers to believe that "there is salvation in Christ for every one of you", an utterance bursts forth by the voice of Henry Drummond:—

"Ah, shut Him not out—shut not out your Saviour! Ah, you are proud of your dignity! Ah, truly your power is fearful! Ah, you have a power of resisting your God! Ah, you are not straitened in your Father; you are straitened in yourselves! Oh, receive Him now! The day is almost closed. Ah, enter now! delay not—delay not, delay not. Ah, wherefore stand you back?"

Several other utterances burst from various "gifted persons". After the intimation of ten weekly services, Henry Drummond's voice again broke out:—

"Ah, be ye warned! Be ye warned! Ye have been warned. The Lord hath prepared for you a table, but it is a table in the presence of your enemies. Ah, look you well to it! The city shall be builded—ah! every jot, every piece of the edifice. Be faithful each under his load—each under his load; but see that ye build with one hand, and with a weapon in the other. Look to it—look to it. Ye have been warned. Ah! Sanballat, Sanballat, Sanballat; the Horonite, the Moabite, the Ammonite! Ah, confederate, confederate, confederate with the Horonite! Ah, look ye to it, look ye to it!"

In March, 1833, Irving was summoned to the bar of the Presbytery of Annan on the charge of holding heretical doctrine as to the "sinfulness of our Lord's human nature" expressed in those books which the General Assembly of 1831 had condemned. But for the notoriety of the "manifestations" it is unlikely that the Presbytery would have gone out of its way to summon him. It must be remembered that he had continued to indulge in the most unmeasured vituperation of the General Assembly in the pages of *The Morning Watch*; what had once been the venerable supreme court of his National Zion was now "the Synagogue of Satan"! The Presbytery might well have spared a fallen man, but as Dr. R. H. Story maintained, "Irving seemed to court deposition."

A formidable printed *Libel* was duly delivered to him by a Westminster lawyer "in the study of his dwelling-house at Newman Street", adjoining the new place of worship. Incidentally, his prosecutors incurred a charge of £18 4s. 2½d. Need Irving have gone to Annan at all? To have been condemned *in absentia* would have made no difference to his position and would have saved him much strain. He went without any intention of appealing to the General Assembly against the verdict which he knew would be adverse. And he had ceased to be the minister of a Church of Scotland congregation for a year. But he must necessarily "go up and suffer persecution like his father". He had his "Ides of March".

On 13th March, 1832, he arrived at Annan in the morning and was taken to the house of Mr. Dickson, his brother-in-law. During the forenoon, people of all classes poured into Annan from the countryside and vehicles from Dumfries, Longtown, and Carlisle converged on the quiet country town.

At midday the trial opened in the parish church (crammed with 2,000 persons, it was computed). Mrs. Oliphant and others have darkened the background by picturing Irving baited and insulted by a handful of ignorant country ministers unfit to discuss theological issues. Carlyle speaks of the Moderator, "one Roddick—one of the stupidest and barrenest of living mortals" and Sloan, the senior member, "who went niddy-noddying with his head" and compared himself to stripling David assailing "even so great a giant as that reverend gentleman". Every Church Court has its weaker brethren who like to air their views in public, especially when there is a large audience. Most of the ministers of Annan Presbytery were easy-going men who did some farming and would not be likely to condemn anyone for metaphysical subtilties in doctrine; some of them were country gentlemen in a small way. The most outstanding was Henry Duncan of Ruthwell, sanely Evangelical, interested in social welfare and scientific progress—the kind of mind that *sees*. Duncan's influence alone was enough to redeem the Presbytery from the charge of being a little obscurantist conclave. Irving's own attitude was bitter and uncompromising. He refused a private conference in the session-house, and to his supporters in London he wrote:—"God gave me grace to refuse to every one of them the right hand of fellowship, yea, and not to eat bread with them and drink wine with them". In his defence he addressed the public rather than the court (tumult might easily have occurred, for he was popular with the people). The Moderator said it seemed to him as if Mr. Irving imagined he was in London, preaching to his people there.

"Remember where you are, Sir!"

"I know well where I now stand," came the reply. "I stand in the place where I was born, in the church wherein I was first baptised and then ordained. . . . Ministers and elders of the Presbytery of Annan! I stand at your bar by no constraint of man. You could not—no person on earth could—have brought me hither. I am a free man on a free soil, and living beyond your bounds. . . . Is it nothing, that ye have taken me away from ruling among my apostles and elders, and brought me three hundred miles to stand before you at this bar? . . . I stand here not by constraint but willingly. Do what you like. I ask not judgment of you; my judgment is with my God" (*Trial of Mr. Edward Irving*, Dumfries, 1833. *Journal* Office).

Reading the account of the trial to-day one is amazed that Irving should have been found guilty of holding the sinfulness of our Lord's human nature. Beyond all doubt he affirmed his belief in his Saviour's divinity. To assert the reality of Christ's temptations, along with His untainted holiness, was that not true orthodoxy? But the religious world a century ago did not realise that to overlook the Master's humanity was as unsound as to question His divinity. Apart from that, Irving's deposition was a foregone conclusion; the Presbytery wanted to bring to a final conclusion its connection with such a "notorious" person.

As the shadows of evening darkened the crowded church, the Moderator asked if he had any objection why sentence of deposition should not be passed against him. "Objection? All objection! I object, not for my own sake, but for the sake of Jesus Christ my Lord, whom I serve and honour. I object for your sakes . . . I object for the Church's sake. . . ." After the defendant's final appeal, the Moderator called on the senior member of Presbytery to lead in prayer before he pronounced the sentence. Suddenly "an utterance in the power" was heard. A voice came out of the gloom "Arise, depart! Arise, depart! Flee ye out of her, flee ye out of her! Ye cannot pray! How can ye pray? How can ye pray to Christ whom he deny? Ye cannot pray. Depart, depart! Flee, flee!" One of the Presbytery lifted the solitary tallow candle and looked with it searchingly into the gloom, to discover the whereabouts of the intruding voice—not an inapt symbol of the clerical mind peering by the feeble light of the understanding into the heart-mysteries of religion. It was a follower of Irving, the Rev. David Dow of Irongray, who rose and proceeded to leave the church. The audience (so far very restrained in spite of occasional applause during Irving's speech) now became confused. The defendant followed his friend, and to the crowd which somewhat obstructed his passage, he cried—"Stand forth! stand forth! What! will ye not obey the voice of the Holy Ghost? As many as will obey the voice of the Holy Ghost—let them depart!"

So in the March twilight Irving made his way through crowds of wondering but respectful spectators, forth from the church of his baptism and ordination. In the darkness, illumined only by their solitary candle, the Presbytery concluded their seven hours' *sederunt* by declaring him no longer a minister or member of the Church of Scotland. In the perspective of thirty years, Carlyle looked back on this

"poor aggregate of Reverend *Sticks* in black gown, sitting in Presbytery to pass formal condemnation on a Man and a Cause which might have been tried in Patmos, under Presidency of St. John, without the right truth of it being got at!"

Mrs. Oliphant (II, 353) pictures Irving afterwards addressing thousands of excited and sympathetic listeners at Cummertrees—on the Sands of Dumfries—and on a hillside in Terregles, the fair *Terra Ecclesiae;* "it was a solemn leave-taking of his native hills and mosses." That romantic way of looking at the tragedy must be corrected by Carlyle's realism. Writing to his brother in Florence on 29th March, he tells of Irving's "heroic-distracted speech, Dow finishing off with a Holy Ghost shriek or two".

"Whereupon Irving, calling on them to 'hear that', indignantly withdrew. He says, in a letter printed in the newspapers, that he 'did purpose to tarry in those parts certain days, and publish in the towns of the coast the great name of the Lord;' which purpose 'he did accomplish', publishing everywhere a variety of things. He was at Ecclefechan, Jean writes us; gray, toilworn, haggard, with 'an immense cravat the size of a sowing sheet covering all his breast;' the country people are full of zeal for him; but everywhere else his very name is an offence in decent society. 'Publish it in the towns of the Coast!' Oh! it is a *Pickle-herring Tragedy:* the accursedest thing one's eye could light on. As for Dow, he must surely ere long end in a mad-house. For our poor friend one knows not what to predict."

"Cracked!" remarked a local spectator after the trial.

"Cracked he may be," replied a neighbour, "but remember a crack often lets in light."

Far from Annan, Coleridge observed:

DARK DAYS

"Perhaps the kirk would not have been justified in overlooking the exhibitions of the Spirit . . . disgraceful breaches of decorum; but to excommunicate him on account of his language about Christ's body was very foolish; his apparent meaning, such as it is, is orthodox."

It is noteworthy that six members of the General Assembly representative of the Church's best legal and theological talent recorded their dissent, including Principal McFarlane of Glasgow. Dr. Chalmers remained silent.

On his return to London he was received at Newman Street, not with extraordinary honours as a martyr but with an immediate interdict, forbidding him to exercise any priestly function. He was admitted as a deacon—the lowest order of the new hierarchy then being brought into being by the circle of "gifted persons", with Henry Drummond as chief hierophant. Not a word of complaint fell from his lips in public. Other men have founded sects to rule them: Irving gave up a position of authority and influence only to serve and obey. On 5th April, says the authorised *Chronicle*, by "the concurrent action in manifested supernatural power, both of prophet and apostle, he was called and ordained Angel or chief pastor of the flock assembled in Newman Street, at the hands of Mr. J. B. Cardale." This nominal re-ordination has been justly named by Washington Wilks—"Irving's baptism for the dead". It was an anointing for his burial though he had nearly two years to live. He published no more books or sermons; he no longer preached in "open places about the city". He became more and more isolated in the little sectarian world that was guided by ecstatic utterances in Newman Street. The new prophets and apostles were puzzled how to manage his reluctance to see the hand of the Holy Spirit in every new development of doctrine and organisation. They sympathised with him as far as they could. With resignation he bowed to the inevitable, yet not willingly, as his brother-in-law, the Rev. J. Brodie of Monimail, testified. Mr. Brodie was present one Sunday at a Newman Street Communion Season in June, 1834. As Irving "fenced the tables", one of the apostles exclaimed: "And if there be any one who does not acknowledge that the Spirit of God is amongst us, let him abstain; let the unbeliever depart." Mr. Brodie explained next day that under such conditions he could never communicate. Irving paused and added,

"Ah, yes, the Spirit hath so enjoined us". His friend then realised that not without a struggle did the "Angel" give up the liberal and catholic feeling whereby he had once regarded all who loved the Lord Jesus as his brethren.

Soon after his return from Annan, his youngest infant, Ebenezer, became ill and died on 23rd April. The state of his mind is indicated by the fact that "in faith" he addressed "words of godliness" to nourish the seed of faith in a child only a few months old; "his patient heed was wonderful", he adds in a letter to Mr. Martin. As Carlyle was crossing Kensington Gardens at the end of May, 1834, he saw a figure start up and stalk towards him. It was Irving, but how changed in two years!

"His head, which I had left raven-black, was grown grey, on the temples almost snow-white; the face was hollow, wrinkly, collapsed; the figure, still perfectly erect, seemed to have lost its elasticity and strength. . . . Friends and doctors had advised him to Bayswater for better air; had got him a lodging there, a stout horse to ride; summer, they expected, would soon set him up again. His tone was not despondent; but it was low, pensive, full of silent sorrow. Once, perhaps twice I got a small bit of Annandale laugh from him, strangely genuine, though so lamed and overclouded; this was to me the most affecting thing of all, and still is when I recall it."

Neither at the Bayswater address nor in Newman Street could Carlyle find him "at home". The Carlyles had just settled in Chelsea and could not yet ask him to their new home. Carlyle felt that perhaps Irving's "poor jealous, anxious and much-bewildered wife had her hand in the phenomenon" of "these perpetual not-at-homes". So he applied to the good William Hamilton, who had married a sister of Mrs. Irving. That resulted in an invitation to dinner at Newman Street.

"None but Irving and his wife besides myself were there; the dinner (from a good joint of roast-beef, in a dim but quiet comfortable room) was among the pleasantest of dinners to me; Madam herself wearing nothing but smiles; and soon leaving us together to a fair hour or two of free talk. I think the main topic must have been my own outlooks and affairs, my project of writing on the *French Revolution*, which Irving warmly approved of; of his Church matters we now never spoke. I went away gratified . . . had not the outlooks on his side been so dubious and ominous. He was evidently growing weaker, not stronger; wearing himself down by spiritual agitations, which would kill him, unless checked and ended. Could he be got to Switzerland, to Italy I thought; to some pleasant country, of which the language was unknown to him, where he would be *forced to silence*, the one salutary medicine for him, in body and in soul!" (*C.R.*, p. 303f).

In the summer of 1834 Carlyle wrote a letter to Henry Drummond suggesting this as a practical necessity, but owing to misgivings did not post it. Mr. Martin was in London at his son-in-law's, but could think of no remedy. All he could say to Carlyle was: "Grows weaker and weaker, and no doctor can find the least disease in him. So weak now, he cannot lift his little baby to his neck!"

"He complains," wrote Carlyle to his doctor-brother John, "of biliousness, of pain at his right short rib; he has a short, thick cough, which comes at the slightest irritation" (15th August, 1834). .

At the beginning of September Irving paid his first (and last) visit at Cheyne Row before starting on a leisurely journey to Wales and Scotland. Towards sunset he came ambling gently on his bay horse to Chelsea and stayed twenty minutes in the ground-floor room where thirty-two years later Carlyle sadly penned his *Reminiscences*. Never could he forget Irving's "fine chivalrous demeanour" to Jane, how he cast his eyes round the simple artistic room and turned to her with a smile—"You are like an Eve, and make a little Paradise wherever you are!" His manner was sincere and affectionate, but there was a suppressed sadness in it; he must not linger. The Carlyles never saw him again, for he died at Glasgow the following December.

In September, 1834, Irving set forth on his last visit to Scotland. Some time before, he had been commissioned "by the power" "to do a great work there as a prophet". His relatives were alarmed at the idea, for he was in no fit condition for any great work. In fairness to the authorities at Newman Street, one must admit that Mr. Cardale and others opposed the idea. The suggestion was made that "it was his own air", and at his own wish Irving set off slowly towards Scotland, eager to do "the Lord's work", if possible by the way. He went northwards against the advice of his doctor, however, who recommended a warmer climate. One is inclined to agree with Carlyle that Mrs. Oliphant's biography is nowhere so true as in this last part, where it is drawn almost wholly from his letters to his wife, *en route*. "A good deal of her narrative is romantic, highly-coloured, pictorial, here and there is perfect *portraiture*" (*C.R.*, p. 305). These letters tell how he rode leisurely through the valley of the Wye, meditating at Tintern Abbey enjoying the hospitality of friends and sometimes addressing meetings ("I am fully persuaded, by experience, that it is the proper exercise of the lungs").

He reassures his wife that all is well with him and sometimes mentions what he has had for dinner, e.g. 18th September:

"Ham and egg, a cold fowl, an apple-tart and cheese, a tumbler of cider, Sicilian Tokay, of which Mr. Brydgeman put two bottles in my saddle (bags). Tell your dear mother I had such a memento of Kirkcaldy Manse—ginger wine in a long-necked decanter. . . ."

To Margaret and Martin, his surviving children, he would give a vivid description of a secret hiding place where Charles I eluded his pursuers.

His descriptions of Welsh scenery are worth recording.

"I rode from Harlech, before breakfast, along the sea shore until we found an inlet to follow up, at the head of which sits Taw-y-bwlch, in such stillness and beauty. . . . Oh! it is a place of peace and repose! Then I crossed rugged and barren mountains with occasional views of the ocean, till the road swept up a mountain pass of great sublimity, and opened at the head of it upon Beddgelert (then he tells the inevitable story of the 'hound Gelert' for Maggie's benefit). Here I had a harper to play to me the choicest of the old Welsh airs, *Of a noble race was Shenkin, The March of the men of Harlech*, etc. The old blind man was very thankful for a sixpence, and I taught him how to use his harp as David had done, in the praise of his God. From thence I set myself to begird the roots of Snowdon, for he covered his head from the sight of man. I had seen his majestic head lifted above the mountains from Aberystwyth, and it is the only sight I have had of him. He is the monarch of many. The mountains stand around him as they shall stand around Zion. That beautiful sunset which I saw at Harlech yielded only wind; and as I rode up these defiles the wind was terrible. It made the silken shroud over my shoulders rattle in my horse's ears till he could hardly abide it. I never endured such a battery of wind."

At Bangor he viewed the Menai Bridge (constructed just eight years earlier); while marvelling at "that wonder of man's hand" he got wet by a sudden gust driven through the straits and had a fevered night, though his inn, the Penrhyn Arms, was like a castle—"the very house of a Shunamite woman". Fever still worried him at Flint, where he tried to shake it off by refusing to stay even a day in bed. At Liverpool he had "a good deal of those cold creepings upon the skin which Dr. Darling used to inquire about". He asked his wife to come to him. "Oh how I have longed after you in heart and spirit!"

Mrs. Irving joined her husband as soon as possible in Liverpool. In spite of the protests of their friends, they insisted on sailing to Glasgow. They arrived after a cold and boisterous passage. A Greenock friend, Mrs. Stewart Ker, described his condition:—

"He is sinking under a deep consumption. His gigantic frame bears all the marks of age and weakness; his tremendous voice is now often faltering, and when occasionally he breaks forth with his former feeling, one sees that his bodily powers are exhausted. Add to all this the calm, chastened dignity of his expression—his patient waiting upon God for the fulfilment of His purposes to himself and his flock through this affliction. . . . In driving through the crowded streets of Glasgow, he laid aside his hat and exclaimed, 'Blessed be the name of the Shepherd of Israel, who has brought us to the end of our journey in the fulness of the blessing of the Gospel of Peace!' and continued for some time praying."

The Rev. Mr. Martin remonstrated with his daughter for bringing a sick man north to Glasgow instead of south to Madeira, with reflections on the folly of the "guidance" they had followed. No notice was taken of this letter for some time; when Isabella did write to Kirkcaldy she referred to it as "awful". As for the patient—"poor good man!" exclaimed Mr. Martin. "That he feels the cold air bracing and refreshing, I wonder not, for the usual state of his pulse is 120 in the minute, and has been higher." Dr. Rainy, a skilled physician, and an old acquaintance of Edward (an elder in St. John's), traced his symptoms not directly to the lungs but to "a deranged state of the bowels".

In spite of his weakness, he gathered together a few followers in the "Lyceum". As he rode or walked (with the support of a stick) the Glasgow people would glance at him compassionately and point out to each other "the great Edward Irving". His face would light up as he recognised someone who had been a fellow-worker in his mission days in St. John's parish. Sometimes he would ride with McLeod Campbell in the country. One cloudless day Irving looked up at the sky and turned to his friend with deep emotion—"Oh that Thou wouldst rend the heavens and come down!" At the end of October he addressed two pastoral letters to the Church in Newman Street.

"It well becometh me, who was the chief instrument of bringing in that sin for which the hand of the Lord hath long lain heavy upon us, to do my utmost part to remove the same, that He may again lift upon us the light of His countenance. . . . We were beguiled to think that the full measure of the tabernacle of the Lord would be given to that church over which I preside as angel, which was no less than the exalting of the angel of the Church into the place of Christ. . . . I do repent and call upon all the flock to repent with me. . . . We sought independence as a Church, and but for the grace of God we had reaped the very independence of Satan. God saw that we had been taken in through our simplicity, and therefore He had mercy upon us, and began to take the veil from off our eyes. . . ."

We read on, however, to find that the veil is to be taken off "by the hands of His Apostles", i.e., the Newman Street apostles, Henry Drummond in particular! His "sin" was having acted, when in London, on a command given by one of the "gifted persons", without the authority of the Apostle! Apart, however, from Newman Street and its paltry sacerdotalisms, we can see this letter is full of questionings and dubieties. If we cannot prove any clear confession of having been deluded, as in the case of Robert Baxter, we can feel an undercurrent of deep disappointment with the hierarchy and its subjective basis. This letter was printed for private circulation among the Newman Street congregation, but afterwards Henry Drummond and his associates laid hands on every available copy that could be destroyed. It was reprinted in the *Gospel Magazine* (May, 1835) and as an appendix to Mrs. Oliphant's *Life*.

Robert Story came to Glasgow to persuade Irving to rest at Rosneath, but found that he had crossed the Clyde to Erskine, to see Dr. Stewart, the physician-minister with whom they used to spend their Saturdays long ago at Bolton Manse. But it was too late. He returned to the house of the kind stranger (an enthusiastic disciple) who had welcomed him at Glasgow, and his last weeks were spent in bed. A prophetic message had announced that he was to recover from his illness. "I desire to depart and be with Christ" once broke from his fevered lips. His wife reminded him of the prophecy. "I have expressed my desire," he answered, "not my expectation." At times he spoke mystically of the "Tongues", adding with pathetic humility, that of these gifts he himself had never been found worthy. His mother and sister, and Mr. Martin and other friends from Kirkcaldy were with him in his last days. The end came on Sabbath evening, 7th December, 1834. His last audible words were—"If I die, I die unto the Lord. Amen". He was only forty-two.

"Who would care for his family if he were taken away? "The elders of the Church, mother." To their credit they provided adequately; Mrs. Irving was afterwards conveyed to London by Mr. Woodhouse, an Apostle, "a gentle, modest and benevolent person".

Mr. Martin wrote to his daughter at Dumfries (12th December, 1834):

"In his monomania Isabella seems completely to partake. . . . Afterwards she may think it a duty to Edward's memory to adhere to the views to which he died a victim; and which there was no sympton perceptible in his death-bed, that he himself doubted or forsook."

"Every other consideration," said the ultra-orthodox *Scottish Guardian*, "was forgotten in the universal and profound sympathy with which the information was received." His funeral was attended by a host of friends, including many of the ministers who had opposed him in his life-time. They buried him in the crypt of Glasgow Cathedral, like his Master, in the grave of a stranger; Mr Laurie, partner of William Hamilton, who had first introduced him to London, came forward to offer a last resting-place. One of the noblest crypts in Europe is partly at least redeemed from being "waste—regions of oblivion" (Scott, *Rob Roy*).

"Know ye not that there is a prince and a great man fallen this day in Israel?" Dr. Black of the Barony church, who was present at the funeral, said that when the mourners retired, they still left standing at his grave a number of young women clothed in white, who confidently expected he would rise again. His grave needs no dusky banners, no tattered escutheons; it is neither obscure not unsought. It is pointed out to visitors—"and sometimes it is asked for by one whose fixed gaze, escaping sigh, or furtive prayer, reveal to him that it exceeds in interest far older shrines". His nephew emblazoned the narrow lancet over him with a representation of John the Baptist.

"What a falling of the curtain," cried Carlyle; "upon what a Drama! Rustic Annandale begins it, with its homely honesties, rough vernacularities, safe, innocently kind, rugged, mother-like, cheery, wholesome, like its airy hills and clear-rushing streams; prurient corrupted London is the middle part, with its volcanic stupidities, and bottomless confusions;—and the end is terrible, mysterious, godlike and awful; what Patmos could be more so? It is as if the vials of Heaven's wrath were pouring down upon a man; yet not wrath alone, for his heart is filled with trust in Heaven's goodness withal. It must be said, Irving nobly expiates whatever errors he had fallen into; like an Antique Evangelist he walks his stony course, the fixed thought of his heart, at all times, 'Though He slay me, yet will I trust in Him'; and these final deluges of sorrow are but washing the faithful soul of him clean" (*C.R*, p. 305f.).

CHAPTER XIV

SHRINES OF MEMORY

" There is no place perhaps where you have such a feeling of blankness when life has gone from it as in a Church. . . . I have often looked at the pulpit whence Chalmers preached in the zenith of his fame; can you bring up again the excited throng and the rush of eloquence?"—A. K. H. BOYD.

THE buildings of the Caledonian Chapel, Hatton Garden, the National Scottish Church, Regent Square, and the Catholic Apostolic Church, Gordon Square, form a triangle, standing out in London as landmarks of the progressive stages of Irving's beliefs. The Caledonian Chapel, a warehouse for a half a century, was burnt down a few years ago. The Gordon Square Church, a Gothic Revival cathedral, is successor to the modest meeting place at Newman Street and the chief centre of the community founded on the credit of Irving's name. Had the Regent Square Church been held by personal tenure, it would have been the home of the new sect. But the faithful office-bearers preserved it for Presbyterianism. Their heroism, if unspectacular, was real. The congregation, reduced to a mere handful, was faced with the difficult tasks of procuring a minister big enough to fill Irving's place and of meeting the interest on the Building Fund debt (£10,000). Some members would have allowed matters to drift to their inevitable result, the sale of the church to satisfy the claims of the mortgagees. Mr. William Hamilton, Irving's counsellor and his wife's brother-in-law, launched a fresh appeal to the religious and patriotic feelings of London Scots. As a result, the church was kept open and continued to be a Scottish church though the Disruption of 1843 severed the link that bound it to the Church of Scotland. The "trust deed" by which Irving had been ousted continued to cause trouble as it required the minister to be one ordained by the Church of Scotland; the congregation was not prepared to revert to its old allegiance, so in 1859 bought the building from the mortgagees for £6,000, thus acquiring its freedom. "Regent Square" became one of the leading London congregations of the Presbyterian Church of England. The Scottish Church Union of 1929 restored cordial relationship with the parent Church of Scotland.

This is not the place to unfold the history of Regent Square Church (See Bibliography, p. 299) but it is relevant to point out that the best traditions of its early days have been upheld. It has had a succession of great ministries. Dr. James Hamilton (who had met Irving in his father's manse at Strathblane) attracted people of rank and distinction in early Victorian days; Miss Margaret Wilson, afterwards Mrs. Oliphant—Irving's biographer, "sat under" him. McCheyne, Duff, Candlish, Guthrie, D'Aubigné and Livingstone preached there from time to time. Dr. Oswald Dykes, the next minister, in the mid-Victorian period was famous through the Presbyterian world as theologian and preacher. And in 1889, with the coming of John McNeill, the church was crowded as it had never been since the days of Edward Irving.

McNeill deviated from the beaten track and often ruffled the spirit of decorum to which the congregation had been used for fifty years. He was a man of great gifts and spiritual power, but the evangelist rather than the settled minister; fortunately, he did not hive off, with the majority of the congregation, to some new tabernacle, like Irving! During his ministry the sounding board of the historic pulpit was removed, and the pulpit reconstructed in the platform style then in vogue. The fact that an organ was not installed till 1902 was a link with the austere days of Irving. Various relics of his ministry are preserved in a museum in one of the church towers. Amidst all the transformations of the church interior and the changes in theology and usage, the clock in the back gallery remains the same faithful recorder as when Irving, divinely commissioned and absorbed in his subject, held on his way in rapt defiance of its silent admonitions. A century after his death, his church fulfils its original purpose of ministering to Scotsmen and their descendants, presenting Christianity in a simple and yet dignified form, and thus making a worthy contribution to the religious life of the metropolis.

Turning from "the noble towers" of Regent Square to the Catholic Apostolic Cathedral of Gordon Square, we feel we are in the region of something approximating to High Anglicanism rather than "Irvingism". Members of the Catholic Apostolic Church never fail indeed to resent the name of "Irvingite", and to some extent they are justified. They were indebted to Irving for much of their theology and to the publicity his reputation gave to the manifestations. But he was the forerunner and prophet of a new dispensation rather than the founder of a new sect. Because the movement started in a Scottish congregation, it took over Presbyterian practices such as the singing of metrical psalms. But the influx of new adherents who had no interest in the Church of Scotland gradually changed all that. *The Morning Watch* repeatedly declared that the majority of its readers were members of the English Church, and discussed the position of the body during Irving's life-time as though it was merely in a temporary refuge; some spoke of "*The Ark of God in the Temple of Dagon.*" New congregations sprang up apart from Irving's, of Anglican and also of Nonconformist origin.

Before Irving finally left Newman Street a congregation had grown up under the Rev. Nicholas Armstrong, an Irish clergyman of the Church of England. In January, 1834, the Rev. H. J. Owen of Park Chapel, Chelsea, also resigned his charge after a lengthy correspondence with Bishop Blomfield, and organised a congregation of his own. A Miss Hughes, afflicted with curvature of the spine, had suddenly been cured on hearing of Miss Fancourt's cure. Owen (who had been a member of the Albury circle), preached and published four sermons upon this, and generally asserted that the gifts of the Holy Ghost should still be possessed by the Church. In Bishopsgate Independent Chapel Mr. Miller, the minister, had been teaching Christ's imminent Second Coming and personal reign on earth, and the bestowal of spiritual gifts. In his church the voices of the prophets were heard from 12th June, 1832, onwards, —expressions of praise, warning and deliverance. On 12th May, 1832, Mr. Miller was forbidden to administer Communion, by an utterance in the Power. He applied to Newman Street for instructions, and was afterwards ordained by Mr. Cardale as an Angel, when his church became the second of "the Seven Churches of London".

A Catholic Apostolic book *The Lord's Work* (1899) also tells of the sympathy shown towards the movement by the Baptist ministers at Oxford, Messrs. Hinton and Bulteel, the latter a man of talent, formerly incumbent of St. Ebbe's.

At Edinburgh Mr. Tait, formerly of the College Church, had espoused the cause. The outpourings in his congregation had been accompanied by some utterances so debased as to be rejected by the better type of "prophet". Irving was sent in January, 1834, to deal with these "unclean spirits" and from all accounts seems to have been effective. But he was a mere shadow of his old self. Mrs. Irving wrote to her mother at Kirkcaldy: "Edward was truly grieved that it was not in his power to go to see you, but truly his time is not his own, neither is he his own master." It was a great disappointment to Henry Drummond that Irving's friend, McLeod Campbell, refused to give a lead "if a sect were establishing in the West of Scotland" (spring, 1834). At Greenock he met Lady Harriet Drummond, Mr. Tapli and other lights of "the New Church" (*Memorials*, 103, 115–125).

"Prophecy" was however destined to be supplanted. It was discredited by its subjectivity. Continual doubts repeatedly arose over Mr. Taplin ("who kept an academy in Castle Street, Holborn") "the chief of the prophets". On rebuking Mr. Irving, he was himself rebuked by utterance through Miss E. Cardale; and after some days confessed that he had harboured unjust thoughts against Mr. Irving and that he had spoken this rebuke "by the power of an evil spirit".

The Sunday after Mr. Irving's burial, Mr. Ryerson in a sermon at Newman Street was showing how a man might have the gift of the Spirit without the gift of God in his heart, alluding, as was generally understood, to Mr. Taplin, when Miss E. Cardale again "broke out in the most appalling utterance"—"He never had it—He never knew it!"

Henry Drummond's Ordination as Apostle and pastor of the Church at Albury (28th December, 1832) marked progress in the abandoning of the "prophetic" leadership. "It is the Lord's will," declared Cardale, in a commanding manner, "that thou proceed to feed this people with the body and blood of Christ. See thou to it." The new Apostle might add, before administering Communion: "I may give you the bread and wine, but *this* is not to have communion with the Lord—*it is the Spirit that quickeneth.*"

The Prophetic Movement had burnt itself out within the next few years. Out of the molten material of healing, prophesying, and speaking with tongues, there emerged the "Catholic Apostolic Church", an institution essentially priestly (though more "apostolic" in framework than the Catholic Church which it so closely resembled), twelve apostles planting and watering churches throughout the world, on whose decease the Second Coming was expected. The historian will notice the rapid transformation from spontaneous enthusiasm to hierarchical and sacramentarian order, which the Irvingite Movement underwent between 1834 and 1842,—a striking contrast to the more gradual and natural evolution of the Apostolic Church from primitive simplicity to ecclesiasticism. Yet it is interesting to note that if the prophecy of the O.T. inspired the Irvingites in their earlier days, later development proceeded on the close and even fantastic analogy of the O.T. priesthood.

We may date the transition from the Irvingite Circle to the Apostolic Church from the winding up of the *Morning Watch*, June, 1833. Few editors have made such a valedictory statement as this:—

"The followers of Christ and the followers of Antichrist are now gathering. Christ is gathering His children into the true Church, to do Him service there, and, in so doing, to be prepared for His coming; Satan is gathering his hosts under the standard of *Liberalism* to become the pioneers of the man of perdition, the personal Antichrist.

"In the progress of this work, Christ hath been calling for the personal services of nearly all the regular correspondents of this journal; and he hath at length called the editor to take the place of an elder in His Church, and hath claimed all his time for the special duties of feeding and overseeing a sixth part of the flock in London. To this higher calling the editor now resolves to devote himself wholly, and at the same time brings the *Morning Watch* to a close, as he will not transfer to any other person such a solemn responsibility."

There is a remarkable parallel to the Irvingite Movement which occurred in South Germany at about the same time, unknown to the "gifted persons" in London. In 1842 a certain Johann Lutz received a letter from his friend Leinfelder, recommending Caird (husband of Mary Campbell):—

"'In England there are churches such as there were in the beginning.' I was much surprised. 'Who directed these churches?' 'Apostles.' 'What! Apostles? I have been waiting for a special work of God in the Church for *fourteen years*.' 'When did these people (i.e., in Germany) speak in prophecy?' asked Mr. Caird. I told him that it was at the same time that persons in Scotland began to speak in the power of the Holy Ghost!" (See Appendix, p. 286ff.).

This intercourse with the Continent led to the establishment of Catholic Apostolic congregations in Germany and Switzerland. North Germany ("the tribe of Simeon") was allotted to Thomas Carlyle (1803–55), like his namesake, an Annandale man. He had been legal counsel for McLeod Campbell in 1831; as an "Apostle" he found ample scope for theological activity. In America, W. W. Andrews, a Divinity student just out of Yale, had his attention drawn to "the work" in 1831. He visited England in 1843, was impressed with the now crystallized Catholic Church and six years after his return to New England joined the new body.

It is tempting to stray into this unfrequented by-way of Church History, and I must forbear. A few interesting facts, however, may be noted. The happy title "Catholic Apostolic Church" was due to the accidental enrolment of a census clerk. A certain householder was asked what denomination he belonged to. He replied, "the Catholic and Apostolic Church worshipping in Newman Street". The clerk registered "Catholic Apostolic Church". This Church is Catholic in its use of the ancient creeds and liturgy, based on Roman, Greek, and Anglican rites; lights, incense and vestments are used. It is Apostolic in its permission of "tongues" (still occasionally heard) and in its deacons, elders, prophets and apostles. It emphasises the "phenomena" of Christian experience and deems miracles and mystery to be of the essence of the spirit-filled church.

In its worship it anticipated many of the ritual developments of Anglo-Catholicism, though its early morning services grew out of the early morning prayer meetings at Regent Square. Its extravagant love of symbolism, allegory and typology seem to be derived from Irving, as also the hope of the Second Coming. It was expected that this would occur on the death of the last Apostle. Since this hope was blighted on the death of the last Apostle on 3rd February, 1901, the Church has abandoned further extension. It publishes no statistics and continues to dwindle. It maintains its position through tithes and several splendid places of worship in London, Edinburgh and Albury, near Guildford, Surrey—the home of the "prophetic movement" and later the seat of the Apostolic College. By "apostolic act" it recognises the "Orders" of such clergy of other branches of the Universal Church as desires it; and during the Victorian era a number of people in sympathy with the movement availed themselves of this, including Presbyterian ministers like Dr. John Macleod of Govan. Mr. C. F. Andrews has given us an attractive picture of the Catholic Apostolic congregation at Birmingham where he was brought up, in *What I owe to Christ* (Chapter IV). In spite of Biblical literalism, obsession with numerical symbols, the "measurements of the tabernacle" and farfetched allegorisation, there was a genuinely apostolic sense of expectation and of self-dedication; at the age of twenty, every member was "sealed" by the laying on of hands and anointed with consecrated oil. Had Irving lived to see the Catholic Apostolic Church as finally evolved, he might have had difficulties over vestments and liturgies, but there is no doubt that its dream-like atmosphere would have appealed to him strongly.

CHAPTER XV

THE IRVINGITE MOVEMENT IN THE LIGHT OF PSYCHOLOGY

" I can neither explain nor account for phenomena so extraordinary."—MRS. OLIPHANT IRVING.

§ 1

The Obscurantist Mentality

IRVINGISM was a child of Millenarianism, that fertile mother of "fancy religions". Millenarianism is like a "recurring decimal" in the history of the Christian religion. It has come in waves, age after age, in the Early Church, in the Middle Ages and particularly in literalistic, unprogressive circles of Protestantism. There was a wave of Second Adventism in Irving's time and another after the Armistice in 1918. There have always been groups of "Bible students", devoid of imagination, who treat the Bible as a book of cryptograms. Much time and zeal is consumed in unwrapping the dark sayings of Daniel and the writer of the Apocalypse.

The mystical "666"—"the number of the Beast"—gives them as much pious entertainment as worldly folk derive from the solution of crossword puzzles! From Nero down to Napoleon and the ex-Kaiser, the beast has been confidently identified. Macaulay was accosted in 1834, without preface, by an Englishman in Mysore: "Pray, Mr. Macaulay, do you not think that Buonaparte was the Beast?" Prof. Eadie, on his voyage to Palestine in 1870, was tackled by the captain . . . he quietly asked, "Which Beast?" Dr. George Matheson answered an interrogator, "The Number of the Beast is *Number One!*" When the voice of Manning, the Romanist, was first heard in Exeter Hall in 1868, *Punch* declared it was "all up with Exeter Hall". "Had we not better call it 666 Strand?" The repeated failure of predictions of the end of the world and the Second Coming of Christ has seldom had the effect of damping the ardour of enthusiasts. Dr. Cumming of Crown Court was typical. In 1861 he declared that 1867 would see the end of chronology.

During the next few years the faithful were kept on tiptoe of expectation. When the alarm proved false, the Doctor cheerfully chose another date; this time it was "positive" (yet the prophet of catastrophe took his house on a fifty years' lease!) Dr. Cumming found a successor in "Prophet Baxter", who lectured at Wolverhampton in a hall draped with lurid pictures. His last prediction of "the end" was 1909; but in 1907 he renewed the lease of his business premises for thirty years!

There was little of the charlatan in Irving, but even if he had lived in our own time it is likely that he might have been lured into some obscurantist cul-de-sac. The advance of civilisation has not prevented the survival of sects and movements of a literalistic, "four-square Gospel" type. Belief in "unfulfilled prophecy" has persisted even in cultured circles. A well-known journalist describes Millenarian gatherings in London in the old Exeter Hall days:—

"Usually there were half-a-dozen retired Indian Generals and Governors of Provinces, along with elderly ladies sombrely costumed, and clergymen of the Evangelical school, mostly incumbents of wealthy parishes or churches at prosperous seaside resorts. I think the authors of Daniel, the Song of Songs and the Seer of Patmos would have opened their eyes in amazement could they have heard their symbolic dives into the future so confidently made applicable to the history of our own time" (H. Jeffs, *Press, Preachers and Politicians*, 1874–1932, p. 155).

In such circles the "British Israel Movement" has gained numerous devotees in our own time. The modern view of the Bible is taught in most Protestant theological colleges in Great Britain, but that has not prevented the persistence of extremely conservative views among certain clergy, whether Anglican Evangelicals, Presbyterians, or Nonconformists. Millenarianism is a "recurring decimal" in history. Had Irving lived in our own time, his movement might have been different in form, but quite likely would have approximated to Millenarianism. In spite of the advance of civilisation and thought, there will always be some people of Irving's temperament who will seek out kindred spirits and form a movement that will make its appeal to a certain public. The Appendix will give some idea of "prophetic phenomena" such as the Gift of Tongues and their persistence through the centuries into modern times.

In this chapter, we approach the Irvingite Movement from the circumference, thereafter proceeding to the core—Glossolalia.

Professor J. B. Pratt, in *The Religious Consciousness*, finds in religion three vital elements, (1) the Traditional, based on the inherited wisdom of the race, and involving institutionalism; (2) the Rational, with a "de-personalising tendency" towards scepticism; (3) the Mystical, opposed to the abstractions of the Thinker, yet, like the Rational element, based upon an immediate personal experience, which tends to be nourished and coaxed for its own sake. All of these elements contribute to the full and harmonious life, but in actual practice there has been a tendency to stress one—to the exclusion of the other two, with disastrous results.

The followers of Irving, as we have seen, laid exclusive stress on the possession of certain religious experience, denouncing both the Intellect (identified with "rationalism") and Tradition (regarded as a departure from Apostolic Christianity).

In discussing Mysticism, William James assigned to it the attributes of Ineffability, Noetic Quality, Transiency, and Passivity.

"This latter . . . connects mystical states with certain definite phenomena of secondary or alternative personality, such as prophetic speech, automatic writing, or the mediumistic trance."

In the Irvingite, as in other similar movements, we find Glossolalia associated with "spiritual healing" (e.g., Mary Campbell, the Macdonalds, Miss Fancourt); prophecy (e.g., Baxter); automatic writing (e.g., Mary Campbell); and telepathy (the inner Irvingite circle). These phenomena were regarded as unique at the time. It was left to William James to impress on the public mind the fact that "you will hardly find a religious leader of any kind in whose life there is no record of automatisms".

"St. Paul . . . and the whole array of Christian saints and heresiarchs, including the greatest, the Bernards, the Loyolas, the Luthers, the Foxes, the Wesleys, had their visions, voices, guiding impressions, and 'openings'. They had these things because they had exalted sensibility, and to such things persons of exalted sensibility are liable."

The result is that "Beliefs are strengthened wherever automatisms corroborate them".

"But when a superior intellect and a psychopathic temperament coalesce in the same individual, we have the best possible condition for the kind of effective genius that gets into the biographical dictionaries. . . . Their ideas *possess* them, they inflict them, for better or worse, upon their companions or their age" (*Varieties of Religious Experience*, p. 478, 1929 ed.).

The last statement is qualified (p. 23). "There is of course no special affinity between crankiness as such and superior intellect, and superior intellects more commonly have normal nervous systems."

Now it cannot be claimed that intellect was characteristic of the Irvingite circle. Baxter's intellect made itself felt in spheres other than religion. Drummond was a shrewd organiser, but had a reputation, which he undoubtedly deserved, of being a "crack-brained enthusiast" in politics and religion. Irving could absorb, but could not digest, the thought of his age; his weak will made him the victim of impulse and circumstances. Of other members of the group it may be said that there was a mixture of simple devout piety, of credulity and fanaticism—sometimes combined with sanity on all other matters except religion. Strong intellect, which can see life steadily and whole, was wanting. The typical Irvingite can be recognised in a portrait sketched by William James:—

"The cranky person has extraordinary emotional susceptibility. He is liable to fixed ideas and obsessions. His conceptions tend to pass immediately into belief and action; and when he gets a new idea, he has no rest till he proclaims it, or in some way 'works it off'. 'What shall I think of it?' a common person says to himself about a vexed question; but in a 'cranky' mind 'what must I do about it?' is the form the question tends to take" (p. 23).

When a circle has conceived a particular animus against the Intellect, we must not be surprised to find credulity leading to insanity.

In all ages, in all lands, in all religions, abnormal religious life has been stimulated by long prayer meetings, vigils, fastings. In the Irvingite circle the more extreme forms of asceticism were not present. But some of the members were people of leisure, who started the day with an early prayer meeting and spent it in conclave or private devotion, frequently obtruding their common obsession even at breakfast and dinner parties. London tended to produce a nervous, excitable type of person, who would seek to be stimulated, either by pleasure or "religion". And in these early days of hygiene, life in a large city was much less healthy than to-day.

It will be remembered that the Gifted Persons from the west of Scotland, Mary Campbell and the Macdonalds, were consumptives. Even Irving, that son of Anak, died of consumption. Physical causes undoubtedly contributed to the "manifestations". St. Theresa declared rightly:—

"That the disquiet of the soul comes most from bodily indisposition. I have had great experience of the matter . . . this poor prisoner of a soul shares in the miseries of the body. The more we force the body, the greater the mischief. The poor soul must not be stifled. Let those who thus suffer understand that they are ill" (*Vita*, XI, 23).

On the other hand, the cures effected (e.g., Mary Campbell and the Macdonalds) in the Irvingite Movement, indicate how a religious joy can enable men and women to transcend the frail limits of humanity. "I cannot help thinking," said General Gordon, "that the body has much to do with religion."

§ 2

Irvingism and "the Herd"

The eighteenth century was a century of Revival. The Irvingite Movement could not help being unconsciously influenced by them. The "bodily effects" (swooning, convulsions, etc.), which made their appearance during "The Great Awakening" in New England, provoked acute criticism and led to Jonathan Edward's penetrating and accurate psychological treatises *On the Religious Affections* and *On the Present Revival*, which attained a wide circulation on both sides of the Atlantic. Many of Edward's frank criticisms of the "work" might have stood as criticisms of Irvingism, with few changes, e.g.:—

IN THE LIGHT OF PSYCHOLOGY

(1) "Undiscerned spiritual pride." It is not beautiful that critics of the Revival should be dubbed "Pharisees, carnal persecutors". "While Peter wounds, Christ heals."

(2) "Adoption of wrong principles."—"That it is God's manner in these days, to guide his saints . . . by inspiration or immediate revelation as to what shall come to pass hereafter. Why cannot we be content with the divine oracles . . . which we have in such clearness since the Canon of Scripture was completed?" They take texts, such as "led by the Spirit", as impressed on their minds, and improve it as a new revelation to all intent and purposes. "A man may have ten thousand such revelations and directions from the Spirit, and yet not have a jot of grace in his heart." "The Spirit of God doth teach the saints their duty in a higher way than ever Balaam or Saul were taught—a more excellent way."

Another error; that external order is but little to be regarded.

That ministers, as Christ's ambassadors, may speak with the same authority as the apostles did, yea Jesus Christ himself. "The principle is absurd . . . there is a vast difference in degree of authority."

(3) "Being ignorant or unobservant of some things by which the devil has special advantage.

"The beam of light as it comes from the fount of light in our hearts is pure; but as it is reflected hence, it is mixt."

"We may not take all for gold that glistens."

The workings of imagination, and a person's "supposed eminency and distinction from others in the favour of God"—constitute the human element which tends to increase in a convert, as the vision fades.

"Bodily effects", "impulses" and "impressions"—are merely incidental (*Thoughts on the Present Revival*, Part IV, p. 403–13).

If "The Great Awakening" occurred among a community that had achieved stability, but inherited the faith of seventeenth century Puritanism (what Davenport calls the "dogmatic-emotional type") the Revival of 1800 took place in the backwoods where law and order scarcely existed. In Kentucky it found uncontrolled expression. As a result of midnight camp-meetings thousands rolled on the ground shrieking, some shaking in every joint ("jerks"), and others "barking on all-fours". By 1803 the "holy laugh" and rather free association of the sexes appeared. In Irvingism motor expressions existed, but in individual cases, not *en masse;* nor was there the slightest tendency towards immorality. But Irvingism was born in a settled community, and the automatisms were generally sensory rather than motor (trance, vision, etc.), as in the Ulster Revival of 1859. (Compare the Methodist Movement, p. 248–52.)

Irvingism developed in relation to certain physical and mental conditions. This is the first "law of Revival" suggested by Davenport (*Primitive Traits in Religious Revival*).

A second law is that of Spread by impulsive social action, through suggestion. Thus Glossolalia broke out in the west of Scotland, was brought into the wider "apostolic" framework in London, and developed in congregations other than Regent Square, both in London and in the country.

Akin to the law of Spread is that of Restraint.

"In the more primitive religious revivals there is little or no restraint until the wave has spent its fury . . . while in others, calmer leadership within and critical judgment from without, combine to hold in leash the natural excesses of the movement" (*See* G. Steven, *Psychology of the Christian Soul*, Ch. VI).

The Irvingite Movement flared up and burnt itself out. It was true that the "Catholic Apostolic Church" issued from the ashes, and that the new polity was conserved. But the dynamic of the movement—the gifts of prophesying and speaking in tongues, was quenched, and the protest against externalism in religion was exchanged for sacramentarianism and sacerdotalism of an eclectic type.

A fourth law is, that while origination of a revival is generally traced to thinkers, the first movement for carrying out the plan is often due to sub-rational elements in society. Crusades were decreed by Councils, but impulsive social action accounted for the ill-fated expeditions of Walter the Penniless, Peter the Hermit, and the pathetic "Children's Crusade". Similarly a stimulus to the revival of "gifts" was given by the preaching of Irving and A. J. Scott: the response was made by Mary Campbell, the peasant girl and the Macdonalds, simple pietists (all three, consumptives), and in London by the ill-balanced Baxter and Taplin, not to speak of the "hysterical women" noted by Carlyle.

The emotions of the crowd are such as can be shared by those whose emotions are crude, by a low order of mind.

Men are "carried out of themselves", experience a feeling of enlargement and liberation; their sense of individual responsibility is weakened; their loss of self-control is impaired. They are at the mercy of any leader who can play with success upon their feelings; they accept with acclamation some assertion or proposal, which individual moral sense or intelligence would be slow to accept, because such an assertion or proposal has behind it the force of herd instinct. Membership of a crowd is demoralising.

This is profoundly true of the public services at Regent Square which exerted a powerful influence over suggestible people. The church was filled not with backwoodsmen or negroes, where one might expect to find "primitive traits". For as "Anti-Cabala" said in his "Morning Visit to Rev. E. Irving's":—(1) Fanaticism at Regent Square developed under sanction of an individual not to be classed with those whose defective Education and consequent susceptibility to erroneous impressions easily accounted for pretended wonders; (2) several persons have become its votaries of whom better things might have been expected.

But we have been struck by the fact, in tracing the evolution of the Irvingite Movement, that an inner junta of "gifted persons" claimed to direct the new Church. An observer would not give an adequate description of the movement who ascribed it purely to herd instinct. He must deal with the conclave—"The Psychology of the Group."

§ 3

Irvingism as a "Group"

Professor Wm. McDougall has laid down five conditions of principal importance rendering possible the formation of a "group mind" out of the raw material of the unorganised crowd.

(1) There must be some degree of continuity in the group, "either persistence of the same individuals or of a system of generally recognised positions, each of which is occupied by a succession of individuals".
(2) "In the minds of the members of the group there shall be formed some adequate idea of the group . . . a sentiment for the group which becomes the source of emotions and impulses to action."
(3) "Interaction (especially in the form of conflict and rivalry)

of the group with other similar groups animated by different ideals and purposes, and swayed by different traditions and customs." This "greatly promotes the self-knowledge of each group".

(4) "A body of traditions and customs and habits in the minds of the members of the group determining their relations to one another and to the group as a whole."

(5) "The organisation of the group consisting in the differentiation and specialisation of the functions of its constituents."

"This organisation may rest wholly or in part upon (a) the conditions of the fourth class, (b) It may be in part imposed on the group and maintained by the authority of *some external power*" (*The Group Mind*, Ch. III, 1920).

In the group, the individual is not "lost" as he is in the crowd. Indeed, he "finds himself". He makes a distinct contribution to the common cause. Fellowship is creative. A number of individuals thoroughly identify themselves with one another in the promotion of their "ideal Ego." In groups of a less primitive type the place of a Leader may be taken by an idea or common tendency in which the members can share.

Interaction between the person who leads the movement and the Idea that gives the movement life may cause friction. In sects, the bond of union may consist of loyalty to a leader. But this may give way to a "secondary leader", the leadership of an organic idea relating to the support of certain principles, doctrines or modes of worship (usually something that has been either overlaid or neglected by the "regular" Churches).

It is surprising to find Irvingism entirely ignored by Dr. R. H. Murray in his *Group Movements through the Ages* (1936).

When there is conflict between a new sect and an orthodox Church, there is the alternative of schism or integration.

In all ages and in most religions, authority has been wielded by the older men, who belong to the order of the "stable-minded"; to them Religion means the handing down, inviolate, through the traditional channels, of "the faith once delivered to the saints"; unfamiliar ideas are obnoxious, largely through their very unfamiliarity; and there is a strong temptation to impose external unity, without any sincere attempt to meet the objections of "heretics and schismatics".

On the other hand, the supporters of the new sect, who are often younger people (or at least, youthful in spirit), are drawn together by the coldness or hostility of the bulk of the community; and fused by a common enthusiasm, they sink for the time being their differences in the glow of an intimate and self-conscious brotherhood. An obvious case is that of those "Oxford Groupers" to whom the Group means more than the Church. In Germany there are "ecclesiolae in ecclesiasia—"in the Church but not of it" (e.g., the *Gemeinschaften*).

Sometimes, schism is averted by concession on the one hand and forbearance on the other. This is the way of integration. The formation of small groups within larger groups is facilitated, the lesser groups being integrated into the framework of the greater, after the figure of a "hierarchy". Thus a rich and variegated unity may be substituted for a barren uniformity, the flourishing of such integrated groups being a sign of vitality.

When schism occurs through the fault of the general body or the schismatics, or of both, the sap no longer unites the tree and the severed branch. The mental life of the sect degenerates. Instead of finding its completion in ministering to the life of the whole body, it becomes self-centred and antagonistic; it becomes exclusive and forgets that truth is many-sided; that undue insistence on matters previously neglected may lead to a similar neglect of other truths.

It must be remembered, on the other hand, that a sect can achieve results of a kind more rapidly than the Churches. The individual satisfies his social instinct in a sect where brotherhood is easy; he gains emotional enlargement and sense of power.

"But the process of organising the social instincts so as to make possible the all-inclusive group is, as it were, cut short; and the psychic energies being detached from their true end and confined to the narrow loyalty of the sect only serve to deepen and intensify group antagonisms . . . The sect may flourish for a time, but cannot endure. It is an attempt to harmonise human nature on an incomplete basis and in the long run must fail" (*Psychology and the Church* [Macmillan]. Essay by E. J. Bicknell, D.D., on "Psychology of Sectarianism, Schism, and Reunion" pps. 283–84).

§ 4

How does the Irvingite Movement conform to the above "laws" of the Group?

With reference to Professor McDougall's conditions of the "group mind", the condition of "Continuity" is fulfilled in Irvingism. At the beginning of the movement we find as leaders Mary Campbell, Irving, Cardale, Drummond, Baxter, Taplin. Irving died in 1834; Baxter recanted in 1832; Taplin later fell from favour. But Drummond and Cardale guided the movement in the transition from prophecy and glossolalia to the order of the "Catholic Apostolic Church". There was no distinct break, in spite of opposition to the "quenching of prophecy", largely due to this continuity of leadership. And at an earlier stage, the inner conclave of "gifted persons" guided the movement, formed in the minds of the Group a sentiment which became the source of emotion and impulses to action, and promoted the self-consciousness of the group by their hostile attitude to all other groups. With regard to Professor McDougall's fifth condition, in the earlier stage of the movement its organisation depended on the authority "imposed and maintained" by some *external power*. In most groups the external power would be a body of persons; in Irvingism it was "THE POWER", as exercised on passive and receptive minds. In the later stage of Irvingism the organisation depended on Professor McDougall's alternative, "a body of traditions and customs"—viz., an "angel" exercising authority over each congregation, and twelve "apostles" visiting the Churches, imposing discipline in the light of "Catholic Apostolic" principles.

Leadership in Irvingism was largely expressed in a "Secondary Leader". It is true that Irving and Scott preached the Restoration of Apostolic Gifts. But when "gifted persons" took him at his word and responded to the stimulus, they merely made use of his church as a convenient centre, and of his name as a means of obtaining publicity for their manifestations. We have already seen that Irving's will was weak. He began by welcoming these manifestations as God's answer to prayer; then treated his doubts as temptations; gave way to the strong representations of the gifted persons that they should be absolutely free to exercise their gifts; and was deprived of his leadership on being finally deposed by the Church of Scotland.

The real leadership was exercised by "a common tendency, a wish in which a great number of people can share". The craving for gifts (speaking with tongues, prophesying, and healing) diffused throughout the Group, and especially concentrated in the inner conclave, was the real dynamic of the movement. A number of "gifted persons" threw their whole energy into the movement, which individuals like Mrs. Caird, Miss Emily Cardale and Taplin must have identified as their "ideal ego". They felt they had a special mission in the world; they were the mouthpieces of the Holy Ghost. Little wonder that Irvingites, like some mystics in every age, found their highest aspirations ecstatically expressed in the language of sex—e.g.

"Oh, but she shall be fruitful—oh, oh, oh, she shall replenish the earth!" Also, the frequent quotation of Isaiah xxviii. 9. "Whom will he teach knowledge? and whom will he make to understand the message? them that are weaned from the milk, and drawn from the breasts!" Note Irving's defence of Miss Hall at his London Trial— "She is one of the lambs of my flock—she is carried in my bosom." Many other examples could be cited. (Compare Samuel Rutherford and the Scottish Covenanting tradition.)

The Irvingite Movement, partly through the hostility of Protestant Christianity, partly owing to the impetuosity of the "gifted persons", failed to become integrated with the organised Church. It is, in fact, a striking example of the "psychology of sectarianism and schism". Within the group itself there was earnestness, continual prayer, genuine religious experience of an intensely ecstatic type, a sense of brotherhood. So much so that we are not surprised to read of telepathic communication between members of the group—a fact in harmony with Professor McDougall's qualified admission that "telepathy occurs sporadically and only between individuals specially attuned to one another, or in some abnormal mental state that renders them specially sensitive to the influence".

It is worth noting further, that Irving, Cardale, Baxter, and Drummond were comparatively young men, susceptible to enthusiasm and jealous of the authority of their elders. One has only to look through the literature of Irvingism to be confronted with crude immaturity, reckless dogmatism, bitter censoriousness.

The presence of women in the movement has already been emphasised. It is true that Mary Wollstonecraft had published her *Vindication of the Rights of Woman* in 1792. But in 1832 the position of women was still far from elevated; in the middle classes social intercourse was the alternative to housework, for politics and religion were closed to them, and slipshod education put intellectual interests in the background for all but a few. We can therefore understand the enthusiasm of Mary Caird (née Campbell, Emily Cardale and others. For them, prophecy and glossolalia proved to be veritably heaven-sent means of self-expression. And how Irving deferred to them!

The waste of genuine enthusiasm and spiritual energy in the Irvingite Movement is to be deeply deplored. Psychic energy, being short-circuited, worked itself out in explosive outbursts within a very limited sphere, instead of making its contribution to the Church at large; and the attempt to make the charismata the primary characteristic of the Irvingite presentation of Christianity was harmonisation on an incomplete basis, the mistaking of means for ends. "They sacrifice unto their net and burn incense unto their drag" (Habakkuk i. 16).

§ 5

Irvingism and the Methodist Revival

But for Methodism, it is difficult to visualise Irvingism. Wesley redeemed "enthusiasm" from the eighteenth century charge of fanaticism. The Romantic Movement, in a different way, helped to release the sluice-gates of feeling, and give the emotions outward expression. The spiritual climate had grown warmer. But the prejudice against Methodism died hard. Irving, strolling through the fields near Craigenputtock, remarked to the Carlyle brothers:—

"Not a good religion, Sir . . . far too little of spiritual conscience, far too much of temporal appetite. Goes hunting and watching after its own emotions, that is, mainly, its own *nervous-system*; an essentially sensual religion, depending on the body, not on the soul!" "Fit only for a gross and vulgar-minded people," I perhaps added: "a religion so-called and the essence of it principally *cowardice* and *hunger*; terror of pain, and appetite for pleasure, both carried to the infinite?" To which he would sorrowfully assent, in a considerable degree. My brother John, home from Germany, said to me next day, "That was a pretty little *Schilderung* he threw off for us, that of the Methodists, wasn't it?" (*C.R.*, 287).

This portraiture of Methodism would have come more naturally from the Rev. Sydney Smith than from one who was at that time indulging in "prophetic" fanaticism with the Albury obscurantists!

Methodism by 1830 had crystallized from a Society into a Church, without forfeiting entirely its fresh and joyous experimental faith.

A new denomination could hardly arise in the early nineteenth century without being to a large extent unconsciously influenced by its organisation and ideals. The Irvingite fellowship was indeed pre-figured by that "love-feast" of Wesley held in Fetter Lane on 1st January, 1739, described by Whitefield as "a Pentecostal season indeed", when the whole day was spent in fasting in prayer, and the brethren parted "with a full conviction that God was about to do great things among them". All around the early Irvingites were Methodist Class-meetings where men and women met regularly in small groups for mutual exhortation and discipline.

"Methodism presented the emotional experience as something within the range of all persons and in comparison with which all other attainments were insignificant. Learning, creeds and doctrines; social station, wealth and achievement, counted for nothing against this immediate sense and evidence of the presence of God. All who possessed this experience understood each other and felt themselves the fortunate members of a mystic company."

This passage from Ames' *Psychology of Religious Experience* (p. 386) bears out the spirit of an early Methodist letter:—

"We find great power from the Lord in our private band, the Love of God shed abroad in our hearts, our souls knit to one another, we drink of one Spirit and the Lord doth meet us, and that It is no wonder that we are Loth to part for we think four hours too little a time for so heavenly a communion" (MS. letter from M. Summerell to John Wesley).

The Methodist Society, however, was successfully "integrated". The tendency towards unbridled individualism was checked by the building up of each Society into a framework of district, provincial, and national synods, and by the appointment of superintendents and other officials; thus was "Scriptural Holiness" spread over the land, instead of being "bottled up" with explosive effect as in Irvingism, where the only discipline was that of "The Spirit" wielded by a small group of "perfecti" slow to admit outsiders to share in "gifts" which they were merely allowed to admire. And while opposition from without held the Irvingite circle together, bitter dissension made itself felt when the new denomination had firmly established itself, on removal from Regent Square.

Professor J. B. Bury (followed by Mr. and Mrs. Hammond) has tried to explain the Methodist Revival as due to "the failure of nerve"—the loss of self-confidence, diseased introspection—a pathological reaction from the "splendid sanity" of the eighteenth century. Dr. S. G. Dimond has proved that this is not the case as far as Methodism is concerned. He quotes Professor Caldecott's opinion of Wesley's early preachers:—

"Though these young men describe unusually intense emotionality, they were not of ill-balanced nervous systems; they all lived vigorously, and most of them continued laborious pursuits until advanced old age; they were not depressed with the ennui of prematurely-worn-out emotions; nor were they of melancholy temperament. . . . They struggled against the sadness they experienced in the first stage they describe, with an irresistible conviction that it need not be if only joy could be obtained" (*The Psychology of the Methodist Revival*, p. 165).

This statement may be supplemented by M. de Fursac's estimate of many converts of the Welsh Revival of 1905 as "grands, bien developpés . . . rien du pseudo-mystique nevrose et debile, avide de sensations nouvelles".

Irvingism might, however, be ascribed to the failure of nerve, though many other causes were at work. Since the middle of the eighteenth century Methodism had been working like leaven in raising the standard of the neglected and ignorant working classes. Apart from a few exceptional people like Lady Huntingdon, the aristocracy and upper-middle classes stood coldly aside from the Methodist Revival, until the upheaval of the French Revolution, the Napoleonic Wars, and the industrial and political unrest which followed stampeded them into Evangelicalism. Many of the Albury circle were Evangelicals of this type; not merely were they afraid of reason, which they connected with radicalism and infidelity—but the spiritual energy which their ancestors had restrained for over a century now seemed to bubble over, seeking an outlet.

I think it is no exaggeration to describe Irvingism as a crack in the earth through which the pent-up fiery vapours gushed. Compressed steam denied a continually open outlet, will suddenly burst through every restraint. And spiritual energy which is repressed will break out in nervous hysteria, glossolalia, and "prophecy". No one could describe Irvingism as a "religion of healthy-mindedness". As a moralist, Carlyle failed to do justice to the deep-rooted causes and genuine spirituality of the manifestations; but he was perfectly right in describing the manifestations as pathological and unhealthy. Methodism was a national movement, affecting the most distant counties of England. Irvingism at the stage at which we are studying it was confined to Regent Square, and a few rather feeble imitations elsewhere; but this very narrowness of area made for intensity.

As regards Wesley himself, it should be noted that he published an English edition of Jonathan Edwards' *Thoughts on the Present Revival*, with Edwards' strictures on bodily effects removed; natural occurrences he ascribed either to God or the devil, as Irving afterwards did. But Wesley's practical and strongly ethical sense, combined with a gift for leadership, made extravagances the exception rather than the rule. "Bodily effects" might be manifested at his revival meetings, but in spite of his stress on experience rather than on ecclesiastical polity or theology, Methodism has remained within the Catholic Church, while making to it a unique contribution of its own.

There was a conflict of loyalties with Wesley; tradition drew him to the Church of England, and practical necessity to Nonconformity. Irving likewise was continually asserting his loyalty to the Calvinistic standards of the Scottish Church, while various currents, Coleridgean, Millenarian, etc., drew him in practice into a welter of ambiguity. Strong practical sense might even then have saved him, but he foundered like a rudderless barque.

There was little conflict between the sex-appetite and other forces in Wesley's case, owing to the sentiment of vocation—for he believed that he was "a brand plucked from the burning", schooled by a mysterious Providence for a superhuman task. His voluminous correspondence with educated women provided some compensation for his lack of a wife who could be a true spiritual and mental companion; he had no family of his own, but his parental emotion was diffused throughout his societies, and his converts were his children by spiritual adoption. Irving likewise threw his whole weight into the work to which he believed he had been divinely called, an attitude intensified by his growing delusion of "grandeur" and "persecution": he had been called by God to restore the dispensation of the Spirit, and that involved being "persecuted like his fathers".

His married life was happy and there is little evidence that his feverish absorption in Prophecy and Tongues was due to a repressed passion for Jane Welsh.

In concluding the comparison of Irvingism with its much greater predecessor, it may be said that the way was paved for the revival of Apostolic charismata by the Methodist insistence on:

(1) God's immediate action upon human nature. The sense of The Divine was recovered—"the transcendent became again immanent to consciousness". "The life of God in the souls of men", was Wesley's definition of religion.
(2) Pronounced emotional sensibility.
(3) The recovery of the Holy Spirit as a dynamic in human experience.
(4) Universal grace: "Assurance": the possibility of "Christian Perfection" (the last of which was held by Irvingites in an exaggerated form).

CHAPTER XVI

THE IRVINGITE MOVEMENT IN THE LIGHT OF PSYCHOLOGY (*continued*)

> "The whole drift of my education goes to persuade me that the world of our present consciousness is only one of many worlds of consciousness; and that although in the main *their* experiences and those of this world keep discrete, yet the two become continuous at certain points and higher energies filter in."—WILLIAM JAMES.

§ I

The Subconscious

SINCE the time of William James study of the subconscious has been deepened and extended, and a flood of light thrown upon such abnormal phenomena as hallucination, hypnotism, automatism, and double personality, which were previously denied, or ascribed to divine or diabolic agency.

The subconscious is

"the abode of everything that is latent, the reservoir of everything that passes unrecorded or unobserved. It contains, for example, such things as all our momentarily inactive memories, and it harbours the springs of all our obscurely motived passions, impulses, likes, dislikes, and prejudices; our intentions, hypotheses, fancies, superstitions, persuasions, convictions, and in general all our non-rational operations come from it.

"It is the source of our dreams. . . . In it may arise whatever mystical experiences we may have, and our automatism, sensory or motor; our life in hypnotic and hypnoid conditions; our delusions, fancies, ideas . . . if we are hysterical subjects; our supra-normal cognitions, if such there be, and if we are telepathic subjects.

"It is also the fountain-head of much that feeds our religion. In persons deep in the religious life, as we have abundantly seen—and this is my conclusion—the door into this region seems unusually wide open; at any rate experiences making their entrance through that door have had emphatic influence in shaping religious history" (*Varieties of Religious Experience*, p. 483f, 1929 ed.).

The subconscious self is the result of the activities of the conscious, rather than the source and fountain head of the conscious, as F. W. H. Myers urged. The subconscious mind is our own mind as we have ourselves built it up. The thousands of impressions that come to us daily (sights, sounds, trivial acts and words) disappear like the dead leaves of the forest, but like dead leaves form the very soil from which the future giants of the forest spring. The subconscious enters into every new experience, and absorbs it, thus modifying the self for good or evil. "We cannot step into the same stream twice, nor can we step into it twice the same man; we have become another man by stepping into it once."

In the mind of man are a number of "systems of thought", sometimes blending, sometimes becoming entirely separate. The appropriate stimulus will call now one system of ideas, now another, from the margin of the field of consciousness into focus.

A man's interests will determine the strength of the various systems of ideas; the appropriate stimulus will tend to draw subordinate interests in the train of dominant interests where possible, inhibiting them where impossible. The very meaning of words such as "home", "love", "religion", "Bible", will differ according to a man's dominant system of thought. Facility and skill tend to become subconscious the more a man devotes himself wholeheartedly to a trade or accomplishment—even, in a sense, to the "religious life" for the more a man prays the easier will he find concentration. Sudden impulses and decisions are the response to a man's total experience of life. The subconscious mind is always in harmony with the personality, different, we may admit, from what we *think* we are, but not from what we really are. Hence, we sometimes look back on some impulsive action and say quite truthfully, "I really don't know why I behaved like that".

The subconscious will now be examined in its bearing on the various abnormal manifestations of the Irvingite Movement. It is an exhaustless fountain head for ever pouring out fresh conceptions as from some unseen laboratory—not merely a storehouse but a workshop.

§ 2

"Dual Personality"—the Case of Robert Baxter

"Dissociation of the mind into logic-tight compartments", says Bernard Hart, "is by no means confined to the population of the asylum. It is a common and perhaps inevitable occurrence in the psychology of every human being." We are each of us many "personalities" in our conscious states. As business men, family men, churchmen, citizens, —we tend to call up different systems of ideas in each sphere, inhibiting other systems. By suggestion and imitation—the herd, the group, personal likes and dislikes—our ideas tend to be irrational (e.g., our political convictions are notoriously inaccessible to argument). Without being consciously a hypocrite, a man may be a good churchman but a "sharp" business man, or an upright business man but a household tyrant. With many men, acute conflict is avoided by keeping the different spheres of life in rigid, water-tight compartments.

Psychologists have noted extreme cases of dissociation. Morton Prince has familiarised us with "multiple personality" through his *Sally Beauchamp*. William James tells of the Rev. Ansel Bourne, an itinerant preacher, who on 17th January, 1887, drew a considerable sum from the bank at Providence, R.I., and entered a tram. On 14th March one A. J. Brown, who had rented a small shop six weeks before and was described by neighbours as not in any way eccentric, woke up in a fright, declared his name was Ansel Bourne, and that the last thing he remembered was drawing money from the bank at Providence.

With normal individuals the field of consciousness resembles a continuous ciné film: in cases of dissociation such as Bourne's, there is as it were an abrupt change to another film.

There is

"a splitting off of the stream of consciousness into two streams. These may be of co-ordinate complexity; but more frequently one of them seems to be a mere trickle diverted from the main stream of personal consciousness. It is not possible to prove that such disintegration of the personal consciousness actually takes place. But the facts appear to many psychologists . . . to demand this interpretation." A division of the nervous system takes place "comparable with the division of the nervous system of a worm by the stroke of the knife, which seems to split the psychical individual in two" (McDougal, *The Group Mind*. p. 32).

The case of Baxter is intermediate between absolute dissociation such as Bourne's and the cases of disintegrated but artificially unified lives which are so much more common.

Baxter was one of those ecstatics who retire into the world of daydreams and immerse themselves with efficiency in an imaginary world.

"The phantasy created by his own mind acquires the tang of actual reality. He has crossed the barrier which separates in the normal man daydreams from the dreams that accompany sleep, and the creations of an idle fancy have become the delusions of the lunatic. A further degree of dissociation has been attained, and the complexes achieve a luxuriant expression undisturbed by the flagrant contradictions which experience everywhere presents to them" (B. Hart, *Psychology of Insanity*, p. 148).

But we have seen that Baxter was not the type of crack-brained enthusiast who is fit for nothing but the "religion" in which he has immersed himself; he was not an introvert absolutely. If he was a successful lawyer, so was Finney, the American revivalist; if in later life he was an able writer on economics, it will be remembered that George Fox and John Woolman were excellent business men. Indeed, Professor J. F. Rees of Birmingham has noted in Economic History the not unusual combination of business aptitude with religious heterodoxy. If Baxter outdid such men in eccentricity, it still remains true that

"a man may have a delusion on one point and be sane on all others . . . where a definite insane delusion exists, it is by no means easy to determine how far its influence extends in the mental sphere" (Lord Justice Cockburn. Quoted, G. R. Jeffrey, M.D., F.R.S.E., *Common Symptoms of an Unsound Mind*).

Baxter seems to have been one of those "educated, widely experienced men" cited by E. S. Ames. Such an individual

"mingles with many classes, and is identified with various groups in business, professional, and neighbourhood life. *Yet the standards of his ideal interests may be those of still another set*" (*Psychology of Religious Experience*, p. 378).

Baxter's *Narrative* gives us the impression that he was typical of his age in his rigid separation of religion from ordinary life. At first, religion was "a mere trickle diverted from the main stream of personal consciousness". Yet he seems to have been a regular churchgoer, devoted to good works all his life, though his horizon was limited to the outlook of narrow Tory Church-and-State Anglicanism. In Chapter XII, Baxter is described as "a fervid evangelical". As the *Narrative* was written after his Irvingite experiences, and without any account of his previous life, beyond a distinct enunciation of his political and ecclesiastical creed, we are not entitled to assume that he was an evangelical before his conversion to Irvingism. It must be remembered that before the Oxford Movement, the High Church Party, of which he was a zealous adherent, was distinctly Protestant in doctrine, while conserving some elements of Laudian Anglicanism: it was "high" in its support of the throne, nobility, and Establishment; its religious temperature was low, its preaching moralist, its enthusiasm confined to attacks on Methodists, Dissenters, and Liberals generally.

Baxter's potential spiritual energies had evidently been repressed; he had a craving for a religion deeper than he could find in his own circle, and he drank deep of Irvingism. At first, curiosity led him to an Irvingite meeting; being "seized in the power", he struggled against it and for many weeks there was an internal conflict, ended only by his whole-hearted surrender to the new movement. Throughout his Irvingite experiences he reached convictions "irrespective of the slow processes by which the mind ordinarily reaches them . . . though an apparently logical chain of proof was always, at the moment, given for the conclusion."

His ordinary professional duties he seems to have performed with the ease of successful practice, enabling him to throw his whole weight into the Irvingite Movement. He almost succeeded in immersing himself in day-dreams which became delusions, cutting him off from the everyday world. Continual brooding on the Second Coming of Christ at the end of three years and a half, and on the Restoration of the Apostolic Age with its gifts and portents of coming doom, which was a matter of immediate urgency, had filled his subconscious mind with a store of varied fancies. There were—first, his former antipathies to Romanism, infidelity, and "liberalism"; images from the Bible (of which he was a zealous student) particularly from Daniel, Revelation, and the Prophets; historical facts, interpreted ecclesiastically (particularly of the last forty years); and Irving's stress on the Spirit working in men, as in a Christ whose humanity was emphasised. Daily happenings "suggested" further material, and though the import of these happenings was not appreciated at the time, the subconscious was at work fitting every event into the predominant scheme of ideas. Thus, "fire" in connection with Carmel, mentioned in Baxter's prophecy regarding the proposed national fast, followed by other references to fire, led to the revelation that *he* would be "baptised with fire". He lived in deadly fear of his reason. The superior faculties, reflection and will, were in abeyance—as far as religion was concerned. Hypnosis was induced by the subject himself. His passive mind received impressions, which were phantastically mingled in the subconscious, placed in the dominant system of ideas, and brought to the surface in the form of revelations. The crude fruit of the subconscious was eagerly accepted by Baxter as the fruit of the Spirit.

The faculty of "rationalising" was developed to a surprising extent in him, as well as in the Irvingite circle generally. When power of utterance failed him at the Court of Chancery, painful mental conflict was ended by the feeling that it was "discernment he lacked". This was followed by a command to "flee away and be separate". The more testing revelation to throw up his professional career, leave his wife and family, opposed by the common sense of the conclave, indeed opened his eyes to the fact that he was not only endangering his "worldly prospects" (of which he had been conscious during his agony in Chancery), but also "sent his wife a lying torture" and "ensured his brother's expulsion from the Church". But this was merely a temporary revulsion. He felt he had again "mistaken" the meaning of the message, and a letter from his wife confirmed his faith. "Baptism with fire" had not taken place on the fortieth day, as prophesied, because the church in London had failed in love towards the Lord; but it would actually occur at Doncaster. And when fulfilment did not even come about at Doncaster, instead of being finally disillusioned, he continued to seek for it for *six weeks*, finally satisfying himself that "fire" signified "the burning out of the carnal mind". And the "exorcism" in Gloucestershire acted as a final confirmation.

The veil is torn from Baxter's eyes again and again. On the brink of stepping over the precipice, his practical sense inhibits action. But he pauses only to re-adjust the veil, and then proceeds to scale even dizzier heights of imagination. It is almost an anticlimax to find him brought to a final halt, not by the failure of his revelations, but by examination of the *bases of the movement*. He suddenly feels that his magnificent structure has been reared on the foundation of Mr. Irving's heresy, and that he, Baxter—the vindicator of orthodoxy—had been led in his blindness by a leader who was a heretic. That leads him to consider utterances made in the Spirit. How could true utterances be distinguished from false? Was there any difference in mode?

The fact is, that the pent-up cistern of overflowing spiritual energy had emptied itself. The intellect which Baxter had so far despised, was brought to bear on the movement, with the result that thoughts coming up from the subconscious were no longer passively received and passed into action; they were now critically examined in relation to the facts of life. The extreme subjectivity of the whole movement was exposed. It is true that he had struggled against "the power"; his *will* had inhibited the extreme steps of leaving his wife and throwing up his profession. But only his *reason* could prove that "the light that was in him was darkness", both in principle and in practice. "For when the will and the imagination are at war, the imagination invariably gains the day" (Baudouin).

At last Baxter's intellect reinforced his will and his strong emotion. "A threefold cord is not quickly broken" (Eccles. iv: 12).

§ 3

Glossolalia Analysed

F. W. H. Myers, in a contribution to *Proceedings of the Society for Psychical Research*, urged that each case of automatic writing or speaking should be carefully examined with reference to the actual message given, so that the automatist might be classed as (1) insane (2) or as a person in whom subliminal uprushes are unusually facile (3) or as a person in some sense inspired with a fuller knowledge than other men, either by their own hidden spirit, or their faculty of transmitting messages from some morally indifferent, sublimely good, or revolting evil source (S.P.R. XII, p. 296).

The Rev. D. Frazer-Hurst, of Belfast, lecturing at the Edinburgh Psychic College on "Edward Irving and the Gift of Tongues", came to the conclusion that Irvingite glossolalia was the result of *unrealised* or *latent* mediumship.

"There were thousands of people who possessed psychic endowment unknown to themselves, and given favouring conditions of emotional fervour, strong suggestion, and contact with many people in a like state of emotional tension, a psychic release took place. The door was off the latch, and some wander-spirit might strive to utter himself or herself. Hence the strange convulsions, the trembling of the body, the closed eyes, the gnashing of the teeth, and the inarticulate sounds. It was the throes of undeveloped mediumship. At times a message of real value and beauty might be transmitted, but at other times only a strange jargon of words" (*The Scotsman*, 29th June, 1935).

Irvingite glossolalia bears the marks of extreme subjectivity, though here and there perhaps there is trace of more objective utterance. It may be emphatically stated that the evidence before us points to the subconscious.

"Under the pressure of great excitement one or more individuals begin to express their emotions by pouring out a broth of meaningless syllables, which they and those around them take to belong to some unknown language. This gibberish of syllables and new-made sounds is of course not all invented on the spur of the moment. Try to talk nonsense for five minutes and you will see. Some real words will now and then come out. Especially will this be the case with those who think they are speaking some language not their own and who happen to know a few words of some other tongue. In the volley of meaningless sounds which they pour forth they will be pretty sure to include specimens of whatever foreign tongue they know and now and then a word of their own language" (J. B. Pratt, *The Religious Consciousness*, p. 183f.).

Overpowering and explosive emotion is often in excess of ideas and words. Thus we find a man crying out at a New York camp-meeting:—"Brethren, I feel—I feel—I feel—I feel—I feel—I can't tell you how I feel, but O

I feel! I feel!" And Davenport quotes an account of early Mormon glossolalia to the same effect:—

"Those who speak in tongues are generally the most illiterate among the 'saints', such as cannot command words as quick as they would wish, and instead of waiting for a suitable word to come to their memories *they break forth in the first sound their tongues can articulate, no matter what it is.* E.g., 'My heart is glad to overflowing—I hope to go to Zion and to see you there and to—to—O, me sontro von te, sontro von terre. O me palassate te . . . etc.'" (*Primitive Traits*, p. 236).

Irving declared that "the utterance in English is far more trying than the utterance in the unknown tongue". He meant, of course, that human associations, feelings and prejudices might mar the divine quality of the utterance. In the former case, his mind would be quasi-passive, sufficiently active to articulate English words with a meaning, yet tortured by doubts as to whether the utterance was really spiritual, or merely "carnal"; in the latter case, granted a passive mind and emotion wrought up to a sufficient pitch of intensity, the subject allowed himself to be borne along by the current.

In Glossolalia the subject may put himself in a hypnotic passive condition, narrowing down consciousness to the smallest possible point, and making the object he desires central in all his thoughts. A suitable stimulus, control inhibited, will produce a sudden shifting of ideas from the subconscious into the focus of attention. This will be greatly facilitated by practice.

Professor Kirsopp Lake has pointed out that one of the most notable advances in pathology is the discovery that movement, sight and speech are under the control of definite parts of the brain (*Earlier Epistles of St. Paul*, p. 247ff.). The impeding of a speech centre will produce dumbness, and in less acute cases aphasia (inability to use certain words) or paraphasia (a tendency to confuse words). On the other hand, anything which will increase activity of the speech centre will increase power of speech. Several glasses of alcohol will remove normal inhibition (instinctive caution, perception of the possibility of misunderstanding, etc.); but when the drinker goes from glasses to bottles, the result will be incoherence, leading to entire paralysis of the working of the speech centre. Any strong emotion has the same result, which is in proportion to the intensity of the emotion. A novice will have difficulty in public speaking. A minister or advocate will speak with the ease that is born of practice and conviction. A red-hot evangelist may rise to address an audience with only a rough outline of his address in the focus of consciousness; as he warms up words and illustrations will surge up from the subconscious, in keeping with his religious experience, though unpremeditated. At the apex of the pyramid, so to speak, we have the man who speaks "in the power"; he is absolutely "worked up", and is carried along by the whirl of emotion; a confused mass of scarcely-formed words run together, and tumbling one after another. There is an ascent; essay-reading, preaching, prophesying, and speaking with tongues. Thus the subconscious operates in conjunction with speech-centres.

The form of utterance will be determined by the particular obsession with which the subconscious is soaked. This may not necessarily be religion, though it very generally is. When religion is the dominant power, the powerful suggestion is naturally that derived from Acts and 1 Corinthians. "To speak in an unknown tongue is Biblical." The N.T. speaks of it as a peculiar sign of the presence of the Holy Ghost. Thus, when a man is sure from the intensity of his feelings that the indwelling Holy Ghost is labouring to get free and thrill others, he is likely to end by speaking in tongues. In every age there have been Pentecostal communities.

The English part of the utterance (in Irvingite circles "four or ten times as long as the unknown" part), as an "interpretation", would depend on intonation, gesture, expression, and the conventional ideas uppermost at the meeting, a few recognisable words acting as a clue. It will be remembered, however, that Pilkington's attempt to translate the unknown part was strongly resented by the conclave as a pervertion of its true end. Pilkington's facile explanation of the tongues as "English, Spanish and Latin" was shallow and crude; the cause might not be the Holy Spirit, but it was certainly preternatural. Yet the foreign language element undoubtedly supplied part of the content of Irvingite glossolalia. Taplin was a teacher. Mr. Cardale was a keen linguist. Baxter knew Latin and French—his wife Italian and a little Spanish. Young men who were teachers used to meet in the evenings in Irving's house. Miss Hall was a governess.

But how can an adequate explanation be offered to cover the cases where the speaker was entirely ignorant of any foreign language? Such cases must have been far less common in Irvingism than in other Pentecostal Communities, confined to less cultured people. At the same time they must be accounted for.

Physiologists as early as Dr. John Abercrombie (1780-1844) had noticed the phenomenon of the preternatural excitement of memory, which tended to be most vigorous and overmastering when its subjects were least cultured. He himself instances the case of an awkward servant, who in sleep imitated elaborate pieces of music clearly and accurately, and could conjugate Latin verbs; it was impossible to waken her, even by bringing a lighted candle near her face; she became immoral and latterly insane.

Coleridge mentioned the case of a woman in a Roman Catholic town in Germany, who was heard talking in Latin, Greek, and Hebrew during a fever. Whole sheets of her ravings were taken down and found to consist of sentences intelligible in themselves, but having slight connection with each other. A doctor afterwards discovered that since the age of nine she had been servant to a great Hebrew scholar, in whose home she had lived till her death. It had been the old man's custom for years to read aloud to himself. Dr. Dawson Walker also tells of a lady placed under an anæsthetic for an operation, who talked voluble French during "suspended consciousness", though it was completely unknown to her; her husband was a teacher of languages.

The more limited the range of the conscious mental faculty, the more potent is preternatural memory when the subject is in a passive state. Thus a simple-looking African repeated with uncommon precision a sermon of Dr. Moffat's on *"Eternity"* and touching his forehead, said—"When I hear anything great, it remains *there*". Thus bands of ignorant Camisard children in 1700 preached sermons in excellent French, which they were quite incapable of doing normally, knowing only the district patois. (*See* R. Heath, "Little Prophets of the Cevennes", *Contemporary Review*, January, 1886). Thus young men and women in the Welsh Revival of 1904, who could not speak a dozen words in Welsh in ordinary conversation, could engage in public prayer for five or ten minutes in idiomatic Welsh, which to the onlooker would suggest familiarity with the language (*Yorkshire Post*, 27th December, 1904).

To seek a solution, we must deal with the questions asked by Edgar Quinet, as far back as 1825:—

"How far do the memories of the species reflect themselves in the individual? How do such memories harmonise with his own impressions? What law do they impose on his personal activity?

"He who would understand history must consent first of all to look into himself and become attentive to the movements of his own mind. He who truly does this will discover buried there the whole series of the past ages."

This theory is borne out by Haeckel and Hering: "We are one person with our ancestors".

The extent to which the memory of the species is unconsciously transmitted will depend on the relative strength of certain traits. When we read of children aged from three to fifteen not merely preaching, but interrogating their elders on their secret motives, in spite of threatened punishment, we must realise that for 150 years the Cevennes had been the scene of Protestant martyrdom; for fifteen years persecution had been intensified—pastors exiled, men executed, women sent to nunneries or hounded to death by dragoons. The children's sermons were mere "composite photographs" of Camisard preaching; certified "sane" by the Medical Faculty at Montpellier the young preachers were treated as "fanatics" by the Government. Their religious consciousness was overflowing with the intense faith of their ancestors. To a much smaller extent, one hundred years of vital evangelical experience surged up in the minds and hearts of the young Welshmen of 1904.

The cases just cited refer to (I) Foreign words soaked in by the subconscious, unknown to the subject, and brought up when the mind is passive. (e.g., Coleridge's and Dawson Walker's case.)

(II) Unusually clear speaking in the case of the Camisard children and young Welshmen, where one would least expect it—attributed to the transmission of religious traits, the reflection of the species in the individual. To "nature" we must add: "nurture".

"The everyday utterances, the likes and dislikes of a man's parents, their social and caste feelings, their religious persuasions are absorbed . . . assimilated and made his own" (Francis Galton, *Human Faculty*).

What light do these parellels throw on Irvingite glossolalia?

(I) It is evident that cases such as those mentioned by Coleridge and Walker are very similar to the glossolalia we are examining. Glossolalia, however (*a*) was induced by emotional stress, rather than by fever or anæsthetics—the common feature being the emptying of the subconscious in a passive state. (*b*) The cases of Coleridge and Walker are isolated: in Irvingite glossolalia we have a collective movement with its psychological implications, not to speak of the fixed ideas which create a channel for the forces at work.

(II) Glossolalia differs from the inspired speaking of the Welshmen and Camisards in being unusually obscure, instead of being unexpectedly clear: the common characteristic is that the words are spoken "in the power". A *direct* parallel is that of the twins in Gloucestershire, which we have noticed in dealing with Baxter's *Narrative;* they spoke in the power and ordered their elders about, partly through inheriting a nervous psychic temperament, partly through the example of their parents and governess; "nature" and "nurture" co-operated pathologically.

In a general sense we can speak of the reflection of the species in the individual, in connection with the Irvingite Movement, though the "reflection" far outdid the original.

Irving himself came of Covenanting stock, as we have seen, attending a Secession meeting house as a boy, entering into a world of imagination and poetry, which served as a relief from the monotony of a dull country town. The confused blend of dogmatism and mysticism, the sense of being "specially called" and being "persecuted like his fathers"—these traits were characteristic of certain Covenanting types. Among the Irving forefathers moreover was a family of French Protestant refugees (the Howys), one of whom had become parish minister of Annan; Huguenot fervour may have at last found expression in Edward Irving. His mother's family, the Lowthers—grazier farmers —were genial giants, essentially "characters".

A. J. Scott and Mary Campbell came from the shores of the Clyde, where the religious tradition of the region was a warm pietistic mysticism. Henry Drummond was of Scottish stock, transplanted several generations before to England. It would be interesting if relationship could be traced between Robert Baxter and his great namesake Richard Baxter: it is worth noting that Richard Baxter had a "settled hatred of fanaticism", made a deep study of the Holy Spirit, but was strongly opposed to the restoration of Apostolic "gifts". But a century of dull moralism separated the two Baxters, and the influence (not always direct) of the Evangelical Revival was the real source for Irvingite converts, in England at least.

§ 4

Conclusion

Professor F. R. Barry has pointed out the present tendency to equate religion with sheer "feeling", to make it a matter of temperament.

"What, then, of those who do not share this temperament? Is there no religious experience for them? This is all a recrudescence of the peril which beset the primitive Church of the first generation. Behind the books of the N.T. one can detect precisely the same tendency to identify the 'Christian experience' with certain psychological phenomena which seem often to have accompanied it. But they are the accident and not the essence. Any religion can make people 'speak with tongues'. It was St. Paul and St. John who saved the Church from so disastrous an equation. They said what needs to be said today with emphasis, that no intensity of feeling guarantees the value of an experience, or gives any real explanation of it. It is the content of experience, not its feeling tone, that matters. We must 'try the spirits, whether they be of God'. To stress religious experience is sound: but it leaves us in a swamp of morbid psychology unless we bring it all to the test of an objective standard of truth and value" (*Christianity and Psychology*, p. 123, 1924).

The truth or falsity of a prophet's message is not decided by his excitability, but by the intrinsic value of what he says. The most that can be said of glossolalia and kindred concomitants of ecstatic religion, is that they are to be expected under certain mental and physical conditions:

IN THE LIGHT OF PSYCHOLOGY

when the crisis is past, the healed and integrated Christian must proceed from the rudimentary and primitive to the rational and spiritual. Davenport has pointed out that those who give way habitually to emotion are the relatively untrained elements of society whose spinal ganglia and *lower* brain centres are more highly developed than the higher rational and volitional faculties that have their throne in the grey matter of the cortex.

"When the sensation passes along the *afferent* nerve, the impulse to action is at once delivered over the *efferent* nerve to the muscle. But if the higher centres of inhibition are well developed, and the current of sensation or a part of it is deflected into the brain, the sensation or complex of sensations is detained, so to speak, and the whole cortical apparatus of the cerebrum may be brought to bear upon the matter in the process of reflection" (Davenport, *Primitive Traits in Religious Revivals* p. 243f.).

(*a*) The brain may decide that it is proper for the muscles to act, and will in that case re-enforce the impulse.

(*b*) Or it may inhibit the impulse, and the whole life of reflective action is begun.

The two processes may be illustrated by the following diagram:—

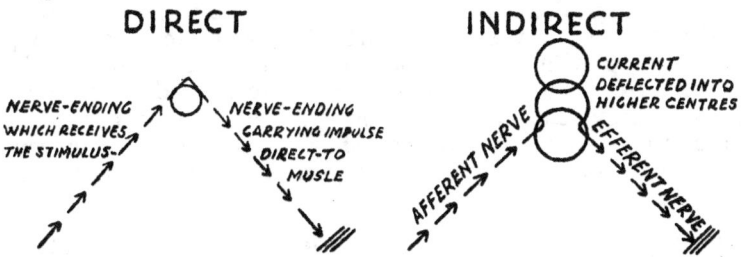

The above process is not hard-and-fast; a glance at the Appendix will show there are varying degrees of facility with which suggestible persons will react to stimuli. But it is undoubtedly the case that in most instances of glossolalia, the higher rational and volitional faculties of the subjects are undeveloped. And in the cases which were so numerous in Irvingism of educated people "speaking in tongues", continual opposition to "the snare of the intellect" combined with absolute passivity when the "power" was about to descend, resulted in a low mental level—in practice. Such people, often with absolute sincerity, believed that they had to become as drift-logs on the current of divine purpose, "as nothing in floods and waterspouts of God", surrendering everything—intellect, talents, social pleasures.

"If the heart, at high tide, swamp the brain now and then,
"'Twill be richer for that when the tide turns again."

But it is difficult to believe that the Holy Spirit deliberately chooses as His field of operations the slime of the subliminal, the lower mystical marshlands of the human spirit, while avoiding the sunlit hills of full rational consciousness. "By their fruits ye shall know them", it was decided nineteen centuries ago. To go back on that is to find ourselves at Delphi or the still cruder shrine of the witch-doctor. And, believe Paul, the mature fruit of the Spirit is not the subliminal uprush, the ecstatic flow of emotion, the rhapsody, the lapse of inhibition, but rational love, joy, peace, long-suffering, kindness, goodness, faithfulness, meekness, self-control.

Bushnell declared that abnormal spiritual phenomena ("these prodigies") were merely signs and tokens.

"Their propagation . . . is therefore no principal interest of Christianity, and the living power of Christianity is never to be tested by their frequency, or the impressiveness of their operations. . . . When the world that ought to be repenting is taken up with staring, the sobriety of faith is lost in the gospel of credulity. And then, instead of a solid, ever-during reign of providence . . . we should have a glittering firework around us, that really governs nothing, has no power to regenerate souls, or strengthen the kingdom of Christ in the earth" (*Nature and the Supernatural*, p. 316f).

And representatives of a very different school of theology have definitely limited the value of special "gifts", e.g., St. Theresa: "There are many saints who do not know what it is to receive one such favour, while others who receive them are not saints at all." The author of *The Cloud of Unknowing*, says:

"All other comforts, sounds, and gladness and sweetness that come from without suddenly and thou wottest never whence, I pray thee have them in suspect. For they may be both good or evil."

Men tend to be quite primitive spiritually, in spite of the advanced political, social and material progress which unconsciously affects their ideas. While a few open-minded theologians endeavour in every age to bring dogma into vital relationship with the needs of the day, and a few secularists (without much sympathetic study of the faith that has sustained millions in the past) reject it in favour of the exact scientific knowledge of the present, the mass of the people accept dogma dully, as transmitted from father to son. When there is a revival, restricted or extended in scope, the body of doctrines which formerly lay inert in the background of consciousness come into the foreground and become realities. "The expulsive power of a new affection" may then become the true dynamic in a man's life, but the doctrinal material which quickly comes into use is too often antiquated and crude. The convert's emotions have been touched, and genuine spiritual life surges up. But the intellect remains unenlightened; arbitrary yet traditional interpretations of Christianity are eagerly and fanatically embraced. Faith is conceived of as the wholesale assimilation of the body of doctrines transmitted, and the use of the intellect is regarded with such horror that the irrational is gloried in, and the way paved for delusions such as Baxter's. "*Credo quia impossibile.*"

Such zealots have no historical perspective. They have a clear-cut stock of ideas to which everything must conform. The Apostolic Age must be imitated in every possible way, regardless of changed conditions. The supernatural was a reality to the men and women of the New Testament: it must therefore be revived in exactly the same form to-day. Those to whom the new life has been vouchsafed imagine that they in particular are the salt of the earth, to whom the restoration of true religion has been entrusted. The mildest criticism confirms them in their views; anything approaching persecution is like wind to their sails; they feel they are indeed on the level of the martyrs and apostles.

These remarks apply to the various attempts to resuscitate Apostolic Charismata in the backwaters of the Christian Church throughout the centuries, particularly to the Irvingite manifestations. It is true that the Irvingite Movement was a protest against a lethargic rationalism which imprisoned God in natural law, had no sense of the urgency of the Gospel Call, and no experience of Christianity at first-hand.

"Let Him now break forth in miracle and holy gifts, let it be seen that He is still the living God in the midst of His dead people . . . They see in His gifts that the Scripture stands, that the graces and works of the apostolic age are also for them. It is as if they had now a proof experimental of the resources embodied in the Christian plan. The living God, immediately revealed, and not historically only, begets a feeling of present life and power, and religion is no more a tradition, a second-hand light, but operative *now*" (Bushnell, *ibid.*, p. 318).

Had the Irvingite Movement broken out in the earlier eighteenth century when the Churches were most dead and conventional and the fresh springs of religion almost evaporated, the sudden reaction would have been natural and welcome in spite of its excesses. But it broke out after the Evangelical Revival had been transforming the character of England for the past sixty years. Even if its base had been broader, it is doubtful whether it could have exerted much influence. It corrected some of the errors of current evangelicalism perhaps, but tended to produce most of its faults in an exaggerated form—fear of the intellect, self-righteousness, a bitter and acrimonious spirit, blindness to the Industrial Revolution which was covering the country with hideous mushroom towns inhabited by an under-paid and brutalised population. Yet one cannot but admire Irvingite fervour, and wish that it had circulated throughout the Churches of Britain, instead of being short-circuited —flaring up to provide food for journalists and the religious psychologists of a later day! The net result was the birth of a posthumous offspring, another new sect, belying in many respect its origin. This critique of Irvingite Glossolalia may be summed up in the words of Dean Inge:—

"The operation of the Holy Spirit must not be looked for in any abnormal, violent or mysterious psychical experiences. Such convulsions have indeed in some cases marked the awakening into a new life; like a volcanic upheaval, they have brought to the surface hidden strata of the subconscious life; but generally it is by the small voice, not by the earthquake or fire, that God speaks to us. And the wish to empty ourselves of our own personality, to empty ourselves that God may fill the void, is a mistake. It is when we are most ourselves that we are nearest God" (*Faith and Knowledge*, p. 167f).

CHAPTER XVII

IRVING'S PERSONALITY

" Edward Irving was a sent man, but they who are sent sometimes go further than they ought."—WILLIAM BLAKE.

IRVING'S heredity was essentially religious. He sprang from a stock soaked in the Covenanting traditions of South Western Scotland. He may be classified as belonging to the "Dogmatic-Emotional" type of Scottish piety, which was nourished on such books as Samuel Rutherford's *Letters*. Dogma was fired by imagination and warmed by unction—a contrast to the hard, unbending Calvinism of the North East.

We have seen that Irving found an outlet for the imaginative and emotional side of his nature in attending the Secession meeting-house at Ecclefechan. The prophetic note, the heroic memories of the past—and also the controversial spirit of the seventeenth century maintained in country places (despite Carlyle's definition of the Secession Church as "*Free Kirk* making no noise ")—all contributed to the bent of the boy's soul. His absorption in old-world writers and divines in his student days further gave him the appearance of having been cast in another mould from that of the age in which he lived. On the other hand, his splendid physique and love of the open-air, his genial spirit, quite removed him from the "narrow-nebs". He would laugh heartily and without malice at some of his "road-companions", e.g., "Wullie Drummond", the little tailor with mournful goggle-eyes, and "Joe Blacklock", the rickety weaver with his protruding chin and one leg too short for the other. No healthy youth could take these people and their "testimonies" too seriously. Irving never seems to have thought of entering the Secession Ministry. As a student he made friends of people who could not possibly be called unbalanced or inclined to fanaticism.

On the intellectual side, the friendship of Carlyle and Coleridge, on the social side, the gentle refinements of the Welshes, and the genial business contacts of Glasgow, would be calculated to adjust any over-balance. The realities of Glasgow slums and the practical idealism of Chalmers would surely correct any bias to visionary notions. Few young Scottish ministers in London have had Irving's opportunity of meeting the greatest minds of the age and of seeing people of culture and influence going out of their way to hear him.

One cannot speak of "intoxicating popularity" without considerable qualification; even in his unpopular Kirkcaldy days, Carlyle could detect a certain inflation, a self-conscious affected manner that gradually became second-nature. His nature was not without a strain of self-esteem and "love of being loved", but this was strangely mingled with humility. He believed himself to be "a prophet of righteousness to the great city," and did not hesitate to attack vested interests and popular prejudice alike. When the tide of success receded, there was little sign of mortified ambition; *that* merely threw him back on the divine resources of a God Whose supernatural intervention would save the world. His humility in the presence of prophetic devotees and "gifted persons" has an element of true pathos. He made no effort to speak in tongues or prophesy; "he aspired to be no more than the humble pastor of the flock". He allowed a group of zealots, many of them outsiders, to fasten barnacle-like on his Church, and with resignation accepted a nominal position in the sect established in Newman Street. His actual management of the manifestations was distinctly muddle-headed. He had prayed for the coming of the "gifts", but never worked out any technique by which true utterances could be distinguished from false—apart from Paul's tests which were not easy to apply in the totally different circumstances of the nineteenth century. Sometimes he thought of the "gifted persons" as mere trumpets who yielded themselves as instruments for the Divine Voice: at other times, he thought of them rather as intelligent and conscious men and women. When he "tried the spirits" in private, he "could not charge his memory" with the particulars. He himself was once publicly denounced "in the power"! On one occasion he expressed his doubts as to glossolalia in church. His assistant David Brown, a close observer of the phenomena, advised: "Don't do it whilst you have a doubt." Whereupon Robert Baxter cried out in a most fearful voice "that if the manifestations were of God, who could hesitate to argue with them?" Inevitably, this led to a credulity that gloried in anti-intellectualism and treated seriously the most feeble utterances.

Canon J. G. Simpson has pointed out that lack of a real sense of humour was one cause of Irving's excesses. He could indulge in "Homeric laughter" of a loud and cheery kind. But he never saw anything incongruous in taking himself too seriously. He would address a casual controversialist, "Who art thou, O man! that smitest me with thy tongue?" He would begin an argument with the words: "Men and brethren, I do you to wit." He would ask such a protracted blessing at a meal that the viands were too cold to eat. Every speech must be an oration, his pulpit a national forum, the "tongues" indisputably the direct work of the Holy Ghost. Luxury, rationalism, and unbelief assumed monstrous forms. The distant ages of faith lured him on irresistibly. His judgement became more and more *absolute;* he became impatient of time and place as limiting conditions. His words and actions reveal a certain lack of both historic sense and common sense. He was one who had trusted friends, but unfortunately he did not follow their advice. Too late, he confessed to Henry Drummond: "I ought to have seen more of Thomas Carlyle, and heard him more clearly than I have done."

He had "a growing mind", as Coleridge said, and found affinities with people of very diverse political, ecclesiastical and theological schools. When he claimed his part in the goodly inheritance of some other school of thought, he was forthwith repudiated by some undiscerning brother— as the cygnet, drawn by its own image to the stream, affrights its brother fowl. "He seemed not one, but all mankind's epitome." One thinks of the glorious eclecticism of an intellect that ranged freely through mathematics and foreign languages, poetry and history. One envies a personality so much at home in the most diverse company and yet not lonely in solitude. He was at home in the open air as in the study. The interplay of action and meditation made his life harmonious. He was no sour misanthrope, like so many religious zealots. "His very enthusiasm was sanguine not atrabiliar; he was so full of hope, so simple-hearted. . . . He might have been so many things; not a speaker only, but a doer; the leader of the hosts of men." There must have been some fatal flaw in his personality that undid the good of all his gifts.

A clever wife, aware of this flaw, might have saved him. (Such as Isabella's sister, Elizabeth, who married Irving's friend and elder, William Hamilton.) One recalls Jane Welsh Carlyle's remark: "There would have been no tongues, had Irving married me." Froude, with his flair for the sensational triumphantly cites this (I, 164) just as he jumped to the conclusion that when Irving first came to London he took to religious excitement as grosser natures take to drink because the Martins would not release him from his engagement to Isabella. Jane Welsh became Carlyle's clever wife, but there is no reason for supposing that she would have made Irving any happier than he was with Isabella, or that she would have succeeded in preventing him from becoming insulated in a circle that did him so much harm; he might easily have continued as he did, "mildly obstinate" (though she might have kept crowds of unwelcome callers from the house!). Jane's mocking wit and fine sense of the ludicrous would have harmonised imperfectly with Irving's simple, devout earnestness.

"And she might have come to despise him for his blind faith; whilst she could never despise Thomas Carlyle. That bitterness, at least, was spared her, in the ill-prospering of her first love" (Mrs. A. Ireland, *Life of J. W. Carlyle*, p. 28).

Isabella was not the true companion of Irving's intellect, though she had been his pupil in the Kirkcaldy days. She was pious, uncritical, "suggestible". Carlyle saw that she needed guidance and, as we have seen, introduced her to Mrs. Basil Montagu—the last person likely to be of use. Carlyle saw that Isabella gave her husband unquestioning support in his abnormal developments. Is it not possible that she may not have been stimulated to do this more or less consciously, knowing that her former rival, Jane Welsh Carlyle, was so opposed to prophecy and "tongues"?

There is abundant evidence that the Irvings were most happy and were closely drawn together by the death of two of their puny children. Jane Welsh was not made for the simple uncomplicated happiness that satisfies so many women. Her friend Geraldine Jewsbury told Carlyle after her death that she was so fascinating that she seemed born "for the destruction of mankind". Carlyle's own opinion was that she was not a *flirt* if the term means one who tries to inspire love without feeling it.

"But she was full of grace, talent, clear insight, playful humour, and also of honest dignity and pride; and not a few young fools, of her own or a slightly higher station, made offers to her—which, sometimes to their high temporary grief and astonishment, were decisively rejected" (*C.R.*, p. 49).

A great many men were made unhappy. What chance had Irving among these suitors? Jane Welsh had an eager, restless nature, which had far more to do with her unhappiness than circumstances. Sir James Crichton-Browne, M.D., LL.D., F.R.S., editor of her *New Letters and Memorials* (1903) suggests in his Introduction that she was something of a neurotic, with her constant sick-headaches and influenza; her malady was emotional rather than mental, and was controlled to some extent by will-power. As a result she must have been "gey ill to deal wi'" no less than Carlyle. Temperamentally, she was no wife for Irving, though his chivalrous nature prompted him to a constant deference to women. He was the centre of an adoring female circle which received his teaching with implicit faith, re-echoed his sentiments, took his vaguest speculations and wildest hopes and gave them form and substance in incoherent utterances. But Jane Welsh was a very different person from Miss Cardale or Mrs. Caird!

Mrs. Oliphant, in the appreciation of Mrs. Carlyle which appeared after her death in *Macmillan's Magazine* (1866), referred to her friend's natural reticence about the preference "which gradually swept Irving out of her girlish fancy, if he had ever been fully established there." But even Jane's keen intelligence could not conceal her dislike to Mrs. Irving.

"This dislike looked to me nothing more than the very natural and almost universal feminine objection to the woman who has consoled even a rejected lover. The only wonder was that she did not herself . . . see the humour of it."

· · · · ·

The real tragedy of the Irvingite Movement lay in the waste of such a noble life as Edward Irving's. Baxter on being disillusioned might devote his energies to his profession. The Cairds might run the new organisation on different lines, when the first springs of glossolalia had run dry. The masterful Henry Drummond might direct the course of the "Catholic Apostolic Church", as one of his many interests. The only great soul in that circle, whose contribution to the Christian Church might otherwise have been so fruitful, was cut off—many believed with a broken heart.

"He set out," said Dr. Cumming in Irving's funeral sermon, "like some warship with streaming pennants and majestic sway; but the storms beat, and the waves arose, and prudence was driven from the wheel and, perchance, the seven spirits that are before the throne, ceased to breathe upon the sails; and battered and tossed and rifted, she foundered amid rocks and shoals. He speaks to us strongly on the danger that environs a lofty intellect. None, with the exception of his illustrious father in Christ, Dr. Chalmers, was so able to arrest the attention, and gain the hearts, and mould the doings of his audience. He knew and felt so well the greatness of his genius, and this made him fancy he could penetrate the arcana of eternity, and gather to his bosom flowers that bloomed not on earth. Like the eagle, he soared too near the sun, and was struck blind. He was misled by sparks of his own kindling."

That is the judgment of a contemporary Scottish preacher who went some way with him in emphasising the Second Coming and apocalyptic outlook generally. Theologically at the opposite pole, is the estimate of F. D. Maurice the Broad Churchman, a fellow disciple with Irving at the feet of Coleridge:—"From God he must begin. . . . In spite of enormous prejudice against him, I was forced, and am now more than ever forced to reverence and love him." Maurice is commemorated along with Irving in a series of stained glass windows installed by Dr. John Hunter in Trinity Congregational Church, Glasgow (1908). The fellowship is completed by the names of McLeod Campbell, Erskine of Linlathen, A. J. Scott—and Carlyle. These were "the men who did most for the widening of religious thought in Scotland during the first half of the nineteenth century".

No one had the opportunity of knowing Irving better than Carlyle:—

"But for Irving, I had never known what the communion of man with man means. He was the freest, brotherliest, bravest human soul mine ever came in contact with: I call him, on the whole, the best man I have ever, after trial enough, found in this world, or now hope to find."

Exactly a century later, the Presbytery of London North in whose bounds Regent Square lies, recorded their appreciation in a minute prepared by Professor Carnegie Simpson, which closes as follows:—

"Edward Irving was a man misled by false lights; but he was not himself false to what he believed to be the light. He was deceived; but he was not dishonest. He listened to voices which were not of truth; but he was sincere when he declared that he was condemned because he 'refused to allow the voice of the Spirit of God to be silenced'. Let us think of his inward faithfulness rather than of his outward failure, as to-day we are reminded of his death. It was less his death than his release; for only thus was his broken heart healed, was his fevered spirit calmed, and was his soul set free from the coils that had so entangled it on earth to escape *ex umbris et imaginibus in veritatem*—out of the shadows of time and the vain imaginings of men into the serene light and the eternal truth of God" (Reprinted, *Presbyterian Messenger*, December, 1934).

APPENDIX

GLOSSOLALIA IN HISTORY: PARALLELS

"Any religion can make people speak in tongues."—
F. R. BARRY.

§ 1

The Ancient World

THE roots of glossolalia lie deep in the past, involving a study of primitive religion, possession, inspiration and prophecy. It is only possible here to touch on these questions. We may note that even Old Testament prophecy, with its spiritual vision and ethical insight, had a primitive origin. Its "enthusiasm" developed from an ἐνθυσιασμός which overpowered the prophet's reason, turning him into a mere instrument on which the Spirit plays. He was most divine when least human. The Spirit of the Lord came upon Saul; he "was turned into another man" and behaved as one possessed. Balaam was a "trance speaker", automatically inspired, disclaiming responsibility for what he said. Amos, Hosea and Jeremiah had to encounter a national tradition that associated prophecy with visions, auditions, psychic power and dervish-like behaviour.

In Greece and Rome, Oracular Inspiration played an important part. One thinks of the Pythia at Delphi, seated on her tripod over a fissure in the ground, with the aid of mantic stimulants delivering unintelligible utterances, afterwards "interpreted" by a circle of "gifted" persons. (Plutarch spoke of the Pythia's "tongues".) Plato declared that "no man in his wits attains prophetic truth and inspiration . . . his intelligence is either enthralled by sleep or he is demented by some distemper or possession" (*Timaeus*, 72). Virgil presents a life-like picture of a prophetess "speaking in tongues". He depicts her quick change of colour, her panting breast, her apparent increase of stature as the god fills her with divine afflatus and her voice loses its mortal ring (*Aeneid*, VI, 46, 98).

Throughout the Roman Empire glossolalia, automatic writing and other phenomena were popular in the "Mystery Religions". Without over-estimating the debt of Christianity to these Mystery Religions, one must recognise that in the Apostolic Age there was a widespread diffusion of the Holy Spirit over the Roman world:—

"It was manifested abnormally and explosively by extraordinary elevation of human faculties, so that miracles, prophecy, glossolalia and visions were abundant; more normally in great enthusiasm, sound knowledge of human character and comfort in suffering" (*Encyclopedia of Religion and Ethics*, art. "Holy Spirit").

Pentecost was the uprush of overflowing vitality that broke the bounds of ordinary speech. A surging tide of feeling swept everything before it.

"We can follow the preparations for a new life . . . but life is always something not accounted for by the sum of what has gone before. The beginning of life is always marvellous. And when men have felt it so, when they look back on such a beginning, still more when they attempt to describe it to others, they almost inevitably call in the marvellous to account for their experience, to confirm and justify their conviction that the miracle of new life *has* happened" (C. A. Anderson Scott, *The Fellowship of the Spirit*, p. 35).

Unfortunately, Christian tradition became more interested in the by-products of Pentecost than in the reality of its experience (as described by Luke the artist in dramatic form—wind, fire and tongues being the usual accompaniments of a theophany). The homiletic mind saw in Pentecost a reversal of Babel; as Grotius put it: "Poena linguarum dispersit homines: donum linguarum disperses in unum populum collegit." And the "permanent endowment theory" (the miraculous gift of preaching in other languages) found supporters like Bishop Wordsworth even fifty years ago. Eighteenth century rationalists and nineteenth century critics disputed the historicity of Pentecost, in their reaction from unintelligent literalism. The modern study of social psychology and of the world of the New Testament restores Pentecost to its proper historic setting and affords less excuse for purely imitative "Pentecostal" manifestations. Apart from any question of tongues as a "permanent endowment", however, it is surprising that even in the past men like Edward Irving have not realised that Paul himself did not admit tongues to a high place among "charismata" at Corinth. He admitted their mystical value as a confirmation of ecstatic experience, but considered public exhibition unedifying. A manifestation might be artifically "worked up", becoming an end in itself rather than a devotional by-product. The test was the heavenliness of the fruits rather than the roots.

Huxley pointed out that hidden in English soil are innumerable seeds of tropical flora, which would spring up amazingly if for one summer we could have the heat and moisture of the tropics. So, when the Christians of the Apostolic Age passed suddenly from the frigid realm of pagan philosophy and the temperate zone of Judaism into the tropical splendours of the Gospel, it is no wonder that the new emotions awoke into life and the Church blossomed with a profusion of strange spiritual phenomena. When "the conquering, new-born joy" subsided and the spiritual temperature sank, there remained groups who sought to keep alive these "charismata" and believed that their dying-out was a sign of degeneration in the Church. But this artificial "forcing" was apt to mean reversion to pagan conceptions. The Gnostics would speak, for example, of the divine plectrum using men's tongues as a harp to reveal heavenly knowledge. Towards the end of the second century A.D. the Montanists tried to restore the purity and enthusiasm of the Apostolic Church. Rigid asceticism was to prepare the Church for the dispensation of the Paraclete, when the Spirit would possess the Church wholly. Millennarian views were proclaimed (modified by the declaration that the New Jerusalem was to be at Pepuza in Phrygia). Charismata were to be abundantly poured out on the elect, —passive instruments to be played on by the Divine Spirit.

The Montanist sectarians, with their (sour) fruits of the spirit, caused a strong reaction. By the time of Chrysostom (second half of the fourth century A.D.) glossolalia and prophecy had apparently died out in the Church. Conyers Middleton dealt trenchantly with the question of miraculous gifts in the Church from the rationalistic view point in his *Free Inquiry* . . . and *Gift of Tongues* (1747–9). A century later Bushnell admitted that there was no likelihood of a miraculous dispensation being restored in the Christian Church, "after being quite passed by and lost".

"But there may be casual suspensions and re-appearances (in one place or another) that are quite consistent with the conviction that the dispensation is perpetual, never withdrawn, and never to be withdrawn" (*Nature and the Supernatural*, 1862, p. 315).

§ 2

Church History

Montanus believed that Christianity had its rudimentary principle in Nature, its infancy in the Law, its childhood in the Prophets, its youth in the Gospel, its full maturity only in the dispensation of the Paraclete. It is interesting to see how this doctrine of development reappears in history, modified according to circumstances. So in the Middle Ages we have Joachim of Floris (1145–1202) teaching that the Christian Faith unfolded in three dispensations:—

(1) The Age of the Father—"The law and the letter" —Obedience (comparable to the stars).="The vestibule."

(2) The Age of the Son, intermediate between letter and spirit, grace and faith (comparable to the moon). An age of Study—the teaching of Jesus enigmatical.="The Holy Place."

(3) The Age of the Spirit, perfect in full-orbed love (comparable to the sun). An age of Contemplation—"Then shall we see face to face."="The Holy of Holies."

The above scheme is fitted into contemporary history. Laymen and clergy are God's instruments in the first two stages, monks in the final culmination. The initiation period begins with St. Benedict: the actual age of the Spirit is to open in A.D. 1260, the Church ("mulier amicta sole," Rev. xii: 1) remaining in the wilderness 1,260 days. Joachim's bias was strongly anti-Papal, and his *Eternal Gospel* exerted great influence over the Franciscan "Spirituals", who found consolation in his fiery Apocalyptic denunciations of the Church.

Similar ideas were held by certain groups of sixteenth century Anabaptists, the framework being scriptural instead of mediæval, and in a modified form the early Quakers during the English Commonwealth embraced "the Gospel of the Spirit".

The Quakers had no elaborate theory as to the ushering in of a Dispensation of the Spirit in such-and-such a year in their own time. They simply believed that the centuries which separated them from the Apostolic Age constituted a gigantic interpolation, which had to be removed. Fox claimed for every soul the privilege of receiving the truth at first hand from the fount; he had "openings"—gleams of light direct from God. Led by the Spirit, and liberated from the letter of the Word and from the authority of man-made Ministry, Creeds and Sacraments, Christians might exercise the gifts of the Apostolic Age, heal the sick, and even overcome sin in this life.

If the *form* of Irvingism was Millenarian, we may say that its *content* at many points recalls early Quakerism.

The experience of Marmaduke Stevenson, a Quaker "Boston Martyr" of 1659, bears a close resemblance to Robert Baxter's numerous revelations, in matter and style:—

"In 1655 I was at the plough in Yorkshire, old England; and as I walked after the plough, I was filled with the love and presence of the living God. As I stood, the word of the Lord came to me in a still, small voice—'I have ordained thee a prophet unto the nations.' I was put to a stand, seeing that I was but a child in such a weighty matter. So, at the time appointed, Barbadoes was set before me, unto which I was required of the Lord to go" (M. D. R. Willink, *The Prophetic Consciousness*, p. 65).

George Fox's Journal is full of picturesque realistic phrases like "The Lord's power broke forth", "those that were in the power". So when on one occasion he was "moved to pray", "the Lord's power was so great that the house seemed to be shaken". As a result we have "burdens" and prophecies on O.T. analogy. "It was winter; but the word of the Lord was like a fire in me. So I put off my shoes and cried, 'Woe to the bloody city of Lichfield!'" Woolman cried—"My heart was like a vessel that wanted vent." And Behmen—"The truth of God did burn in my bones." Compare the agonised cry of a "gifted sister" at Regent Square: "Do you not know that it burneth in the bone—burneth in the bone?"

Fox seems to have had an uncanny insight into the future, for many of his predictions came true: Baxter's, on the other hand, fell flat—except in minor cases of likely coincidence. Thus in 1653:—

"Being one day at Swarthmore Hall . . . I was moved to tell Justice Fell and Justice Benson . . . that before that day two weeks the parliament would be broken up, and the speaker plucked out of his chair. And that day two weeks, Justice Benson coming thither again, told Justice Fell that now he saw George was a true prophet, for Oliver (Cromwell) had broken up the parliament."

Again, "When some forward spirits among us would have bought Somerset House for meetings, I forebade; for I then foresaw the king's coming in again" (1658).

Yorkshire was a stronghold of the Friends. Baxter, whose phraseology resembles so closely Fox's at times, was a Yorkshireman. It would be interesting if Quaker blood could be proved to have run in his veins some generations earlier. For it was in the eighteenth century that the Society of Friends for a time decayed. Both among the Friends and in Irvingism, messages delivered in the power, which had no obvious occasion, must often have been eruptions from the subconscious; e.g., Fox gave *a* reason for his judgment on Lichfield—a thousand martyrs had fallen there under Diocletian. *The* reason was a horror of the city probably arising from what he must have heard in childhood from his mother (of martyr stock), concerning a woman burnt at Lichfield during the reign of "bloody Mary", who came from a locality where he once lived. Baxter's sudden outburst, when the Court of Chancery was mentioned, "There go I, thence to the prison house!" was likewise so unexpected, that the Court must have had some unpleasant personal associations (family litigation? "sharp practice?"—something subconsciously "repressed").

The Quakers, in spite of occasional fanatical outbreaks, provoked to no small extent by their persecutors, seem to have brooded in silence before breaking out "in the power", seeking to ascertain the will of God. Irvingite revelations, rebukes, and injunctions were too facile, too subjective. We find no Irvingite parallel to the action of Woolman, the eighteenth century American Quaker:—

"One day, being under a strong exercise of the Spirit, I stood up and said some words in a meeting: but not keeping close to the Divine opening I said more than was required of me. Being soon sensible of my error, I was afflicted some weeks. . . . Being thus humbled, my understanding became more strengthened to distinguish the pure spirit which inwardly moves on the heart, and which taught me to wait in silence sometimes many weeks together, until I felt that rise which prepares the creature to speak like a trumpet through which the Lord speaks to his flocks. . . . I was taught to watch the true opening, and take heed lest my own will get uppermost, and cause me to utter words from worldly wisdom" (*Journal*, p. 140, Swarthmore Edition).

Irvingites tended to accept utterances "in the power" as divine, simply because of the manner in which they had been uttered—ascribing them to the flesh or the devil when not in accord with the general feeling of the conclave, or when too absurd or too blasphemous.

Quakerism is curiously connected with the Camisards (p. 263ff). Primitive traits of a motor type (fits, trembling, staggering) had made their appearance during the persecution which followed the Revocation of the Edict of Nantes.[1] The stages were: (1) avertissement, (2) soufflé, (3) prophétic, (4) dons. The subject, after several fasts, three days in length, became pale and fell insensible on the ground. Then came violent agitations of limbs and head, as Voltaire said—"quite according to the ancient custom of all nations and the rules of madness transmitted from age to age". Then the patient would say in the French of the Huguenot Bible—"Mes frères, la fin du monde approche, *le jugement général sera dans trois mois;* repentez-vous du grand péché que vous avez commis d'aller à la messe; *c'est le Saint-Esprit qui parle par ma bouche*".

The discourse might go on for two hours; after which the patient could only express himself in his native patois (a Romance idiom) and had no recollection of his "ecstasy". This inspired speaking was associated with guiding lights in the sky, encouraging mystical voices; wounds were often harmless. "The supernatural was part of their life." An intense and living faith, accompanied by fasting and absorption in apocalyptic literature, and stimulated by ceaseless persecution had produced these by-products of sensory and motor automatisms (See art. "Camisards", *Ency. Brit.*, 11th ed.).

In 1706 several of "the French Prophets" visited London

[1] After the publication of the Bull *Unigenitus* in 1713, and the consequent flight of the Jansenist leaders to Holland, those who remained in France suffered persecution. The result was apocalyptic prophecy, speaking in tongues, the excesses of the *convulsionnaires*, and the alleged cures at the grave of deacon Pâris. Thus persecution aroused fanatical ecstasy—whether the victims were Protestant or Catholics.

and excited much curiosity. On the protest of the consistory of the French church at the Savoy against "cette secte impie et extravagante", they were tried at the Guildhall, and in spite of Misson's defence that the spirit which caused Balaam's ass to speak, could speak through these prophets from the Cevennes, several were condemned to the pillory and stocks. Speaking in unknown tongues, miraculous healing, and foretelling were associated with their activities. They made several hundred converts, among them Fatio, a member of the Royal Society of London but "with a great fondness for astrology and tinctured with enthusiasm", and John Lacy a member of Dr. Calamy's congregation, whose eccentricity stopped short of surrendering an income of £2,000 per annum. Dr. Calamy gave the following account of Lacy:—

"I went into the room and taking him by the hand lifted it up, when it fell flat upon his knees. He took no notice of me; but I observed the humming noise grow louder and louder by degrees, and the heaving in his breast increase, till it came up to his throat, as if it would have suffocated him. And then he at last began to speak, or, as he would have it taken, the Spirit spoke in him. The speech was symbolical, and there was a distinct heave and breathe between each syllable; but it required attention to distinguish the words. When the speech was over, the humming and heaving gradually abated, and I again took him by the hand, and felt his pulse, which moved pretty quick, but I could not perceive by his hands anything like sweating."

In the early eighteenth century an offshoot from Quakerism adopted the principles of the "French Prophets", and organised a society at Manchester under James and Ann Wardley. But the real founder of "Shakerism" was Ann Lee, daughter of a Manchester blacksmith (1736–84). She was frequently imprisoned for shouting and dancing in ecstasy on the Sabbath, and when examined by four clergymen spoke for four hours in seventy-two languages! Acknowledged by 1770 as "the Mother in spiritual things" of "The Millennial Church" or "United Society of Believers in Christ's Second Appearing", she took a select band to America in 1774, following a "revelation". A community was then organised on a communistic basis in New York State. "Ann—the Word" was regarded as the female manifestation of Christ—the bride ready for the bridegroom at the Second Coming, God being regarded as bisexual.

In 1838 the Gift of Tongues appeared, but the spirits, after warnings, are said to have left the Believers. (See art., "Shakers", *Ency. Brit.*, 11th ed.) Dr. Dwight describes a visit to a Shaker village in the western part of New York State (1799).

"They believed themselves to be under the immediate guidance of the Spirit, made known to them by an involuntary extension of the right arm, which they followed (one man being thus directed to a hog-trough, where he regaled himself). In their worship they sang in an 'unknown tongue'; it was a succession of unmeaning sounds, frequently repeated, half-articulated, and plainly gotten by heart, for they all uttered the same sounds in succession (tune 'Mary Dawson'). The gesticulations of the women were violent, and so often practised that it made them goggle-eyed, suffused their eyes with blood, and made them appear like persons just recovering from a disease. The motions of the men were very moderate—rather condescendingly than earnestly made. I observed 'that the sounds could not be *words*, as they were not articulate'. One woman replied 'How dost thee know, but that we speak the Hotmatot language?' The language of the Hotmatots is said to be made up of such sort of words. I challenged them to speak Greek or Latin or French—but they were silent." (Quoted in *Anti-Cabala's Morning Visit to Rev. E. Irving.*)

Notice the parallel between the woman last mentioned and Mary Campbell—"the language of the Hotmatots and Pelew Islanders"!

We have already referred to Johann Lutz, in Southern Germany (p. 233f). Born in 1801, he became a Roman Catholic priest and was influenced by the saintly Bishop Sailer. At Karlshuld on the Donaumoos, he felt that his flock was craving for spiritual nourishment which the Church did not provide. He had preached a Revival sermon on New Year's Eve, 1827. At 3.15 a.m. next day he was awakened by a crowd wanting to confess. A peasant woman urged him to rely more on the Spirit. Many spent the night of Ash Wednesday in prayer, when a man and woman suddenly spoke under the influence of a higher power. "We know nothing of that which we utter until we begin to speak; a power comes upon us, and the words which we are to speak are given to us."

Words were spoken *in the power* in Church and in the people's homes. No record was taken of the utterances, but Lutz distinctly remembered the following:—

APPENDIX 287

"Ye are living in the time when Jesus will awaken the sleeping ones." "This generation shall see it! The Lord gives again Apostles and Churches as at the beginning!" "The Lord will pour out His Spirit as at the beginning!"

There were visions, dreams, but also demoniacal attacks. Lutz believed that treasure was contained in earthen vessels (2 Cor. iv: 7). The gift was not always manifested in a pure form; he noted the case of a "gifted" young woman, who from want of proper control, miscarried herself with one of the men who idolised her.

Lutz's biographer then refers to the movement in Britain in 1830: Here also it was connected with (1) The preaching of the love of God in Christ; (2) The true human nature of Our Lord; (3) The prophetic study of Scripture; (4) Prophecy pointing to the speedy coming of the Lord, and to preparation for this through apostles.

"That shoot within the Roman division, being touched by the frost, withered; the one in the more favoured Protestant part of the Church was able to gain strength and thrive."

It was only till July, 1828, that speaking in the power flourished in Lutz's parish; after that it was occasional. He did not then consider supernatural gifts absolute essentials. Only later did he attain the conviction:

(1) "That the Holy Ghost Who dwells in the Church, would by means of these gifts *continually* testify to Jesus, and illuminate the path of the Church.
(2) "That these gifts are absolutely essential if the Church is to be built up for the habitation of God *through the Spirit*, and to be prepared for the coming of the Lord."

It is interesting to note that his congregation were continually complaining of the burden of ceremonies, officially petitioning Lutz for the Scriptures. He was supported by the Government, and opposed by the Chapter; sought a refuge in the Protestant Church, but was appalled by its rationalism and returned to Romanism (1832). When priest at Oberroth, he met Caird. The result of intimacy with Caird was an accusation of "Irvingism", for which he was eventually excommunicated (26th February, 1856). The rest of his life he spent in the service of the "Catholic Apostolic Church", after his reception by Henry Drummond acting as "Angel" at Berne. (*See* L. W. Schoiler's *Life of J. E. G. Lutz*, E.Tir., Longmans, Green, 1894).

The life of Lutz shows that in the third decade of the nineteenth century there was something in the *Zeitgeist* favourable to the revival of Apostolic charismata, which found expression both in Britain and on the Continent, in Protestant and Roman Catholic Churches, and which would probably have developed in the latter on Irvingite lines but for Lutz's caution and ecclesiastical opposition. In both cases the gifts tended to be the hot-house fruit of a warm pietism, stimulated by ascetic practices. In Germany there was a revolt of the Spirit against the bondage of ritual; in Britain against the bondage of idolised Confessions and Biblical literalism (though the exegesis of the Irvingites was generally grotesque). In both Britain and Germany, the murmur of revolutions, wars and industrial conflict seemed to be signs of the Last Days.

§ 3

The Twentieth Century

America is proverbially notorious as a breeding-ground of peculiar sects, arising from a thin "mental atmosphere" that seems to stimulate sensationalism. It is not therefore surprising to find that "the gift of tongues" has been revived in communities not pre-eminent in culture and historical perspective.

Glossolalia has been facilitated by the mixture of races and languages so characteristic of the American "melting pot". Thus, trappers would identify the "unknown tongues" of Mormon ecstatics as snatches of Indian dialects. In the case of Mormonism, the chief factor was the hypnotic personality of leaders like Joseph Smith and Rigden. In other circles the manifestations have not been closely linked to commanding personalities.

A wave of Pentecostal enthusiasm swept over certain communities in 1906, starting with a negro prayer-meeting in Los Angeles. So far, glossolalia had been described either by "gifted persons" or by common-sense critics who could only gauge the manifestations bluntly. America was fortunate in possessing a rising school of religious psychology. Mr. Frederick G. Henke in 1906 collected valuable facts from five places in Chicago relative to glossolalia. ("The Gift of Tongues and Related Phenomena at the Present Day", Vol. XIII, *American Journal of Theology*.)

A short service of song would provide a suitable atmosphere. No sooner had a man started exposition of Scripture than the manifestations began. Suddenly the leader, working up automatic action of his head and shoulders, seized the reader by the shoulder and said he would now "take over". There were requests for prayer for individual cases, (e.g., "for a man who don't believe anyone"). A coloured man rises:—"I feel a burning inside in the inner man like a coal of fire!" There is an ecstatic response from the congregation, numbering about 300—shouting, "jerks", screaming. A woman begins in a "tongue", and passes into singing in a "tongue", improvising her tunes; an "interpretation" is then given in Scriptural phraseology—"The Lord is my light and my salvation, whom shall I fear?" After fifteen or twenty testimonies, the leader preaches—dwelling on the mechanical nature of the power. Like Irving, he stresses baptism in the Spirit. "The head, the understanding cannot perceive the Holy Ghost. He must enter the heart, the fleshly valvular heart. The Holy Ghost came in through my legs, November 20th, 1901."

Those seeking for "the Baptism of the Spirit" were then asked to gather in a back room for prayer; those seeking for conversion or healing to kneel at the "altar".

Henke concluded that like Pentecost, this Chicago outpouring of the Spirit was a genuine result of "expectation, preparedness and fellowship in prayer", combined with primitive belief in "possession". As far as "unknown tongues" were concerned, he could not recognise one of the six languages with which he was acquainted. The novice would babble or screech "yah-yah-yeh-yeh-yeh-yah-yah": the expert would form syllables which he would tend to repeat, e.g., "kak-tah-lah-see-ah, oh-nee-see-nee-nah." There were degrees of suggestibility—those in the lowest stage of culture being the first to give way to "the power". There was a constant tendency to imitate leaders or moving spirits who had the most violent automata. The atmosphere was electric. A stove fell with a crash as "Elder" Sinclair was preaching. (He claimed to be the first in Chicago to be baptised with the Spirit.) He stopped. On his way back to the pulpit he remarked: "We can expect 'most anything these days. I wouldn't be surprised if Jesus would come just as unexpectedly."

Excitement is raised to the highest possible pitch, and

there is screaming, laughing, and shouting in "tongues". One man felt the Holy Spirit coming through his side, another through his mouth.

Henke's account of the "Pentecostal Experience of the Rev. A. E. Street" is illuminating. "Some twelve years ago I began to long for Pentecost as described in the Bible and all these years have been praying for that baptism. . . . About a year ago the burden of prayer became greater, night after night." He had a determined struggle *to stop his own thoughts and desires*, "to reach the lower part of the valley of humiliation and be empty in thought."

He finally went to the Mission at 328 W. 63rd Street, Chicago, asking but one question, Why did he not receive baptism? He was prayed for, and told that he need only wait. As he knelt at the altar on Sunday afternoon, 17th March, the "power seized" him and he laughed through the following Communion Service. About 11 p.m. he knelt with a few friends when his "body was *used*" to laugh at the top of his voice for over half an hour. On rising, he found he had rolled over, on to the floor. Kneeling, he felt his jaws being worked by a strange force.

"In a few seconds some baby gibberish was uttered, then a few words in Chinese *that I understood*, and then several sentences in a strange tongue. This turned into singing.

"On Wednesday morning . . . I began to sing the heavenly music at the top of my voice the entire half hour while I was in the bathtub (!).

"On Thursday night I was awakened out of my sleep and began to pray for the gift of Interpretation. After a few words the prayer was taken out of my mouth. For an hour I received a lesson in interpreting. A word was given in a strange tongue. This was followed by its English meaning and the two were repeated until it was plain that they meant the same. From that hour whenever anyone speaks in tongues the interpretation comes if I ask it."

Henke concludes that the phenomena he describes— (1) Agree both as to the origin and experience with the description of similar phenomena in the N.T.; (2) They are a recrudescence of psychic phenomena on a low stage of culture.

In 1907 a revival in Cassel and other parts of Germany produced the common bodily effects. There, insistence on the Holy Spirit's activity was combined with Biblical literalism, e.g., Abnormal phenomena were attributed to evil spirits because those seized with the "power" fell on their backs, while David, Paul and John fell on their faces.

Pastor Paul (editor of *Die Heiligung*) had heard of speaking in tongues in Norway and America. He visited Norway, was impressed, and as the result of a fresh study of 1 Corinthians, was himself "seized with the power" (15th September, 1907).

Singing in tongues became one of his accomplishments, the tune of some familiar hymn (as in the case of the Shakers) getting filled out with new syllables in rhythm.

For example:—
>Schua ea, shua ea,
>   O tschi biro ti ra pea
>   Akki lungo ta ri fungo
>U li hara to ra tungo
>   latschi bungo ti tu ta.

Pastor Paul's mentality may be gauged by the fact that comparison of these hymns "in Zungen" with the German of the hymn usually sung to the given tune, convinced him that—"ich habe etwas von der himmlischen Sprache gelernt" (Mosiman, *Das Zungenreden*, p. 79).

Glossolalia has not always been limited to ignorant and credulous people. Bushnell bears evidence:

"A Christian friend, intelligent in the highest degree, and perfectly reliable to me as my right hand, who was present at a rather private gathering assembled to pray, relates that after one of the brethren had been speaking in a strain of discouraging self-accusation, another present shortly rose, with a strangely beaming look, and, fixing his eye on the confessing brother, broke out in a discourse of sounds, wholly unintelligible, though apparently a true language, accompanying the utterance with a very strange and peculiarly expressive gesture, such as he never made at any other time; coming finally to a kind of pause, and commencing again, as if at the same point, to go over again in English, with exactly the same gestures, what had just been said. It appeared to be an interpretation, and the matter of it was a beautifully emphatic utterance of the principle of self-renunciation.

"'There had been no conversation respecting gifts of any kind, and no reference to their possibility.' The circle were 'put out' by the demonstration, 'not knowing what to make of it.' 'The instinct of prudence threw them on observing a general silence.'"
(*Nature and the Supernatural*, p. 336.)

An individual and unexpected case such as Bushnell's is much more baffling than glossolalia in mass movements, in polyglot communities—such as the French village near the Swiss frontier where "speaking in tongues" was popularly ascribed to demoniacal possession but proved by Professor Tissot of Dijon Medical Faculty to be simply the upsurge of fragments of Latin (the Mass) and German (contact with German-speaking Swiss over the border). (A. D. White, *A History of the Warfare of Science with Theology*, I, p. 159ff.).

An interesting case from England is that of the late Rev. A. A. Boddy, F.R.G.S., Vicar of All Saints, Monkwearmouth, near Sunderland. Mr. Boddy was a highly educated and widely travelled clergyman. For several years he practised as a solicitor in Manchester and after entering the Church, "ministered for thirty-eight years beside a steam-hammer". Successful church work in an industrial district was not incompatible with "Pentecostal" phenomena. From 1907 till the outbreak of war in 1914 numerous cases of speaking in tongues were reported at his meetings.

"Visitors from all over Britain, Australia, America, Germany, Holland, Syria, and even China were drawn to the meetings.

"Mr. Boddy often used to say that he had a good deal of Methodist blood in his veins for he was a descendant of Mrs. Bazeille, a Huguenot who married John Wesley." (*The Sunderland Echo*, 11th September, 1930.)

§ 4

The Mission Field

It is in Eastern lands that the original conditions of Pentecost have been most approximately fulfilled. News of the revival in Wales in 1905 reached the Welsh missionaries in India among the Khassia Hills. Whereupon Pandita Ramabai, a high-caste widow, organised girls' prayer meetings twice daily, which were attended by 550; soon she persuaded thirty girls to preach in the villages round about. At last a tongue of fire was seen to rest on the head of a senior girl, whose companions ran for water, thinking she was on fire. Both natives and missionaries experienced a "burning within"—"the fire of the Holy Spirit". An American missionary at Mukti wrote (17th November, 1905):—

"This morning a little girl gave me the verse Luke xii, 49, which was greatly blessed to me. A flood of fire poured on my head, and this afternoon it burned inside. I am having it now. . . . The burning inside is rather hard to bear. It has taken my physical strength away, but I am thankful for that."

To Mr. Ellis, Special Correspondent of the *Chicago Daily News*, Pandita Ramabai replied, in answer to a question:—

"I have heard girls who know no English at all utter beautiful prayers in your language. I have heard others pray in Greek and Hebrew and Sanskrit, and others again in languages that none of us understand" (Henke, *American Journal of Theology*, XIII, p. 93ff.).

The revival spread in W. and S. India, glossolalia being associated with visions, special revelations, trances, exorcism and falling to the ground. The obscurantism, so often associated and entwined with Pentecostal Movements in Europe and America, was evident also in India. Missionaries of ability and tested piety were set aside in favour of illiterates whose sole qualification was corybantic frenzy.

But the symptoms so characteristic of glossolalia have occurred in places where no imitation of N.T. models has been possible, e.g., in the interior of China. There, once the spirit enters the body—

"The man's eyes close tightly, his whole body trembles, his hands and feet continually move, his hair loosens from the braid —then he begins to speak, and is able to talk, *not only in his own dialect, but in others as well*" (*Fukhien Witness*, June, 1904).

In the Qua Iboe district of S. Nigeria, the "shakers" or "spirit people" caused much commotion (1927), going about in bands, singing senseless verses, shouting and performing such feats as climbing trees backwards. Miss Lois Beveridge, a missionary, describes the symptoms:—
"Violent trembling, eyes staring vacantly, outstretched arms, a strange floating movement as if flying, lying exhausted on the ground till the paroxysm passes." Children and non-church natives were more easily affected than church members, and the Primitive Methodist Missionaries had more trouble with the movement than the Presbyterians. (Kindly communicated by the Rev. John Beveridge, M.B.E., B.D.)

§ 5
Cases of Psychic Automatism

We have seen that glossolalia has appeared not merely in Europe and America in the nineteenth century and in Christian Communities, but also among pagans in ancient times and in our own day, where no knowledge of Pentecost has existed to act as a lever. We must add to these, cases on the fringe of the domain of Psychical Research. We may take as example the study of the medium Hélène Smith, described by Professor Flournoy of Geneva—"Des Indes à la planète Mars . . . un cas de Somnambulisme avec glossolalie (1900). Here we have "secondary personality", combined with what F. W. H. Myers called "Retro-Cognition"; Hélène considered herself a reincarnation of Marie Antoinette, and of a Hindoo princess, giving vivid descriptions of the scenes in which she had figured, in the latter case indulging in glossolalia in which certain Sanskrit words could be recognised. She also uttered, with "interpretation", words purporting to be Martian, e.g.,

"Men mess Astane ce ames e vi itech li tes alize Ami grand Astane, je viens a toi toujours par cet element neumi assile ka inanine ezi atev ni le tazie e ri mysterieux immense qûi enveloppe mon etre et me lance à toi . . ."

This "Mars-Sprache" has been described as "disguised French".

"Cet idiome fantaististe est l'œuvre d'une imagination enfantine qui s'est mis en tête de créer une langue nouvelle, et qui, tout en donnant à ses elucubrations des apparences baroques et inedites, les a coulées sans s'en douter dans les moules accoutumés, de la seule langue réelle dont elle eût connaissance."

William James communicated to the Society for Psychical Research an interesting "Case of Psychic automatism, including 'speaking with tongues'" (S.P.R. XII, 277–97). Mr. Le Baron, a literary man of forty-nine, in an autobiographical narrative, describes how he spent the summer of 1894 in "Shelter Island" in a camp of mystics and spiritualists, whose leader was a lady named Evangel. "The World's Congress of Religions had re-awakened the hope of a new chemistry of civilisation" —a synthesis of East and West. But Le Baron could not be described as a dreamy enthusiast. He had fortified himself by bringing a copy of Kant's *Critique*. "Of practical spiritualism I knew nothing."

At a séance held at midnight under a pine tree

" . . . suddenly an entirely new and strange psycho-automatic force shook through me like a gust of fierce wind through a tree. *I willed myself* into a state of passivity *in order to observe the phenomena.*"

He went into no trance, but motor violence affected his limbs and he was brought down on the flat of his back.

"My mouth made automatic movements; till, in a few seconds I was distinctly conscious of 'another's voice—unearthly, awful, loud and weird—bursting through the woodland from my own lips, with the despairing words: 'Oh! My People!' Mutterings of semi-purposive prophesy followed. I was so dazed that I had to be assisted to my feet."

(There were several witnesses).

On another occasion, as he was lying on a sofa where Evangel's mother had lain on her last illness,—a woman's voice came through his lips. Her dead mother's dog, Barry, at once began smelling his face. "He smells her!" whispered Evangel. In a few minutes the voice of the psycho-automatism changed from a woman's into a man's. "It's father!" whispered Evangel again.

The result was a "conversion". Le Baron exchanged Kant for Zoroaster. [Pilkington likewise reacted from Deism, and Baxter from conventional Anglicanism to an "exciting" charismatic cult.]

On leaving Shelter Island, Le Baron had a number of revelations, to go to certain places at certain hours. There, he would break into speech "in the Power" in the grave deific style known to the occidental English-speaking world—resonant utterances such as:—

"I have seen thee in glory, and I have seen thee in shame! I have seen thee in light, and I have seen thee in darkness! I have seen thee in peace, and I have seen thee in terror," etc.

It seems that Le Baron had an intense craving for the vague, optimistic, philosophy-and-water popularised by R. W. Trine and other less eminent writers, just as the Irvingites craved for the "gifts" of the Apostolic Church.

"Can I, *via* psycho-automatism, ascend into the uncreated essence of thought—to the Mind of Minds—and perchance snatch down some new metaphysical conception helpful to the lower world?" His experiences differed however from "dédoublement de la personalité" in that it did not appear to be a case of subliminal consciousness, nor of supra-normal intellectual faculty, but rather a "purely extraneous psycho-physical spontaneity or automatism".

On Sunday morning, 30th September, 1894, while receiving a message, in a New York suburb, he suddenly broke off into an unknown tongue.

Frequent messages were received that suggest a reincarnation of an Egyptian God-King, parallel to Hélène Smith's reincarnation of the Hindoo princess—Simandini:

"Egypto-Mome su u Ra. Ere mete su onko inte. Ama tu telee. Oumbe te senete su u Ra. Inter pelee te tete. Ombo O sceuntri. Inteneo duru sinte. Mome su u Ra. . . ."

The interpretation being:—"O son of Ra! I have come to thee! The truth has come! I have come to thee, O son of Ra! See the truth in me. . . . The truth has long been hidden from thee!"

It is significant that Evangel possessed a talisman ring from Egypt.

Le Baron, remarked William James, was by no means willing to abandon the idea that his unintelligible vocal performances were involuntary reproductions of some ancient or unknown tongue. The phonetic elements again in his case seemed English.

"I tried to make him believe (but all in vain) that the whole thing was a decidedly rudimentary form of motor automatism analogous to the scrawls of an 'undeveloped' automatically writing hand. He spent hours poring over grammars and vocabularies of African and Asiatic tongues. First it was Coptic, then Romany, then something Dravidian. I corresponded with various philologists on his behalf, sending them specimens, phonetically written out, of his discourse. But no light came. . . ."

Glossolalia has, however, differed in form in different communities. In America snatches of Red Indian dialects and of the languages of the various nationalities have been "brought up". The glossolalia of Hélène Smith betrayed its French origin. Irvingite glossolalia bore a very obvious resemblance to Latin and Romance languages: this could not be said of the glossolalia of Le Baron which seems to be definitely non-Aryan. While factors other than subliminal operated in the case of Mr. Le Baron, the subconscious also played its part. In Irvingite glossolalia the predominance of the subconscious over other factors at work in producing glossolalia, was very marked. Examination of phenomena drawn from varied sources leads us to conclude that glossolalia (and cognate phenomena) are in no sense uniquely Christian, but are to be found in every age, land, and stage of culture. The great fact of Pentecost, however, has so stamped itself on the Christian consciousness, that in practice such manifestations have followed its example in the majority of cases that have been properly investigated.

"One cannot but note," says F. W. H. Myers, "the different way in which these so-called tongues were treated in Irving's time and in our own. Several, at least of the speakers with tongues in Irving's congregation were, I have no doubt, perfectly sincere; and Irving himself was, as all know, a man of probity and elevation.

"Yet his ignorance—his unavoidable ignorance of the phenomena of automatism landed him and his flock in natural mistakes, but at last in obstinate credulity, and spoilt the close of a noble and high career.

"In Mr. Le Baron's case, the automatist himself had the courage and candour to estimate his utterances in the calm light of science, in spite of strong subjective inducement to continue to assign them a value which they did not possess. He had the good fortune, I need hardly add, to meet with a wise and gentle adviser, and the phenomenon which, if differently treated, might have led on to the delusion of many, and perhaps to the insanity of one, became to the one a harmless experience, and to the other an acquisition of interesting psychological truth. If our Society shall continue thus to tend to convert enthusiasm into science and peril into instruction, it will not have existed in vain" (S.P.R., XII, p. 297).

BIBLIOGRAPHICAL NOTE

"Irving" in the *Dictionary of National Biography*, Chambers's *Biographical Dictionary*, *Encyclopedia Britannica* and Hastings' *Encyclopedia of Religion and Ethics*.

The Collected Works of Edward Irving, edited by his nephew, Rev. Gavin Carlyle, M.A. (5 vols., London, 1864-65).

Miscellanies, extracted from *Works*, with reference to volume and page. (London, 1866—"third thousand".)

List of Irving's books and pamphlets in *Bibliography of Parish of Annan*, by F. Miller, F.S.A., Scot. (Dumfries, 1925).

Jones' *Biographical Sketch* (1835) is slight but has contemporary interest.

Washington Wilks' *Life* (1854) marks a revival of interest in his career. It was overshadowed by

Mrs. Oliphant's biography which immortalised Irving in literature (2 vols., London, 1862; three successive editions). Carlyle criticised it as "a loyal and clear but feeble kind of Book, popular in late years".

For able "Irvingite" critique, v. W. W. Andrews' review in the *New Englander* (July and October, 1863)—Reprint, Glasgow, 1900 (2nd edition).

Carlyle's *Reminiscences* (1866) correct the sentimental bias and present us with "the authentic Irving". The two chapters on Irving and Jane Welsh are miniature biographies. Re-edited by Professor C. E. Norton, who repaired the damage done by Froude's inaccuracies, they reveal Carlyle's deep sympathy and broad humanity. The book was for many years inaccessible, but is now in the Everyman's Library.

Jean Christie Root embodied some material accumulated by the American Irvingite, Rev. W. W. Andrews, in *Edward Irving, Man, Preacher, Prophet* (Boston, Mass., 1912). This short life reveals Irving's personality, but is weak in knowledge of the Scottish background and Presbyterian polity.

Some contemporary appreciations, appearing in periodicals after Irving's death, by Gilfillan, Carlyle, and Jas. Hamilton (his successor from 1841 in Regent Square) are conveniently assembled in Nimmo's *Treasury of Modern Biography* (1878). See Hazlitt's *Spirit of the Age* (1823) (Everyman).

Irving's Centenary was celebrated by the following articles:—

BIBLIOGRAPHICAL NOTE

The Quarterly Review, July, 1934 (Miss E. S. Haldane, C.H., LL.D.).
The Modern Churchman, January and February, 1935 (Dr. A. J. Carlyle).
The Hibbert Journal, January, 1935 (Miss Muriel Kent).
The Times, 7th December, 1934 (A. L. Drummond).
The Scotsman, 7th December, 1934 (W. Forbes Gray).
Annandale Observer, 14th December, 1934.

For Irving in relation to his friends, see:—
Biographies of Carlyle by Froude and D. A. Wilson; Letters of Carlyle and Jane Welsh Carlyle (various editions); R. H. Story's *Memoir* of his father (1862); H. F. Henderson's *Erskine of Linlathen—Selections and Biography* (1899); McLeod Campbell's *Memorials*; W. Hanna's *Chalmers* (1849); J. F. Leishman, *Matthew Leishman of Govan* (1924), first half of the nineteenth century, with the "Middle Party" in the foreground (viz., those who tried sincerely to avert the Disruption and afterwards kept alive the Evangelical spirit in the "Auld Kirk").

Principal Tulloch placed Irving in his century in *Movements of Religious Thought* (1875).
Principal Story, in the *St. Giles Lectures* (1883) appraised him among twelve outstanding "Scottish Divines."
Dr. John Stoughton assigned him a niche in the English ecclesiastical scene. (*History of Religion in England*, vol. VII, ch. 16.)
Edward Miller, M.A., from an Anglican viewpoint, saw Irving as heresiarch in his *History and Doctrines of Irvingism* (1878).
Professor P. E. Shaw, of Hartford Theological Seminary, U.S.A., sees him as Herald of "The 'Catholic Apostolic' Church (sometimes called 'Irvingite')"—accepted Ph.D. Thesis, 1935, Edinburgh University Library. It is hoped that this exhaustive study will be published.
Paul E. Davies examines Irving's views "concerning the Person and Work of Jesus Christ" in an accepted Ph. D. Thesis (Edinburgh University, 1928).
James Hair, in *Regent Square* (1889) revealed Irving as the founder and pastor of a congregation. ("The ablest and wisest treatment I have read of the life of Edward Irving"—Alexander Whyte.)

GLOSSOLALIA AND KINDRED PHENOMENA

J. B. Pratt, *The Religious Consciousness* (Macmillan, 1926).

Mr. D. R. Willink, *The Prophetic Consciousness* (S.P.C.K., 1924).

F. M. Davenport, *Primitive Traits in Religious Revivals* (Macmillan, 1906).

A. L. Humphries, *The Holy Spirit in Faith and Experience* (S.C.M., 1917).

A. Machie, *The Gift of Tongues—a study in pathological aspects of Christianity* (Doran, 1921).

G. B. Cutten, *Speaking in Tongues, historically and psychologically considered* (Yale, 1927).

Dawson Walker, *The Gift of Tongues* (T. & T. Clark, 1906). Includes other theological essays.

G. Stanley Hall in *Jesus . . . in the Light of Psychology* (vol. II, pp. 424 and 690) cites books on Pathological Aspects of Religion.

E. Lombard, *De la glossolalie chez les premiers chrétiens* (Lausanne, 1910).

Weinel, *Die Wirkungen des Geistes und der Geister im nachabostolischen Zeitalter* (Leipzig, 1899).

E. Mosiman, *Das Zungenreden—geschichtlich und psychologisch Untersucht* (Tubingen, 1911).

Pfister analyses some interesting cases of "Glossolalie v. der Automat. Krytographie" (*Jahrb. f. Psychoanalyse*, Bd. 3, 1912).

Schmiedel, *Ausführingen*, II, 1 (Freiburg, 1912). Philological approach to Glossolalia.

INDEX

Abercrombie, Dr. John, 263
Albury, Surrey, 133ff, 148f, 232, 235
Albury Circle, 133–6, 142, 152f, 165, 221f, 226, 231ff, 243–8
America, "manifestations" in, 240f, 286, 288–91, 294–7
Ames, Prof. Edward Scribner, 249, 256
Anabaptists, 281
"Andrew," a pastoral "case", 97ff
Andrews, C. F., 235
Andrews, Rev. W. W., 70, 234, 298
Anglo-Catholicism, 231, 234
Annan, 1–18, 20, 32, 36, 42, 81, 116, 217–21
Anti-Cabala, 166f, 243, 286
Apocrypha, The, 108f
Arabian Nights, The, 20
Armstrong, Rev. Nicholas ("Mr. A."), 134, 167f, 171, 174, 176, 231
Arnold, Dr. Thomas, 132

Babylon and Infidelity Foredoomed, 129ff
Badams, Mr., 84
Baptism, 110f, 139f, 159, 164, 194–9, 201, 205, 258, 290
Barry, Prof. F. R., 266, 278
Baxter, "Prophet", 237
Baxter, Rev. Richard, 63, 183f, 266
Baxter, Robert 165, 175f, 185–207, 209, 216, 226, 239, 242, 246f, 255–9, 262, 266, 273, 283
Baxter, Robert D., 185
Beauchamp, Sally, case of, 255
Behmen, Jacob, 282
Bensley, Mr. (printer), 124
Beveridge, "that thrawn baker", 28
Beveridge, Miss Lois, 293
Bicknell, Rev. Dr. E. J., 245
Birmingham, 84, 122, 235, 256
Black, Rev. Dr., 227f
Black Bull Hotel, Glasgow, 43, 80
Blacklock, "Joe", 271
Blacklock, Thomas, 18f, 22
Blake, William, 271
Blantyre, Lord, 22
Blunt, Rev. Henry, 181
Blyth, David, 105
Boddy, Rev. A. A., 292
Bolton, East Lothian, 21f
Bonar, Rev. Horatius, 132, 179
Bourne, Rev. Ansel, case of, 255
Boyd, Rev. Dr. A. K. H., 19, 44, 229
Boyd, Rev. James, 44, 47
Breadalbane, Lord, 81, 103
Brewster, Sir David, 125
"British Israel" Movement, 130, 200, 237
Brodie, Rev. J., 221f
Brougham, Henry (Lord), 50, 62, 97
Brown, Rev. David, 156, 158, 209, 273
Brown, Mr. (teacher, Haddington), 27
Browne, Sir Thomas, 60, 84f
Buller, Charles, 80, 82f, 88
Buller, Mrs., 61f, 82f, 88
Bulteel, Rev. J., 232
Bunyan, John, 64
Burns, Robert, vii, 51
Bury, Prof. J. B., 250
Bushnell, Rev. Horace, 268, 270, 281, 291
Byron Lord, 38, 51, 61f, 129

Caird, W. R., 148f, 159, 233f, 276, 287
Calamy, Rev. Dr. Edmund, 285

Caledonian Chapel, London, 41, 44–53, 88, 104, 229
Calvinism, 26, 86, 110–14, 135n, 136f, 251
Camisards, 263ff, 284
Campbell, Rev A. D. (U.S.A.), 57n
Campbell, Isabella, 138f, 149, 151f
Campbell, Rev. Dr. J. Macleod, 65, 110f, 117, 136f, 140, 226, 232, 234, 276, 299
Campbell, Mary (Mrs. W. R. Caird), 139–51, 160, 196ff, 240, 246ff, 266, 286
Campbell, Nanny, 36
Campbell, Samuel, 145, 149
Campbell, Thomas, 86
Canning, George, 48f, 52, 62
Cardale, J. B., 142, 152n, 165, 193, 221, 232f, 246f
Cardale, Miss Emily C., 157, 186, 190, 197, 204f, 208, 211, 232, 248, 262
Carlile, Sir Anthony, 85
Carlyle, Rev. Dr. A. J., 13, 299
Carlyle, Rev. Gavin, 15, 298
Carlyle, Dr. John, 38n, 88, 184, 223, 248f
Carlyle, Jane Welsh, 22f, 31, 37ff, 45, 75–9, 88–96, 169, 223, 252, 274f
Carlyle, Thomas, vii, 15ff, 20, 25–8, 34, 37–41, 43, 61, 67, 76, 79–95, 103f, 106ff, 116, 124ff, 132, 168f, 184, 222ff, 228, 248f, 271–5, 298
Carlyle, Thomas (advocate), 234
Catechisms, 59f, 134
Chalmers, Dr. Thomas, vii, 22, 32ff, 48, 54f, 59, 65ff, 102, 105, 118, 125, 195, 221, 299
Chalmers, Mrs. Thomas, 42, 48
Charteris, Rev. Prof. A. H., 13
Chicago, "manifestations" in, 289f
China, manifestations in, 293
Christison, Prof., 21, 25
Christ's Holiness in the Flesh, 113
Church, Dean, 134n
Churches
 Catholic Apostolic, 153, 229, 231–6, 242–8
 Continental Protestant, 126f, 130f, 284f
 English, 47f, 70f, 73, 123, 133, 135n, 179ff, 185ff, 191f, 202, 231, 257, 292
 English Nonconformist 73, 107ff, 113, 120, 231f, 237, 248–52, 282f
 Roman Catholic, 99, 121, 129, 131, 138, 286ff
 Scottish, 16, 26, 41, 51, 71–4, 102–6, 110, 113ff, 117–20, 131, 136f, 210, 217–21, 230f
 Scottish Secession, 14, 16f, 26, 109, 131, 271
Clapperton, Hugh, 18
Cloud of Unknowing, 268
Cole, Rev. Henry, 112f
Coleridge, S. T., 50, 66ff, 105, 108, 128, 131, 163, 220f, 263ff, 272f
Collins (publisher), 124, 213
Communion, 158, 188, 199, 211, 221f, 290
Confession, The Scottish, 110, 112, 135
Confession, The Westminster, 110
Consumption (connection with "gifts"), 139, 151ff, 222f, 225
Conway, Moncure D., 92f
Covenanting tradition, 14, 16f, 26, 59, 247, 265, 271
Craigenputtock, 116, 248
Crichton-Browne, Sir James, 23, 275
Cumming, Rev. Dr. J., 179, 237, 276
Cunningham, Allan, 86, 123
Cutten, President, Colgate University, 300

Dalgliesh, Rev. William, 16
D'Arblay, Rev. A. C. L., 179

301

INDEX

Darling, Dr., 225
Davenport, F. M., 147f, 242, 261, 267, 300
Davies, Paul Ewing (Thesis), 299
De Fleury, John, 46f
De Quincy, Thomas, 52
Dialectic Society of Edinburgh, 19
Dickson, Provost, 15, 218
Dimond, Rev. Dr. S. G., 250
Dinwiddie, William, 86, 104
Discipline, First Book of, 113, 210
Discipline, Second Book of, 114
Dods, Rev. Marcus, 118
Dow, Rev. David, 168, 219
Drummond, Lady Harriet, 148f, 232
Drummond, Henry, 125ff, 133, 165, 211, 213, 215, 217, 223, 226, 232f, 239, 246f, 266, 273, 276, 287
Drummond, Rev. Thomas, 22
Drummond, "Wullie", 271
Dryden, John, 152
Dumfries, 116, 218f
Duncan, Rev. Dr. Henry, 218
Dunscore, 116
Dwight, Rev. Dr. Timothy, 286
Dykes, Rev. Dr. J. Oswald, 230

Eadie, Rev. Dr. John, 236
Ecclefechan, 16f, 39, 220, 271
Ecclesiastes (quoted), 18f
Edinburgh 19–22, 28, 30ff, 37, 40, 79, 105, 110f, 115f, 232
Edwards, Rev. Dr. Jonathan, 240f, 251
Encyclopædia Britannica, The (11th ed.), 129f, 185, 284, 286
"Enthusiasm", origin of the word, 278f
Erskine, Thomas, of Linlathen, 117, 128, 131, 137, 140, 142–5, 276
Exeter Hall, 31, 236f
Ezra, Ben, 131

Fancourt, Miss, 152
Fausset, H. l'Anson, 66
Finney, C. G., 256
Fletcher, Phineas, 89
Floris, Joachim of, 130, 281
Flournoy, Prof., 294
Fox Caroline, 203
Fox, George, 256, 282f
Frazer-Hurst, Rev. D., 260
"French Prophets", 284f
Frere, Hatley, 125, 129, 133
Froude, J. A., 38f, 77, 79, 274, 299
Fuller, Thomas, 84

Galton, Francis, 265
Germany, 234, 245, 286ff, 290f
Gibbon, Edward, 28
Gilfillan, George, 50ff, 298
Gillespie, Alex. (last survivor of Irving's Session d. 1884), 49
Gladstone, W. E., 49f
Glasgow, 32–6, 42f, 47, 86, 116, 225–8, 276
Glen, Rev. and Mrs., 27
Godwin, William, 50f
Goethe, 38n, 125
Goode, Rev. W., 180
Gordon, Margaret, 75f
Gordon, Rev. Dr. Robert, 60, 79, 107, 115
Gordon Square Church, 229, 231, 233ff
Graham, of Burnswark, 47
Grant, Rt. Hon. Charles, 102
Gray's Inn Road, place of worship in, 214
Gray, W. Forbes, 48, 299
Greek Youths, Irving's protégés, 100
Greenock, 136, 138, 141, 225, 232
Grenville, George, 167
Greville, *Journals. The*, 215
Grotius, Hugo, 279
Group Movement, Oxford, 244f

Haddington, 21–4, 31, 37, 39, 76
Hair, James, 44, 55, 212, 299
Haldane Miss Elizabeth S., 299
Haldane, James A., 113, 127
Haldane, Robert, 126f
Hall, Captain Basil, 30
Hall, G. Stanley, 300
Hall, Miss, 153, 157, 209f, 247, 263
Hamilton, Mrs. Wm. (Elizabeth Martin), 87, 121f, 158, 209, 274
Hamilton, Rev. Dr. James, 117, 230, 298
Hamilton, William, 86f, 104, 208–11, 222, 227, 229, 274
Hanna, Rev. —, 32
Hanna, Rev. W., 299
Harding, William, 183
Harness, Rev. William, 178f
Hart, Bernard, 255
Hazlitt, William, 50–4, 58, 298
Heath, R., 263
Helensburgh, 142, 149
Henke, F. G., 288ff, 293
Henderson, Rev. Dr. Henry F., 299
Herford, Prof. C. H., 60, 66
Highgate, 66f
Hinton, Rev. J., 232
Hooker, Richard, 20, 60, 110
Hope, Adam, 16, 20
Hope, David, 42, 47f
Hope Park Chapel, Edinburgh, 116
Horn, Archibald, 104, 213
Horn, T. H., 128
Horne, Bishop, 128
Howys, Rev. Thomas, 15, 265
Hughes, Miss, 231
Huguenot tradition, 15, 47, 284f, 292
Hume, David, vii, 28
Hunt, Leigh, 52, 62, 108
Hunter, Rev. Dr. John, 119, 276
Huxley, T. H., 280

India, "manifestations" in, 292f
Indians, Red, "manifestations" among, 199f, 288, 296
Inge, Dean, 69, 270
Ireland, Mrs. Alexander, 39, 274
Irving Family:
  Gavin, 15, 17
  Mrs. Gavin, 15, 17, 36, 227
  Agnes (m. Warrand Carlyle), 15
  George, 15
  Janet (m. Provost Dickson), 15
  John, 15, 17–19
Irving, Edward (1792–1834):
  Environment, 14; ancestry and home, 15; baptised, 16; school days, 16; Secession influence, 17, 271; open-air life, 17f; student life and graduation, 19; revisits old school (Carlyle still a pupil), 20; studies Divinity, 20; schoolmaster at Haddington, 21; tutor to Jane Welsh, 22f; schoolmaster at Kirkcaldy, 24f; Carlyle comes as friend, not rival, 25–8; licenced by Kirkcaldy Presbytery, 28; preaching experiences, 28f; meets Isabella Martin, 29, 31; literary interests, 20, 30f; early friendships, 18, 21f, 26ff, 32, 36–43, 45, 47f; assistant to Dr. Chalmers in Glasgow, 33–6; introduces Carlyle to Jane Welsh, 37; encourages Carlyle, 39ff; his own prospects unhopeful, 41; unexpected Call to London, 41f; ordained by Annan Presbytery, 42; inducted minister, Caledonian Chapel, 44ff.
  Becomes suddenly famous, 48f; impressions of his preaching, 50–7; publishes *Orations*, 59f; and *Judgement to Come*, 60ff; his style criticised, 62–5; influence of Coleridge, 66–9; is easily caricatured, 69f; his *Ordination Charge* at London Wa'l, 71–4; engagement to Isabella Martin, 75ff; correspondence with Jane Welsh,

INDEX   303

Edward Irving (1792-1834):—*contd.*
77ff; marries Isabella Martin, 80; on honeymoon, meets Carlyle, 8of; sets up house in London, 81; daily routine, 82f, 86; secures a tutorship for Carlyle, 82f; new friends, 83-6, 89; Carlyle and Jane Welsh, 90-5; Irving's interpretation of baby Edward's death, 96; extracts from Letter-Journal (pastoral experiences), 96-100; helps his father-in-law v.
  Building of Regent Square Church, 102-6; well filled, but no longer crowded, 106f; new orientation in preaching, 107; quixotic L.M.S. sermon, 107f; Charles Lamb, 108; Apocrypha controversy, 109 ; commends early Reformation *Standards*, 110, 112-15; views on Baptism determined by personal experiences, 110f; views on Incarnation lead to controversy, 112f; preaches in Scotland and meets Scott, 115f; further controversy over Person of Christ, 117ff; his congregation withdraws from Presbytery, 119; his books censured by General Assembly; grows reactionary, politically, 120f; preaches in Ireland, 121f; writes *A Tale of the Martyrs* and *Loss of the Abeona*, 123f; seeks D.D. by Thesis, 125; with Carlyle, meets Henry Drummond, 125ff, 165; influence of "unfulfilled prophecy" in C.M.A. sermon, 129f; translates "Ben Ezra", 131; obscurantist influences, 128-32; the Albury Conference, 133ff.
  His interest in "Tongues" (W. of Scotland)—A. J. Scott, Erskine and Story, 136-51; prophetic prayer meetings in Regent Sq., 153-6; "manifestations", 157ff, 166ff; his interpretation—*Fraser's Magazine* (1832), 159-64; Carlyle's opinion, 168f, 184; relations with Pilkington, 171-8; and Baxter 188, 193,196, 200f, 203-7; the "Group", 170-8, 186, 189, 193, 196f, 201, 204-7, 215f, 221f, 226, 231ff, 243-50; his elders and deacons, 86f, 104f, 107, 119ff, 158, 210f, 213; controversy with trustees, 209-13; ejected, preaches out-of-doors, 211f; physical exhaustion, 213f; with 600 followers, forms new congregation, 215-9; obeys summons to Annan, 217; trial and deposition, by Presbytery, 218ff; re-ordained at Newman St., 221; last meeting with Carlyle, 222f.
  Travels through Wales to Liverpool, 223ff; sails to Glasgow, 225; last days, 225ff; death and burial, 227; tributes, 227f, 276f; personality, 271-7.
Irving, Mrs. Edward (Isabella Martin), 29, 31, 37, 75-99, 121, 184, 213f, 222, 224f, 227, 274f
Irvings' Children, The:
  Died in Infancy—
    Ebenezer, 222
    Edward, 88, 90, 96, 111
    Mary, 111
    Samuel, 122
  Margaret (1825-53), 121ff, 224
  Isabella, married S. R. Gardiner, the historian
  Martin (1831-1912), 13, 122, 224
"Irvingites", 25

James, William, 238f, 253f, 294-7
Jansenists, "manifestations" among, 284n
Jeffrey, Francis, 125
Jeffrey, Dr. G. R., 256
Jeffs, H., 237
Jewsbury, Geraldine, 275
Johnston, Rev. John, 17
Jones, W., 123, 298
Judd Street East (Irving's house), 81

Karlshuld, Germany, 284
Keate, Dr., 49f
Kelley, Miss Lillian W., vii, 212
Kent, Miss Muriel, 299
Ker, Alan, 162
Ker, David, 162

Ker, Mrs. Stewart, 225
Kirkcaldy, 24-33, 37, 80, 96, 100f, 115, 153, 224f, 227
Kirkpatrick, Kitty, 83, 89
Knox, John (11n), 58, 117

Lacunza, the Jesuit, 131
Lacy, John, 284
Lake, Rev. Prof. Kirsopp, 261
Lamb, Charles, 52, 108
Last Days (pamphlet), 134, 179
Laurie, Mr., 227
Laurie, Sir Peter, 86, 96
Lee, Ann, 285
Lee, Dr., 146
Leishman, Rev. J. F., 299
Leishman, Rev. Matthew, 36, 299
Leslie, Sir John, 21, 24, 125
Le Baron, Mr., 294-7
Liverpool, Lord, 49
Liverpool, 105, 133, 225
Lockhart, J. G., 30
Lorimer, Rev. Dr., 21
London University (11n), 120
Lowther, George, 18
Lowther, Mary (v. Irving, Mrs. Gavin)
Luther, 182
Lutz, Rev. J. E. G., 233f, 286ff

Macaulay, T. B., 50, 84, 97
Macaulay, Zachary, 48, 97
Macbeth, Rev., 99f
Macdonald, George and James, 139-47, 150f, 240, 242
Macdonald, Margaret, 140
Macdonald, Rev., Birmingham, 122, 158
McDougall, Prof. W., 243f, 246f
Machie, Rev. A., 300
Mackenzie, Duncan, 104, 121, 213
McKerrell, Archibald, 162, 170
Mackintosh, Sir James, 49, 62
Maclean, Rev. Hugh B., 71, 117, 119
Macleod, Rev. Dr. John, 235
Macnaughton, Rev. Allan, 45
McNeile, Rev. Hugh, 133, 148, 169, 178
McNeill, Rev. John, 230
Martin, Anne, 153, 227
Martin, Elizabeth (v. Mrs. William Hamilton)
Martin, Rev. John, 29, 31ff, 42, 100f, 117, 153, 208f, 223, 225, 227, 274
Martin, John (painter, 1789-1854)
Martin, Isabella (v. Mrs. Edward Irving); b. 1797, oldest of a family of nine
Masson, Prof. David, vii
Matheson, Rev. Dr. George, 236
Maurice, Rev. Prof. F. D., 58f, 276
Melbourne, Lord, 120f, 215
Methodism, 248-52, 293
Middleton, Rev. Dr. Conyers, 183f, 280
Millenarianism, 107, 129-35, 179, 233, 236, 251, 280ff, 287
Miller, Rev., 231
Miller, Rev. Edward, 134, 299
Miller, Frank, 14, 16, 298
"Miss Augusta", 37
Milton, John, 25, 60, 63f, 97
Mission Field, "manifestations" on the, 107f, 147, 263, 292f
Moffat, Rev. Dr. Robert, 263
Moncrieff, Rev. Sir Henry, 43
Montagu, Basil, 65, 84
Montagu, Mrs. Basil, 84f, 92-5, 274
Montanism, 165, 182, 280f
Moore, Thomas, 129
More, Hannah, 97
Mormons, "manifestations" among the, 147, 165, 261, 288
Mosiman, E., 291, 300
Muir, Rev. Dr. J. Macadam, 64

INDEX

Murray, Rev. Dr. R. H., 244
Myddelton Terrace, Pentonville (Irving's house), 81, 83, 88
Myers, F. W. H., 254, 259f, 294, 297
Mystery Religions, 279

Napoleon, 132
Newman St., church, 215ff, 221ff, 226f, 231f, 234
Newman St., Irving's house in, 217, 222f
Nichol, friend of Irving's, 26
Nigeria, S., "manifestations" in, 293
Nisbet, James, 104
Noel, Hon. Rev. Baptist, 153
"Noble Lady", The (v. Mrs. Basil Montagu)
Norton, R., M.D., 139f, 147, 165, 182f
Notes on English Divines (Coleridge), 68

Oliphant, Mrs. Margaret, vii, 14, 16, 18, 22, 44, 96-9, 110f, 118, 212, 215f, 218, 220, 223f, 230, 236, 275, 298
"Oriel School", The, 130f
Orme, William, 108
Orthodox . . . Doctrine . . . (pamphlet), 113, 118, 133
Ossian, 20
Overall, Bishop, 96f
Owen, Rev. H. J., 231
Owen, Robert, 27, 215

Pack, Faithful C., 211f
Paine, Peggy, 16
Paine, Thomas, 16, 130
Pamphlets, 69f, 108, 113, 118ff, 133, 139-47, 166-84, 185-207, 218f, 226, 232, 255-9, 280, 286
Paul, Pastor, 291
Pears (friend of Irving), 27
Peel, Sir Robert, 50, 105
Perceval, Spencer, 126, 133, 153, 195, 213
Periodicals:
  Christian Instructor (Edinburgh), 117, 180
  Edinburgh Review, 97, 129, 142f, 150
  Expositor, The, 119, 156f
  Fraser's Magazine, 84, 106, 138f, 159-64, 177
  Macmillan's Magazine, 275
  Morning Watch, 133, 135, 147, 150, 152f, 169, 213, 215, 217, 231, 233
  Quarterly Review, 62
  Westminster Review, 62f
Perth, 115
Pilkington, George, 165f, 170-8
Plato, 278
Powerscourt, Lady, 121f
Pratt, Prof. J. B., 238, 260, 300
Presbytery of Annan(dale), 3, 42, 217-20
Presbytery of Kirkcaldy, 28
Presbytery of London, 44, 154f, 205, 209ff, 214
Presbytery of London North, 13, 277
Prince, Morton, 255
Proctor, B. W. ("Barry Cornwall"), 68, 84
Prophecy, 114f, 125-35, 139f, 148, 153, 168f, 178-84, 187-207, 215ff, 231-4, 236-9, 247, 257f, 278-97
Prophecy, Dialogues on, 133
Punch, 236
Pythia, of Delphi, 278

Quakers, 211, 281-4
Quinet, Edgar, 264
Quixote, Don, 35, 99

Rainy, Dr. (St. John's elder and physician), 225
Ramabai, Pandita, 292f
Rees, Prof. J. F., 256
Regent Square Church, 102-7, 119, 154ff, 166ff, 183, 209-13, 229f, 299
Rosneath, Dumbartonshire, 21, 36, 100, 133, 136, 138, 148, 226

Rhu, Dumbartonshire, 136, 140
Ritchie, Rev. Prof., 20f, 28
Ritchie, D. G.,editor, Jane Welsh's *Letters*, 37, 75
Robertson, Rev. A., 141f, 170
Robertson, Andrew, 45ff, 102
Robinson, H. Crabb, 11, 84, 108
Roddick, Rev., 218
Root, Jean C. (Biographer of Irving), 298
Rousseau, J. J., 38
Ruskin, John, 44
Rutherford, Samuel, 247, 271
Revivals:
  On the Continent, 126f, 129f, 234, 245, 281, 284f, 286f, 290f
  In America, 147, 240f, 251, 260f, 286, 288ff
  In England, 49-55, 105, 108, 129, 132ff, 152-8, 179, 214-7, 230, 236f, 248ff, 282f, 292
  On the Mission field, 292
  In Scotland, 13, 26, 115f, 136-44, 220, 232
  In Wales, 250, 263

St. Andrew's church, Edinburgh, 115
St. Cuthbert's church, Edinburgh 115
St. John's church, Glasgow, 33-6
Schleiermacher, 67, 128
Schiller, J. F. von, 38
Scholler, L. W., 287
Scott, Rev. Prof. Anderson, 279
Scotsmen in London, 44ff, 73, 99
Scott, A. J., 110, 118f, 136, 138, 168, 242, 266, 276
Scott, Sir Walter, vii, 70, 116, 227
Sedgwick, Prof. Adam, 112f
Sermons, Thirty (Irving's published), 57
Shaftesbury, "Letter concerning Enthusiasm' 178
Shakers, The, 285f, 293
Shaw, Rev. Prof. Plato Ernest, 299
Shoemaker, the infidel, 35
Simpson, Rev. Prof. P. Carnegie, 277
Simpson, Canon J. G., 273
Sinclair, Sir John, 125
Sloan, Rev., 218
Smith, Héline, case of, 294, 296
Solway Firth, 14, 17f
Sottomayor, the brothers, 99
Southey, Robert, 51, 61
Sparrow, Lady Olivia, 148, 165, 213
"Sponging-house", visit to a, 197f
Stanley, Dean, 132, 181
Staunton, Sir George, 146
Sterling, John, 66f
Steven, Rev. Dr. George, 242
Stevenson, Marmaduke, 282
Stewart, Rev. Andrew, M.D., 22, 226
Stoddart, Miss Bess, 37
Story, Rev. Robert, 21, 36, 42, 100, 110, 133, 136-9, 145f, 148ff, 154, 226f, 299
Story, Rev. Dr. R. H., 68f, 70f, 217, 299
Stoughton, Rev. Dr. J., 44, 58, 299
Strachan, Rev. Dr. John, 86
Strachey, Edward, 85, 89
Strachey, Mrs. Edward, 82f, 85, 89
Street, Rev. A. E., 290
Stuart, Hon. Margaret, 22
Sugden, Sir Edward, 213
Sumner, Bishop, 123

Tait, Rev., 232
Taplin, Mr., 157, 165, 169, 186, 190, 211, 232, 246, 262
Taymouth, 80f
Teignmouth, Lord, 109
Terregles, 220
Theresa, St., 240, 268
Thirlwall, Rev. Connor, 128
Thomson, Rev. Dr. Andrew, 31, 116f
Times, The, 62, 69f, 103f, 157, 177, 214
Tisset, Prof., 292
Tite, Sir William, 103

INDEX

305

Tongues, in relation to:
  Automatic Writing, 141f, 146, 238, 279, 296, 300
  Children, 202f, 263ff, 292f
  Group Consciousness, 133ff, 142, 145, 152ff, 171–6, 180f, 193, 196f, 204, 215ff, 221f, 231–40, 243–52, 269f, 280, 284ff
  Mass Movements, 128f, 137f, 157f, 214, 240–3, 249ff, 260–5, 269f, 284–93
  Motor Automatisms, 147, 166–9, 196, 202f, 239–42, 250f, 253, 267f, 278f, 282, 284ff, 289f, 293, 295ff
  Pentecostal Movements, 114f, 138–51, 153–84, 191ff, 201, 204–7, 210, 231ff, 249ff, 262, 266–70, 279–93
  "Permanent Endowment Theory", 145–8, 160, 164, 262ff, 279f, 292f
  Philology, 143f, 146, 160, 169–78, 261–5, 278ff, 288ff, 292–7, 300
  "Possession", 146f, 157f, 166–9, 196, 202f, 232, 260, 264, 268, 278, 284–7, 289–93
  Singing, 160, 170, 290f
  Spiritual Healing, 139f, 152f, 195f, 215, 231, 284*n*, 285
  Psychic Automatism, 141f, 260, 294–7
  Women, 138–51, 165–8, 184, 193, 204, 232, 240, 248, 263, 278, 285f, 292, 294
Tudor, Editor *Morning Watch*, 126, 133, 233
Tulloch, Rev. Principal, 128, 137, 299

Vaughan, Rev. E. T., f. of C. J. Vaughan, the Broad Churchman, 135
Virgil, 278

Walker, Rev. Dr. Dawson, 263ff, 300
Walpole, Lady Georgina, 100
Wardly, James and Ann, 285
Waugh, Rev. Dr., 109
Wellington, Duke of, 123
Welsh, Dr. John, 22f, 28, 37
Welsh, Jane (v. Carlyle, Mrs. Thomas),
Welsh, Mrs. John, 37f, 77ff, 91
Wesley, John, 65, 182, 249, 251f, 292
White, A. D., 292
Whyte, Rev. Dr. Alexander, 30, 65, 299
Widow, case of a "prodigal", 97
Wilkie, Sir David, 11, 46
Wilks, Washington, 66, 221, 298
Willink, M. D. R., 282, 300
Wilson, Bishop Daniel, 133
Wilson, David Alec, 75, 92, 299
Wolff, Joseph, 100, 133
Wellstonecraft, Mary, 248
Woodhouse, "Apostle", 227
Woolman, John, 256, 282ff
Wordsworth, Bishop, 279
Wordsworth, Dorothy, 52
Wordsworth, William, 124, 136

www.ingramcontent.com/pod-product-compliance
Lightning Source LLC
Chambersburg PA
CBHW071933240426
43668CB00038B/1416